WEALTH:
How to Achieve It!

WEALTH:
How to Achieve It!

W. Thomas Porter
Partner, Touche Ross & Co.

Durwood L. Alkire
Partner, Touche Ross & Co.

Reston Publishing Company, Inc.
A Prentice-Hall Company
Reston, Virginia

Library of Congress Cataloging in Publication Data
Porter, W   Thomas.

    Wealth : how to achieve it!
    Bibliography: p.
    Includes index.
    1. Finance, Personal. I. Alkire, Durwood, 1916-
II. Title.
HG179.P573   332'.024   75-34272
ISBN 0-87909-878-3
ISBN 0-87909-877-5 pbk.

© 1976 by Reston Publishing Company, Inc.
A Prentice-Hall Company
Reston, Virginia 22090

10 9 8 7 6 5 4 3 2 1

Printed in the United States of America

To Dorys and Dixie,
who have provided so
much wealth to us.

CONTENTS

PREFACE

This book was written purely on the basis of our conviction that many successful people in business or the professions spend little or no time managing their personal finances. A variety of factors contribute to this somewhat sorry state of personal financial planning. One of the most important factors is the lack of an easy-to-read, easy-to-understand, how-to-do-it book on financial planning. Hopefully this book fills a void.

In this book, we will emphasize the HOW-TO-DO-IT approach for several reasons:

1. You cannot entrust financial planning entirely to financial advisors.

2. Even if you wish to use financial advisors, you need to perform some analysis in order to ask the right questions and critically examine advice of others; in short, to most effectively employ the services of advisors.

3. You cannot learn financial planning solely by listening to others. It takes a little listening and a lot of *doing*.

4. In the event of your spouse's death, you should be in a position to handle financial affairs. Unfortunately, many spouses who are uninformed about financial matters are one *heartbeat* away from total financial *dependence* on others.

This book is not written for everyone, although everyone may find something of value in the book. In our discussions, we will center mostly on those people who have substantial degrees of freedom in making investment decisions primarily because they have high earnings capability and/or substantial net worth. If you are earning over $25,000 per year, we think you should read this book. Remember, you could be one of over a half a million people who could be millionaires in the years ahead. We think it is possible with some effort on your part.

The book is organized to first help you to collect some information about yourself and to develop a financial profile for cash planning, investment analysis, net worth planning and tax and estate planning.

The second and third sections of the book cover investment alternatives. We believe an investment program needs to be related to the major periods during a lifetime—period before marriage, period before children, period before children are in college, period after children have completed their education and no longer require support, and retirement. In each of these periods the objectives of liquidity, income, appreciation and safety are normally different. Therefore, we believe you must analyze many types of investment alternatives. Sections II and III cover:

- Life insurance
- Savings accounts and short-term money market investments
- Stocks and bonds
- Investment trusts or mutual funds
- Real estate
- Investment partnerships commonly known as tax shelters
- Pension and profit sharing plans
- Your own business
- Silver and gold
- Gold mining shares

Section IV of the book discusses *tax and estate planning*. As inflation goes up, tax planning gets more and more important to you. If your "real" income (in purchasing power) stays the same or even goes down, you are getting more and more dollars and therefore climbing higher and higher in the progressive income tax brackets. You must therefore scrutinize and manage your tax dollars to make sure your after-tax dollars are as high as you can legally make them.

Section V provides references as to *additional information* on various types of investments and discusses *investment advisors*—types of advisors, services they provide, fees involved, selection criteria, and how to most effectively use them.

Our discussions and examples throughout the book focus on people—people in various stages of life who have financial opportunities and problems. We introduce you to 15 real people in Section I and proceed, through the remainder of the book, to look at their financial requirements, their alternative investment opportunities, and a process they can go through in selecting among alternatives. We think that you can identify with one or more of the individuals or families presented in the profiles and apply some of the financial recommendations we present in Section V for each of the profiles to your own financial planning process.

We had a lot of fun writing this book. We hope you have a lot of fun reading it and we wish you success in the accumulation of wealth, whatever that is for you.

A great deal of help came from many people in the writing of this book. We owe a special debt of gratitude to our New York partner, Eli Gerver, who read our entire maunscript with great care and gave us thirty-three pages of suggestions and recommendations. We followed most of them, but not all, and want to make it clear the opinions expressed here are those of the individual authors, and not those of our firm, Touche Ross & Co.

We want to also express our thanks to Fred Easter and his crew at Reston, who all exercised great patience and understanding during the processes of review, revision, editing, galley proofs, and finally mechanical production.

We want to thank Mrs. Else Homen, who did so much in preparing the manuscript for one of the authors while he was in Norway; on the other side of the world the thanks go to Terry O'Neil in the Seattle office of Touche Ross & Co., not only for her work and that of her typing crew, but more importantly for her unflagging interest from beginning to end of the project.

W. THOMAS PORTER, JR.
DURWOOD L. ALKIRE

GET YOUR ASSETS IN SHAPE

"Hey—I've got a deal for you!"
"What you need is $100,000 more of life insurance."
"You better get yourself a tax shelter, man!"
"You mean you don't have a will?"

This may be cocktail or clubhouse discussion, but it is realistic talk when one thinks of the overwhelming volume of financial "advice" that surrounds many people today. As much as we like cocktail parties and lockerroom chats, it is useful to have an easy-to-read, easy-to-understand book on an often-neglected area of personal planning—financial planning.

In the past, financial planning may have been simply a virtuous activity. In the decades ahead, with continued inflation, intermittent shortages, and slower growth rates, hard-headed personal financial planning will become an absolute necessity.

Personal financial planning may be defined as the *accumulation* and *utilization* of financial resources to obtain the maximum utility for the individual and the family during the lifetime of the planner and the effective *distribution* of resources after death.

Discussions and examples in this book will focus on people—people in various stages of life who have financial opportunities and problems. Some of the discussion will center around people who are single or married without children—in mid-twenties with most of their life still ahead. Some of the discussion will involve the financial matters faced by people in mid-fifties or over, with children grown and retirement a near-term prospect or reality. Most of the discussion will focus on people in between— in their thirties and forties—some where the husband and wife are planning jointly for themselves and the needs of their children; some where a divorce has changed the financial situation; some where earnings and net worth prospects are extremely favorable; and some where the prospects are not so bright.

To help you identify with some of these people and, hopefully, to help you *do* some financial planning, we will present 15 profiles of people—real people who are disguised in name only. We will look at their financial requirements, their alternative investment opportunities, and the various processes they can go through to select their course of action. We will emphasize the "How-to-do-it" approach which we believe is important for the following reasons:

1. You cannot entrust financial planning entirely to financial advisors because many advisors don't completely understand your requirements, are too busy or specialized to attend to all of your requirements, or are incompetent.

2. Even if you wish to use financial advisors, you need to perform some analysis in order to ask the right questions. Critically examine advice of others to most effectively employ the services of advisors.

3. You cannot learn financial planning solely by listening to others. It takes a little listening and then some *doing*. The analysis we will ask you to perform on *your* financial situation will enable you to know more about your goals and financial consequences than any analysis performed by an attorney, CPA, banker, or the like, can provide.

4. You should be in a much better position to turn your affairs over to your spouse or other trustee in the event of death. And, if your spouse goes through this

book with you, he or she will be in much better condition to handle financial affairs after your death. Unfortunately, many spouses who are uninformed about financial matters are one *heartbeat* away from total financial *dependence* on others.

In the discussions, we have centered mostly on those people who have substantial degrees of freedom to make investment decisions, primarily because they have high earnings capability and/or substantial net worth. The person we are focusing upon is the one who is *now* or *soon expects* to be earning at least $25,000. An individual or family with an income below this level may have very limited possibilities and may find the financial planning ideas discussed in this book not very relevant at the present —in the future, hopefully.

Present State of Personal Financial Planning

Information on personal financial planning indicates many successful people in business or professions spend little or no time managing their personal finances.

A survey of all Americans who earn in excess of $25,000 reveals:

— 25 percent have no written will;

— among the 75 percent with a will, only one-third periodically update their wills;

— 40 percent do not use any type of tax advisor;

— of the 60 percent who receive some tax advice, less than one-half receive it from CPAs or attorneys;

— 80 percent buy life insurance without seeking any form of independent advice;

— less than 10 percent receive any meaningful, organized estate planning assistance.[1]

---

[1] Joseph L. Wiltsee. Business Week's Guide to Personal Business. (New York: McGraw-Hill, 1970.)

The Internal Revenue Service has estimated from Federal estate tax returns that there are in the United States the following numbers of estates of the various amounts shown.[2]

Net Worth	Number of Estates
$ 50,000 to $ 70,000	1,475,144
70,000 to 100,000	2,022,102
100,000 to 150,000	1,639,385
150,000 to 300,000	1,297,638
300,000 to 1,000,000	642,732
Over 1,000,000	120,652

A variety of factors contribute to this somewhat sorry state of personal financial planning. One of the most important factors is lack of knowledge coupled with procrastination. Many are unaware of the information required and techniques involved, to do a decent job of planning. In addition, many have not made the commitment to effectively manage their personal finances. Some believe that too much time and money is involved. This is baloney! It has been estimated that the cost of lawyers, tax men, or other competent professional advisor required to assist someone in the $25,000 to $35,000 income range would be $250–$1,000 per year. In addition, the individual would only have to spend approximately 50 hours per year of his or her own time—one hour per week! We have found that such an expenditure is returned many times in benefits. For example, one well-planned session with a competent tax advisor can save a person the entire cost of the tax consultation.

Another factor contributing to the neglect of personal finances is the overwhelming volume of financial "advice" that comes from all directions today. Such advice might include the hot tip at the cocktail party, the brother-in-law,

---

[2] From Supplemental Statistics of Income, 1969, published by Internal Revenue Service, October, 1973.

the successful corporate executive at the club luncheon, life insurance ads during the Sunday TV football games, or the tax shelter promotions in the financial pages. As a result, the individual often doesn't know where to begin. He either only looks at part of the financial picture, or he suffers from information overload and tunes out all financial advice.

Developing the Personal Financial Plan

Good planning requires good information, so the best place to begin in the development of *your* personal financial plan is to collect some information about *yourself* to determine the following:

1. *Your* present net worth;
2. *Your* present income and expense flows;
3. *Your* financial goals and projections based on the time period before a major life change event—i.e., marriage, children, children's education, retirement.

We emphasize *your* plan because we think any personal financial plan must begin with *you* and information about *yourself* before any analysis can be made of what specific course of action should be taken. The information developed must be comprehensive enough to provide a financial profile for cash planning, investment analysis, tax planning, net worth planning, and estate planning purposes.

In the remainder of this first section of the book, the process of developing a personal financial plan is described with easy-to-use worksheets and illustrations of how to complete the worksheets. We suggest you remove the worksheets in Appendix A and complete them as we go along, so that you can get the maximum *practical* use from reading this book.

Chapter 1

NET WORTH ANALYSIS

Before you decide to start on your personal financial plan, try to assemble some basic financial records, or at least the records you have.

After you have arranged these documents, turn to Worksheet 1 in Appendix A. Worksheet 1 asks for a list of some basic information about yourself, your family, your trusted personal advisors, and the identification and location of some very important financial documents. We suggest you complete this process with your spouse. We suggest this joint process for several reasons:

1. Both of you, or at least one of you, may learn something about each other, your children, your parents and in-laws, and certainly your financial records.

2. You both will have a much better picture of your financial situation for planning purposes and be much better prepared in the event one of you are called upon to act as the beneficiary of the other's estate.

To assist you in the preparation of the worksheets, we have selected one of the 15 profiles that is used in the book—the Stonestons. The worksheets for the Stoneston family are completed to illustrate how to fill them out. So just follow along. But first let us introduce the Stoneston family.

William Fitzgerald Stoneston is a 40-year-old management consultant who heads up a firm called Stoneston & Associates. His associates are his wife and three children. They live in a large city on the West Coast and enjoy the combination of cultural and recreational activities provided by

7

a metropolitan environment close to mountains and water. More information on the Stoneston family is shown in Section I of Exhibit 1.

EXHIBIT 1

BASIC INFORMATION

I. YOU AND SPOUSE

Stoneston

Name	Age	Birth-date	Marital Status
You William Fitzgerald	40		Married X Single
Stoneston			
Spouse Sally Brown	37		Divorced ___ Widowed ___
Stoneston			Head of Household ___

Residence 2272 Watercress Lane   Phone   532-7401

Occupation Management Consultant

Business Address 1404 IBM Building   Phone   426-0301

Social Security Number: Husband 174–62–6192; wife 524–34–4379

Military Identification Number 00403443

II. CHILDREN

Name	Age	Birthdate	Spouse	Age	Occupation	No. of Child.
Paige	14					
Michael	13					
Amy-Ann	3					

III. PARENTS OF FINANCIAL PLANNER AND SPOUSE
List names, dates of birth, and whether you are providing support for parents of either spouse.
Dean Stoneston — 1/10/08
Sarah Stoneston — 3/31/09

IV. OTHER DEPENDENTS

Name	Relationship	Age	Residence	Occupation

V. ADVISORS

	Name	Address	Telephone No.
Attorney	Gary Prince	Prince & Pringle	262-7050
Accountant	Mike Anderson	Touche Ross & Co.	282-1900
Bank Officer	Harry Hopkins	National Pacific Bank	292-1111
Insurance Agent	Ben Johnson	Universal Security Life	454-3993
Investment Advisor	Steve Hooper	Hooper & Dickensen	622-6633
Broker	Peter Kovats	Blyth, Peabody	446-2611
Tax Advisor	Same as accountant		
Trust Officer	Paul Powell	First National Bank	578-3280

Others (with nature
of data involved) _____

VI. DOCUMENTS

	Identification No. (where applicable)	Location	Date
Your Will		① ②	7/25/74
Spouse's Will		① ②	7/25/74
Trust Agreements	Thomas Brown Trust	②	3/18/60
Mortgages	2272 Watercress Lane (297875)	①	9/ 8/66
	6247 45th N.E. (23054159)	①	8/29/73
Property Deeds	Lot 15, Sandy Shores	①	1/30/73
Car Titles	1972 Kingswood Estate Station Wagon	①	7/22/74
Stock Certificates	Some held by Blyth, Peabody. See list on Schedule 2 of net worth statement	①	
Stock Purchase Agreements	Universal Security Life (expires 5/1/76)	①	10/29/71
Bonds & C.D.'s	Bankers Acceptance Notes (National Pacific Bank)	①	
Checking Accounts	See list on Schedule 1 of net worth statement	③	
Saving Account		③	
Passbooks			
Life Insurance Policies	See list on Schedule 3 of net worth statement		
Other Insurance Policies	Auto, medical, homeowners, fire on rental properties	③	
Contracts	Real estate contract—Lot 16, Sandy Shores (payment book in desk)	①	11/17/72
Set of Last Instructions			
Retirement Agreements	Keogh KO-1575	① ②	
Pension or Profit	Pacific Trust & Savings		

| EXHIBIT 1—Continued |
| BASIC INFORMATION |

VI. DOCUMENTS

	Identification No. *(where applicable)*	Location	Date
Sharing Plans			
Birth Certificates		①	
Marriage Licenses	A352687	①	
Divorce and			
Settlement Papers			
Notes Receivable			
Notes Payable			
Employment			
Contracts			
Income Tax Returns		④	
(last 3 years)			
Personal and Business		②	
Income Tax Returns			
(if applicable)			
Gift Tax Returns			
Military Discharge		④	
& Documents			
Financial or Insurance		②	
Surveys			
Other Records and			
Valuables			
Investment partnerships (real estate)			
Professional Realty, Ltd.		① ②	8/ 5/70
Samuel Mead Forty One		① ②	6/17/69
Contracts on publications			
Books		①	Various
Video Tape Program		①	6/10/71
Credit card list		① ②	1/ 1/75

① Safe deposit box; ② Loose-leaf notebook in fireproof cabinet at home; ③ Desk at home; ④ Fireproof cabinet in attic at home.

Basic Data Collection

The first four sections of Worksheet 1 will be easy to complete for most of you. For some of you with more than three children, you may have trouble remembering their names or birthdates and you may wish to assemble them at this point. Some of us have trouble with remembering our parents' ages so a phone call to them may be useful prior to this phase.

As to "Other Dependents," there may be many, many people dependent upon you—the UGN, the League of Women Voters, the University Congregational Church, your favorite charity, the cute blond secretary at your office—but the dependents to be listed in Section IV would be dependents for whom you are contributing more than half the financial support.

Section V of Worksheet 1 enables you to list some information about your financial advisors—if you have any.

In Section VI, you should identify, using names and numbers where applicable, the important documents you have related to financial transactions. The illustration (Section VI, Exhibit 1) indicates the major documents for the Stoneston family, which most of us have, and indicates where the documents are located.

Once you have determined where you wish to keep the documents, be prepared to show the locations. In our example, the Stonestons records are kept in four locations:

1. Safe deposit box;

2. Loose-leaf notebook organized by financial asset category which is stored in fireproof cabinet in personal residence (with duplicate copy in safe deposit box);

3. Desk in home or office used to store current operating records;

4. Fireproof cabinet in attic of personal residence used to store prior years' tax return data necessary to satisfy legal requirements for record retention.

Present Net Worth

Now we come to the exciting part of the basic information-gathering process—the determination of your present net worth. Of course, after you determine your present net worth you may not be excited at all; in fact, you may be downright depressed. But give it a try for several very important reasons.

1. You may be surprised that you indeed have a substantial net worth.

2. You have a base or starting point from which to develop realistic net worth plans for the future and measure accomplishment according to your plan by comparing your present net worth with your net worth next year, two years from now, and so forth.

3. You have a basis for determining realistic goals (children's education, retirement income, starting your own business) and what financial requirements (income, return on investments) are necessary to accomplish your goals.

Worksheet 2 provides a structured approach to accumulating information to prepare your net worth statement. If you have any financial training you will know that:

ASSETS — liabilities = NET WORTH

So we will begin with the asset list first. Sections I and II of Worksheet 2 illustrates a summary of assets and liabilities which should be completed after analysis of each of your assets and liabilities. We will present a completed summary for the Stoneston family and then discuss how each of the categories was computed. Exhibit 2 summarizes the Stoneston's net

---

EXHIBIT 2
PRESENT NET WORTH

AS OF 12/31

I. ASSETS	Estimated Current Value	
Liquid:		
Cash (checking and regular savings accounts)	$ 1,700	
Term savings accounts	$ 3,300	
Short-term investments—Treasury bills, certificates of deposit, etc.	$ 15,000	
Marketable securities	$ 33,300	
Accounts receivable	$	
Cash value of life insurance	$ 6,500	$ 59,800
Not so Liquid:		
Real estate	$111,000	
Investment partnerships—Real estate	$ 54,000	
Special situations—Stoneston & Associates	$ 35,000	
—Other	$ 16,400	$216,400
Retirement Funds:		
Keogh Self-Employment Trust	$ 27,100	$ 27,100
Personal:		
Residence	$ 95,000	
Furnishings	$ 36,000	
Automobile	$ 3,000	
Boats	$ 2,000	$136,000
Other: Thomas Brown Trust	$ 65,000	$ 65,000
TOTAL ASSETS		$504,300

II. LIABILITIES
    Short-Term Obligations:

Current bills	$ 1,500	
Borrowings on life insurance	$ 5,600	
Automobile(s)	$ 2,000	
Notes and contracts payable	$	
Other	$	
Personal loans (give details on back)	$	
Accrued taxes	$ 6,500	$ 15,600
Long-Term Obligations:		
Mortgages on real estate investments	$ 42,000	
Mortgage on personal residence	$ 33,000	
Other obligations		$ 75,000
TOTAL LIABILITIES		$ 90,600
ASSETS — LIABILITIES = NET WORTH		$413,700

worth of $413,700. Let's briefly examine each of the asset categories first to enable you to prepare *your* asset summary.

Liquid Assets. Liquid assets are assets that are in the form of cash or convertible into cash in the near future—say within three months.

Most of you will have a variety of checking and savings accounts which provide liquid assets. In Section I of the net worth worksheets (Worksheet 3), you should provide information on the details of:

1. Regular demand deposit checking accounts;

2. Regular savings accounts—funds on deposit payable on demand;

3. Term savings accounts which provide a higher interest rate because of the need to keep funds on deposit for some period of time, such as three months;

4. Short-term investments which provide higher rates of return than regular and term savings accounts and which require funds to be invested for short-term periods. The major categories include U. S. Treasury Bills, Certificates of Deposit, Banker's Acceptances, and Commercial Paper.

Exhibit 3, Section I shows the details for the Stoneston's cash, regular, and term savings accounts, and short-term investments. This schedule

EXHIBIT 3
ASSET DETAILS

I. CASH & SHORT-TERM INVESTMENTS

Checking and Regular Savings Accounts

Institution	Type (Regular = R 90 Day, 1 Yr.)	Rate of Interest	Restrictions on Withdrawal
University Mutual Savings & Loan 0200 00634 4 0200 01170 8	R 1 yr.	5¼ 6	None
National Pacific Bank 023 8504 5 022 1489 8	R (also checking) Checking		

Certificates of Deposits/Treasury Bills/Bankers' Acceptances

Institution	Type of Investment	Maturity Date	Rate of Interest
National Pacific Bank	Bankers' Acceptance	1/2 (3/4) 3/11	9–10%
Other Savings/Checking First National Bank (Stadium Br.) 3043 9076589	Checking		
Highline Savings & Loan 21000210	Savings (R)	5	

II. Stocks & Bonds

(Indicate if stocks are common or preferred. Give interest rate and maturity of bonds.)

No./Shs. or Par Value	Name of Issue	Exchange	Date Acq'd	Cost	No./Shs. or Par Value	Name of Issue	Exchange	Date Acq'd	Cost

All securities except those in special situations are managed by Hooper & Dickensen (investment counsellors) and securities are held by Blyth, Peabody.

III. Life Insurance

Company & Policy Number	Issue Date	Plan	Face Amount	Special Provisions	Date Acq'd	Cash Value
1. Insurance Co. of North America KYO 9571 Cert. 2902-B	6/ 1/66	Group	150,000	(0)		None
2. Olympic Universal Life G-1800 Cert. 3963	6/ 1/66	Group	133,000			None
3. Northeastern Mutual #3 572 705	7/ 8/61	Straight Life	10,000	(1)		$2,006
4. Northeastern Mutual #3 585 270	11/30/63	Straight Life	15,000	(2)		$2,548
5. Pacific Prudential #91 377 274	6/19/54	Straight Life	5,000			1,220
6. Universal Security Life #333	1/ 7/71	Straight Life	50,000	(3)		800
						$6,574

Summary: Straight Life   80,000
Group Term   133,000
Reducing Term   62,900
275,900

(0) Accidental death & dismemberment only
(1) Reducing term of 7500 to age 46
(2) Reducing term of 16,500 to age 49
(3) Reducing term of 38,900 to age 52

EXHIBIT 3—Continued
ASSET DETAILS

IV. REAL ESTATE

Description, Street No. and Location	Title in Name of	Cost	Present Valuation		Mortgages or Liens			Annual Taxes	Lien Holder
			Land	Improvements	Monthly Payment	Interest Rate	Amount		
Lot 15, Sandy Shores Estates	H/W	$32,500			—	—	—		None
Lot 16, Sandy Shores Estates	H/W	43,500			$651	7½%	24,000	500	WMSB (Earl Wright)
6247 45th N.E.	H/W	25,500			144	7¾%	18,000	425	National Pacific

V. INVESTMENT PARTNERSHIPS

Name of Partnership	Nature of Partnership	Original Investment		Annual Contribution	
		Date	Amount	Years	Amount
Professional Realty	Real Estate	1970	$25,000	6	$5,000
Samuel Mead	Land	1969	15,000	6	2,500

VI. SPECIAL SITUATIONS

Stoneston & Associates—Book value of consulting business Investment in closely-held companies:

No. of Shares	Name of Issue	Date Acquired	Cost
2½	Hooper & Dickensen	March 1974	$5,000
200	Universal Security Life	1970	8,000
450	Advanced Systems	1971	3,400

contains information which does not change too often—account number, type of account, etc. To get totals shown on the net worth summary, Bill or Sally Stoneston had to add up the various regular accounts ($1,700), term savings accounts ($3,300), and bankers acceptances ($15,000). Short-term investments are discussed in Chapter 5.

Marketable securities represent another form of liquid assets, since any stock or bond listed on one of the organized stock exchanges can be liquidated rather easily. It is important to know how and where the securities are safeguarded. You may have the securities kept by your brokerage house and a record provided to you at the end of each month by the brokerage house listing the securities held. If you elect to safe-guard the securities, they should be kept in a safe deposit box, with a listing made of the securities as shown in Section II of Worksheet 3. As Exhibit 3, Section II indicates, the Stonestons have Hooper & Dickensen manage their securities, because Bill and Sally Stoneston do not have the time or information to devote proper attention to managing the funds they have allocated for securities investments. In addition, the Stonestons have not been happy with the performance of their investments during the period when they managed their own investments.

Hooper & Dickensen provide the Stonestons with a quarterly report on the portfolio's performance. The brokerage firm used to buy and sell the securities sends the Stonestons a monthly statement of transactions and the securities held by the firm. In Chapter 6, we will discuss stocks and bonds; in Chapters 16 and 17, we will discuss investment informa-tion and counsellors.

The cash surrender value of the life insurance is the next item of the net worth summary, and this value is determined from information sup-plied by your insurance broker(s). This value, in our illustration, is shown for each insurance policy listed on the insurance summary—Section III of the Worksheet 3 and Exhibit 3 for the Stoneston family. We will dis-cuss types of insurance and how to determine your insurance needs in Chapter 4.

Not-So-Liquid Assets. These assets would be those where you may need some time to convert the asset value into cash. Such assets would include real estate, investments in partnerships, and special situations. Special situations might include investments in your own business; investments in closely-held businesses in which you have some interest; investments in gold and silver, art, antiques, etc. We will discuss the not-so-liquid assets in Chapters 8, 9, 10, 11, and 13.

Section IV of Worksheet 3 can be used to list real estate portion of this asset category; Section V to list investment partnerships; and Section VI to list the special situations. Comparable Sections in Exhibit 3 show the completed schedules for the Stoneston family.

Retirement Funds. Next, you should include the death benefits of any retirement program in which you are currently included. The death benefits should be available from the program administrator or trustee. The Stoneston family's retirement program is in the form of a self-employment retirement trust, the trustee being a bank which permits maximum investment flexibility for such trusts. Bill has contributed $2,500 each year since 1966 to the trust. In Chapter 10, pension, profit-sharing, and retirement programs are discussed.

The remaining assets on the summary usually do not need any detailed analysis. They include the fair market value of your residence, the estimated replacement value of your furnishings, "bluebook" value on your automobiles, and any other assets you may own of a personal nature.

We have separated these assets because typically they are not income-producing assets. Obviously, they have a value and can be sold or used as collateral when borrowing money. Chapter 8 on real estate illustrates the significant financial aspects related to home ownership.

Liabilities

We trust that for most of you, the liability side of your net worth statement is a somewhat simple one. Most of the entries on the liabilities worksheet (Worksheet 2, Section II) should be self-explanatory, but a few comments might be useful.

1. "Current bills" would include estimated amounts due on charge cards and other bills due in the next month.

2. "Other Notes and Contracts Payable" would include the total payments due on installment contracts for appliances, boats, etc.

3. "Personal loans" would include amounts due on short-term borrowings from banks, credit unions, finance companies, and maybe even friends and relatives.

4. "Accrued taxes" would include amounts due on Federal and State income taxes.

Net Worth Analysis

One of the most interesting analyses that can be performed with present net worth is the "What If?" game.

"What if I don't invest any more, what will my net worth be in 10 years?"

Using the Stoneston family, their net worth in 10 years would be:

$741,000 if the assets returned 6 percent per year compounded
893,000 if the assets returned 8 percent per year compounded
1,073,000 if the assets returned 10 percent per year compounded

"How long will it take to be a millionaire?"

For Bill Stoneston, it will take about:

15 years at 6 percent
12 years at 8 percent
10 years at 10 percent

"How many years would it take to deplete my net worth assuming I only earn $20,000 per year and want to spend $35,000 and net worth remaining returned 6 percent?"

For the Stonestons, it would take forever, because at 6 percent the increase in assets would exceed the capital depletion—of $15,000.

Such calculations are based on the rather unrealistic assumption that no more investments are made and there are no tax consequences. Typically, you have additional funds being invested through:

- Payments on the mortgage on your residence;
- Contributions by yourself and/or your employer in a pension and profit-sharing program;
- Investment partnerships;
- Retained earnings in your own business;
- Funds in excess of committed expenses to support your present standard of living.

So what is necessary in addition to a net worth statement is an analysis of your present income and expenses, and what future income and expenditures might look like in light of some goals you and your family have. The next chapter discusses income and expense analysis.

In addition, the rates of return used in our net worth projections are not certain—the rate of return could be better or worse depending upon the types of investments you make. Investment alternatives are discussed in Chapters 4 to 13 and rates of return are analyzed for different types of investments.

Chapter 2

INCOME AND EXPENSE ANALYSIS

Up to now one aspect of your present financial situation has been discussed—your net worth. The other aspect is your income and expenses.

The analysis of income and expenses will provide a useful tool to determine whether your standard of living will permit additional accumulation of financial wealth in the future, to pinpoint areas for financial counseling, and to determine what income and expense pattern in the future is required to accomplish your net worth objectives.

Income Analysis

Worksheets 4, 5, and 6 in Appendix A enable you to collect some information on your income. We suggest you refer to your tax return to obtain the information required. The worksheet is set up to enable you to provide information, not only for the current year, but the previous year and next year as well. This allows you to do some trend analysis of the sources of income available to you.

The sources of income shown on the worksheet are self-explanatory. However, we suggest revising the amounts on your tax return for any noncash expenditures and to record the amounts of income on a cash basis. For example, any income from rental property would obviously be reduced by the amount of depreciation on your tax return, so we would want you to record the rental income prior to depreciation but net of cash expenses. The same would be true of any royalties that you collect. So, the total for income you provide in each of the columns on the worksheet would be income on a cash basis. Your salary, however, would be shown on a "gross" basis, prior to any deductions for taxes, health insurance, or any other deductions that could be classified as an expenditure of the type which we'll cover in a few moments.

Exhibit 4 is the completed income worksheet for the Stoneston family. A few explanatory comments are useful. We mentioned Bill Stoneston

---

EXHIBIT 4

INCOME & EXPENSE ANALYSIS

12	MONTHS ENDED DECEMBER	31,	1974
(Number)		(Month)	(Day) (Year)

The analysis of income and expense will provide a useful tool to determine whether your standard of living will permit additional accumulation of wealth. Some financial counseling may be beneficial at this time to pinpoint areas requiring attention so that you may rearrange your affairs in a more advantageous manner. The analysis for a particular year, not necessarily a calendar year, should also provide the basis for budgets and forecasts of requirements in future years.

	Previous Year	*Current Year*	*Estimated Next Year*
INCOME:			
Salary–			
Yourself			
Your spouse			
Other persons			
Self-employment income–	$ –	$ –	$ –
(Net of expenses)	38,300	49,200	30,000
Other income–			
Interest	250	1,030	1,600
Dividends	370	2,750	2,000
Capital gains and (losses)	80	(5,540)	5,000
Rents (net of expenses)	–	1,070	4,000
Royalties (net of expenses)	11,650	7,770	14,700
Partnerships, estates, or trusts	–	1,100	1,200
Other	–	–	–
	12,350	8,150	28,500
TOTAL INCOME	$50,650	$57,350	$58,500

owns Stoneston & Associates from which he derives his principal source of income. He has built up the consulting practice over the last five years, and the practice has an excellent reputation. The reason for the drop in income in the next year is due to the Stoneston's objective of taking a four-month leave-of-absence from the practice for an extended trip to Europe with the entire family.

The other income relates to the Stoneston's assets presented in the previous chapter. You may wish to turn back to Exhibit 2 of Chapter 1 to again see the asset mix. The Stonestons expect interest of $1,600 or a return of 9 percent from short-term investments and 6 percent from savings accounts. Dividends represent a yield of 6 percent from the marketable securities. The Stonestons expect their investment counsel to improve their own performance in managing their securities and anticipate a capital gain of $5,000. The rental income reflects cash income from rent before mortgage payments—$200 per month from a single family dwelling which they rent to Bill's retired parents; $100 per month from a young couple who occupy, from September through May, their summer cabin on 3 acres of waterfront property. The young couple will also occupy the cabin during the next summer at a rent of $700 for the summer while the Stonestons are in Europe—the total rent from the cabin being $1,600.

Before Bill Stoneston started his consulting firm, he was a faculty member of a major university in the area. He published three books and developed a video tape program on computer concepts. These projects are continuing to provide a significant income stream, and Bill estimates that they will continue to do so for about two more years, at which time he plans to revise the publications.

The income of $1,200 is from the Thomas Brown Trust, which is managed, under the provision of the will of Mrs. Stoneston's father, by the local bank, which has invested the funds in a pooled growth fund.

The real estate investment partnerships are tax-sheltered investments and do not, as yet, provide any cash income.

Expense Analysis

Disbursements analysis is important for several major reasons. First, by analyzing what we call committed expenses, you can determine the expenditures associated with your current standard of living. Second, by analyzing what we call discretionary expenditures, you can pinpoint areas where desirable but not necessary expenditures are being made, areas where possible reductions in expenditures can be made in the future, and areas where the desire for expenditure is so strong that perhaps income requirements have to be maintained or increased to allow these discretionary expenditures to be made.

Third, by associating committed expenditures with the income shown on the income analysis, you know the level of income required to maintain a desired standard of living and also the excess funds available for discretionary purposes. Such an association of income and committed expenses may also indicate an income deficiency which may require borrowing, liquidation of assets, or a reduction in the standard of living.

Committed Expenditures

Many expenditures are certain in nature since they result from commitments made in the past. Such committed expenditures are disbursements for mortgage payments, for insurance premiums, for purchase contracts on automobiles, boats, major appliances, and for repayment of borrowings. Other committed expenditures can be reliably estimated for the year. Such disbursements include contributions to church, civic organizations and charitable agencies, taxes, major personal expenses for entertainment, Christmas gifts, etc. And then there are normal living expenses associated with a certain life style such as utilities, food, gardening, fuel, household goods and supplies, basic transportation associated with commuting and normal everyday living, and recreation.

Sources of information for such expenditures, of course, come from the documents and contracts that are drawn up for certain commitments and also from prior years' tax returns and the analysis of your checkbook. We have found it useful to annually prepare a worksheet by listing the amount of each check written during the year. Although this may seem like an onerous task to some of you, it is surprising how much can be accomplished during the time lapses that occur during a Sunday, whether it is an afternoon football game in early January or the first three quarters of an NBA basketball game in the same time period.

Worksheet 5 provides a way of summarizing your committed expenditures. Most of the objects of expenditures are self-explanatory; some are arbitrary in their grouping. Note that we have included investments and loan repayments under committed expenditures. We strongly believe such expenditures are committed either because they represent a contractual obligation or a commitment to an objective—i.e., retirement fund, purchase of a boat, purchase of an income-producing property, or investment in a tax-shelter partnership.

Note also that we have separated taxes, interest, and installment payments from the other committed expenditures. The "total" before taxes, interest, and installment payments represents an amount that will remain relatively fixed given a continued standard of living being maintained.

Taxes, however, will fluctuate according to income. Interest is a financing charge and will fluctuate according to borrowings. Installment payments also may fluctuate since presumably, as in the Stonestons' case, payments end or even may be discontinued as in the case of the investments. We have shown investments under committed expenditures, however, because we feel strongly that investments should represent planned commitments.

Exhibit 5 shows the committed expenditures for the Stoneston family.

EXHIBIT 5 COMMITTED EXPENDITURES			
	Previous Year	*Current Year*	*Estimated Next Year*
Committed Expenditures:			
Housing (includes mortgage or rental payments, repairs, insurance, taxes, fuel, and utilities)	$ 7,260	$ 7,600	$ 7,900
Transportation (includes payments on installment purchase, insurance, licenses, gas and oil, and repairs)	1,320	2,080	2,200
Food	2,750	2,400	2,700
Household supplies and furnishings	1,000	900	1,000
Phone	340	430	400
Clothing and personal	4,130	4,630	5,000
Education and recreation	3,500	2,400	2,800
Medical (includes health insurance)	2,160	1,650	1,800
Insurance (life)	2,280	2,130	2,100
Total before taxes, interest, and installment payments	$24,740	$24,220	$25,900
Taxes (Social Security and income)	7,600	9,700	7,000
Interest (other than in installment payments)	1,000	1,120	500
Installment payments			
Major purchase (other than automobile)			
Repayment of principal on borrowings	10,000	10,000	–
Investment plans			
Real estate	16,800	14,800	10,500
Investment partnerships	7,500	7,500	7,500
Self-employment trust	2,500	2,500	2,500
	$70,140	$69,840	$53,900

Before going any further let's analyze more closely the Stoneston situation and see what conclusions can be drawn from their case.

Exhibit 6 shows some information we believe is important for you to develop for yourself. First, it shows (line 3) the current amount provided by your major source of income, your occupation, as related to committed expenditures other than interest and installment payments. This analysis is important because it shows whether you are living within your basic income. The Stonestons have been living well within the income provided by Bill's occupation, except for the next year when they have planned to take an extended trip to Europe.

When you add income from royalties and the trust, the Stonestons are generating a significant amount for accumulating additional net worth and/or discretionary expenditures which may not generate additional net worth (lavish entertainment, more clothing, expensive vacations, etc.). We strongly recommend that you live within your income and be disciplined to keep your committed expenses below the income from your occupation(s). If not, you can be in trouble very quickly.

EXHIBIT 6

ANALYSIS OF EARNINGS AND COMMITTED EXPENDITURES

	Previous Year	Current Year	Estimated Next Year
1. Income from employment	$38,300	$49,200	$30,000
2. Committed expenditures other than interest and installment payments, but including taxes	32,340	33,920	32,900
3. Excess (deficiency)	$ 5,960	$15,380	$(2,900)
Income from sources other than investments			
Royalties	11,650	7,770	14,700
Trust	–	1,100	1,200
4.	$11,650	$ 8,870	$15,900
5. Excess (deficiency)	$17,610	$24,250	$13,000
6. Interest and installment payments other than investments	11,000	11,120	500
7. Excess (deficiency) for investment and other discretionary expenditures	$ 6,610	$13,130	$12,500

If you find that your committed expenses (line 2) exceed the income from your occupation, look at ways by which you can cut back on some expenditures. Some expenditures can be reduced rather quickly; some may take longer. For example, clothing expenditures can be reduced in the short-run; public transportation could be used instead of owning a second car. Housing expenditures might be reduced by owning a smaller home; if the smaller house was closer to work, transportation might be reduced as well. Perhaps insurance premiums could be reduced by using built-up cash surrender value to pay premiums or changing from straight life to term insurance.

Of course, you might also look at ways by which income can be increased. Perhaps, there are opportunities in your present job to increase your earnings; perhaps your spouse can start a career or seek part-time employment. Such opportunities should be evaluated carefully.

Note we have not included any income from capital assets such as interest, dividends, and capital gains primarily because we believe that these amounts should be reinvested for maximum accumulation of net worth— at least when you are in a period where substantial income is generated from your occupation. When you choose to curtail your income production—retirement (early or otherwise), partial work year, or change in occupation—you may wish to look at your net worth to help finance your new way of life. If, however, you wish to accumulate capital for some period of time, do not include return from capital as part of your income.

If you find yourself, like the Stonestons, with an amount available for investments and other discretionary expenditures (see line 7 of Exhibit 6), then you are fortunate and will be able to complete worksheet 6 of the "Income and Expense Analysis" worksheets without threatening to jump out the window. At some risk, then, we ask you to turn to worksheet 6, which covers "Discretionary Expenditures."

Discretionary Expenditures

Discretionary expenditures are ones about which you typically have a good deal of discretion as to the expenditure, and the timing of the expenditure. For example, you have a great deal of discretion in determining how much entertaining you will do, when that entertainment will take place, and how much the expenditure will be. On the one hand, you can have Le Canard a l'orange dinner for fifty; on the other hand, you could have a small wine and cheese party for six. The difference in the amount is somewhat significant in terms of the entertainment expenditure. As another example, you may decide to take a ski vacation for two weeks in the Canadian Rockies or a backpack trip in the Olympic Mountains along the Duckabush River. Again the difference in expenditure is rather significant.

Discretionary expenditures are classified into two categories: somewhat discretionary, and very discretionary. Our classification is somewhat arbitrary, we admit, but it is useful to make the classification since certain discretionary expenditures are much more regular and frequent than others. For example, typically you do not make a home improvement every year, nor do you buy a new automobile or boat. Exhibit 7 shows

EXHIBIT 7			
DISCRETIONARY EXPENDITURES			
	Previous Year	*Current Year*	*Estimated Next Year*
Discretionary Expenditures:			
Somewhat discretionary–			
Entertainment	$ 500	$ 450	$ 1,000
Regular vacations	1,500	2,000	–
Church and charities	1,260	1,250	1,200
Hobbies			
Organizations:			
Fraternal			
Civic			
Social	250	250	600
Personal Gifts	500	670	500
Emergency fund (support of			
parents)	–	1,000	1,500
TOTAL	$ 4,010	$5,620	$ 4,800
Very discretionary–			
Home or home improvements	3,900		
Auto, boat, etc.			
Personal property			
(home furnishings)	3,780	940	
Trips—extended			20,000
Investments			
Special goal			
Other			
TOTAL	$ 7,680	$ 940	$20,000
TOTAL DISCRETIONARY			
EXPENDITURES	$11,690	$6,560	$24,800

the discretionary expenditures for the Stoneston family. Some of you may argue with our classifications. For example, some may wish to put church and charities under committed expenditures.

Let's do some more detailed analysis at this point. From Exhibit 6, line 7 we arrived at an amount available for investments and discretionary expenditures. Let's start with that amount and finish our analysis of the Stoneston situation in Exhibit 8. What this analysis suggests is that the Stonestons, over a three-year period, will have required the use of capital of $10,810 ($5,080) + $6,570 + ($12,300): See Line 3, Exhibit 8.

Obviously, they could have changed the amount available for investment or the amount of capital required by exercising a different set of choices requiring financial expenditures. They could have chosen not to take vacations during the last two years and saved $3,500; they could choose not to take the extended European trip and save $20,000. We are not advocating that you forego such plans—because sometimes such plans are foregone forever—but merely mentioning the financial consequences and suggesting that you plan for such expenditures as part of an overall income and expenditure plan.

EXHIBIT 8			
FINAL ANALYSIS OF STONESTON SITUATION			
	Previous Year	*Current Year*	*Estimated Next Year*
1. Excess (deficiency) for invesments and other discretionary expenditures	$ 6,610	$ 13,130	$ 12,500
2. Discretionary expenditures	11,690	6,560	24,800
3. Excess (deficiency) for investments	$ (5,080)	$ 6,570	$(12,300)
4. Investments	26,800	24,800	20,500
5. Amount available for use or (required) from sale of assets or borrowings	$(31,880)	$(18,230)	$(32,800)

Analysis of Where You Are and Where You Are Headed

You first prepared a statement of net worth, and hopefully you were pleasantly surprised as to what you have. You next did an analysis of your income and expenditures and most importantly determined your level of committed expenses.

If your current income exceeds your committed expenditures, you are to be congratulated. If your income greatly exceeds your expenditures, then either you have made an error in arithmetic or you have some funds that are available for alternative investments. If any of the above situations are true, you may wish to do more analysis, seek counsel, or read on.

If your expenditures exceed income, you may wish to analyze the ways by which income can be increased and/or expenditures reduced. We suggest you read on for some help.

Now that you have determined "where you are at," it is time to think a little about the future or "where you are headed." Obviously, your future is yours, and the kinds of things you want to do are largely up to you. We will come back to some specific alternatives later on in this book. Suffice it to say at this time that there are some questions that deserve some attention in answering:

• What changes do you anticipate in the future that will significantly affect your:
    income?
    committed expenditures?

• What major discretionary expenditures (other than education) do you plan to make?

• What will be the estimated cost of educating your children?

• When will the expenditures be required? How will you fund the expenditures?

• What plans do you have for retirement?
    When do you plan to retire?
    At what income?
    What is minimum income required?
    How will retirement income be funded?

• Do you desire to provide support for anyone during his/her lifetime, until marriage, remarriage, maturity, or death?

• Do you desire to place any of your property in trust during your lifetime for the benefit of a potential heir or heirs?

• Do you desire to transfer by gift during your lifetime fixed sums of

of money, specific items of property, or other assets to charitable organza-
tions, relatives, or other individuals?

To illustrate the types of goals and financial consequences of goals, let
us examine the background of our illustrated client, the Stonestons, and
their prospects. As we discovered in Chapter 1, the Stonestons' net worth
is $413,700, largely accumulated in the last decade. Ten years ago, the
Stonestons' net worth consisted of $10,000 equity in a $50,000 Summit,
N.J. home; a 1955 Chevy sedan; $5,000 of furnishings, and a savings ac-
count of $1,000. Bill's salary as a staff associate in a New York based
management consulting firm was $15,000.

Reared by low-income parents, Bill and Sally had, at an early age, received the values of thrift and careful budgeting and had been motivated
to succeed by hard work. Bill worked his way through undergraduate and
graduate schools. As his salary rose to $25,000 at age 32 and current
level of $50,000 at age 40, the Stonestons were able to accumulate their
present net worth by careful cash budgeting, keeping committed expenses
low, managing tax dollars, and having substantial after tax dollars available for investment purposes.

Although the Stonestons are not financially insecure by any means, they
are concerned about whether their assets can withstand the erosion possibilities of inflation; whether they can continue to withstand social pressures to spend; and whether they will have sufficient income-producing
assets to enable Bill to pursue non-professional interests on a more leisurely
basis after he has reached 50. His consulting practice is a demanding
one and, although he has always taken vacations with his family and spends
several long weekends with them at their summer cabin, he has the un-
comfortable feeling from time to time that he does not have sufficient uninterrupted periods of time to delve into his interests in oceanography, the
wilderness, and landscape architecture. He knows, however, that Sally enjoys the relative security and financial freedom of her present life and is
interested in additional education and a possible career as the two older
children reach college age and the youngest child starts school. Bill also
knows that during the next 10 years, educational expenses for their oldest
daughter and son will be considerable.

After much thought and deliberation, the Stonestons have determined
their goals to be as follows during the next 10 years:

• *Income and Committed Expenditures*
   Mr. Stoneston has decided to continue his present work habits and professional involvement until at least age 50, with the prospects of income
from his consulting business to increase about 3 percent in real growth
for the next 10 years; royalties to stay at current levels for 3 years and drop

to $10,000. The Stonestons do not foresee any major shifts in committed expenses, except that the annual payments of $7,800 on the summer waterfront property will be completed in four more years.

• *Discretionary Expenditures*
— The Stonestons plan a major family trip to Europe during the next year which will require an estimated $20,000.
— Mrs. Stoneston plans to work on an advanced degree beginning in two years when the youngest child begins elementary school full-time. The proposed education program will take approximately four years to complete at a cost of $1,000 tuition per year at a local state university.
— They plan to buy, in two years, a water ski boat to be used at the summer cabin at an estimated cost of $5,000.

• *Educational Expenditures for Children*
— They plan to enroll their son in a private high school a year from now for four years at a cost per year of $2,000.
— Their oldest daughter will begin college in four years at an estimated cost of $5,000 per year at that time. Their son will enter college a year later, and Mr. and Mrs. Stoneston plan to fund the educational expenditures for six years for each child.
— They would like to set up a ten-year revocable trust fund for the smallest child in ten years—the fund amount to be $25,000.

• Since Mr. Stoneston has plans to change his professional occupation at age 50 and possibly reduce his earnings capacity, he is interested in having a net worth capable of producing a return sufficient to cover committed expenses at that time.

• Mr. and Mrs. Stoneston plan to provide some support for Mr. Stoneston's parents during their lifetime and expect those expenditures to be $1,000–$2,000 during the next 10 years.

To illustrate the financial consequences of these goals and plans, it is necessary to prepare a worksheet using data from Exhibits 4 through 8. Exhibit 9 is such a worksheet. A few comments about some of the data on the worksheet are in order and are listed as follows:

1. The $26,000 of committed expenditures "before taxes, interest, and installment payments" (line 4) should be looked upon as a control amount. In other words, no matter what *types* of committed expenditures are made, the *total* is planned not to exceed $26,000. The food bill might decrease as children go off to college; real estate taxes might go up; but the total is planned to be no more than $26,000. Control is extremely important to the realization of any plan.

2. Taxes will increase as income increases but at a much greater rate. The effective tax rate in the first year is approximately 17 percent; in the 10th year, it is 28 percent. Income during the 10 years will have grown

66 percent; income taxes will have grown 180 percent. The importance of managing taxes and doing effective tax planning is quite evident from the analysis.

3. When one couples the marginal tax rate associated with increased income, it becomes even more important to keep committed expenses low. At a marginal tax rate of 50 percent, every additional dollar of expenditures requires 2 dollars of income.

4. The amounts projected are in current dollars; obviously inflation could be significant in the future, but our assumption in preparing the projection is that increases in income would be comparable to increases in the cost of living. However, this assumption may not be valid, and committed expenses may rise more rapidly than income in periods of rapid inflation. Also, if income is increased to offset inflation, taxes increase significantly.

5. The existing Thomas Brown Trust is planned to be used for the children's educational expenditures.

Some significant financial aspects of this project include:

• Income during the period is planned to be $658,800; committed expenses, including taxes of $166,500, are planned to be $426,400; thus $232,400 is available for discretionary purposes and investments.

• Investment expenditures are planned to be $158,200.

• Discretionary expenditures are planned to be $165,000, of which $20,000 is for extended travel and $92,000 is for education.

• The cumulative capital requirement from net worth or borrowings is planned to be $27,800.

Let's look at the impact of the additional expenditures, both for investment purposes and to meet the Stonestons' goals, on the Stonestons' net worth. Remember one of the Stonestons' goals was change in professional occupation at age 50. Exhibit 10 presents an estimate of net worth in ten years based on the present net worth statement developed in Chapter 1. The analysis uses the data developed in Exhibit 9—namely, the amounts planned to be invested in various categories of investments and the amount required to finance the deficiency of $27,800. The analysis also is based on estimated rates of return for the different asset categories.

The estimated net worth ten years from now would be $944,500 (Exhibit 10). Assuming the Stonestons stay in their present residence or purchase a residence of equivalent value, assets of $739,400 ($944,500 less $205,100) would be available for income production. Assuming a modest return of 6 percent from a relatively safe investment, the Stoneston income from capital assets would be approximately $44,000, an amount in excess

	EXHIBIT 9			
	LONG RANGE INCOME AND EXPENDITURES ANALYSIS			
	Next Year	*2*	*3*	*4*
1. Income from consulting practice	30,000	50,700	52,200	53,700
2. Royalties	14,700	14,700	14,700	10,000
3. Income	44,700	65,400	66,900	63,700
4. Total committed expenditures before taxes, interest, and installment payments	25,900	26,000	26,000	26,000
5. Taxes and interest	7,500	10,000	17,000	15,000
6. Real estate investments	10,500	10,500	10,500	10,500
7. Investments partnerships	7,500	7,500	7,500	7,500
8. Self-employment trust	2,500	2,500	2,500	2,500
9. Committed total	53,900	62,500	63,500	61,500
10. Excess (deficiency)	(9,200)	2,900	3,400	2,200
11. Somewhat discretionary expenditures (Exhibit 7)	4,800	4,800	4,800	4,800
12. Extended travel	20,000		–	–
13. Education—Wife			1,000	1,000
14. Education—Son		2,000	2,000	2,000
15. Education—Daughter(s)				
16. Trust for daughter				
17. Boat			5,000	
18. Discretionary total	24,800	6,800	12,800	7,800
19. Excess (deficiency)	(34,000)	(3,900)	(9,400)	(5,600)
20. Trust contribution for education		2,000	2,000	2,000
21. Excess (or deficiency)	(34,000)	(1,900)	(7,400)	(3,600)

5	6	7	8	9	Age 50 10	Total
55,400	57,000	58,700	60,500	62,300	64,200	
10,000	10,000	10,000	10,000	10,000	10,000	
65,400	67,000	68,700	70,500	72,300	74,200	658,800
26,000	26,000	26,000	26,000	26,000	26,000	259,900
16,000	17,000	18,000	19,000	20,000	21,000	166,500
2,700	2,700	2,700	2,700	2,700	2,700	58,200
7,500	7,500	7,500	7,500	7,500	7,500	75,000
2,500	2,500	2,500	2,500	2,500	2,500	25,000
54,700	55,700	56,700	57,700	58,700	59,700	584,600
10,700	11,300	12,000	12,800	13,600	14,500	74,200
4,800	4,800	4,800	4,800	4,800	4,800	48,000
						20,000
1,000	1,000					4,000
2,000	5,000	5,000	5,000	5,000	5,000	33,000
5,000	5,000	5,000	5,000	5,000	5,000	30,000
					25,000	25,000
						5,000
12,800	15,800	14,800	14,800	14,800	39,800	165,000
(2,100)	(4,500)	(2,800)	(2,000)	(1,200)	(25,300)	(90,800)
7,000	10,000	10,000	10,000	10,000	10,000	63,000
4,900	5,500	7,200	8,000	8,800	(15,300)	(27,800)

EXHIBIT 10
ESTIMATED NET WORTH

Asset Category	Current Value	Contemplated Changes	Estimated Rate of Return	Projected Value
Liquid Assets	$59,800	To finance deficiency on Line 21, Exhibit 9	6%	$44,300
Not-so-liquid:				
Real Estate	111,000	Mortgage payments	8%	239,600
Investment partnerships	54,000	7,500 annual contributions	10%	{ 140,600 119,500
Stoneston & Associates	35,000	Slow growth	3%	47,000
Other	16,400		15%	66,300
Self-employment trust	27,100	2,500 annual contributions	8%	58,500 36,200
Personal residence	95,000	Mortgage payments	8%	205,100
Thomas Brown Trust	65,000	Used to finance children's education See Line 20, Exhibit 9	6%	37,000
ESTIMATED TOTAL ASSETS:				993,500
LESS LIABILITIES:				
Short-term			$16,000	
Mortgages			$33,000	49,000
ESTIMATED NET WORTH:				$944,500

of estimated expenses of $26,000. Of course, taxes would have to be paid on the income.

Obviously, different projections would be generated based on different assumptions and objectives of the future. We could change the estimates of income, investment expenditures, rates of return, asset mix, and so forth. Once you have developed the information discussed in these two chapters, you have a model which is simple to use in analyzing different assumptions about the future.

Once you determine your plan for the future, all you have to do is to *work your plan.* The remainder of the book will give you some useful ideas about the investment opportunities to evaluate in making *your plan work.*

Chapter 3

INITIAL GUIDEPOSTS AND FINANCIAL PROFILES

No economic forecast of the future suggests that risks and uncertainties will disappear. Because of the substantial problems confronting the world's economy—oil and food shortages, cost-push labor contracts, etc.—inflation may be a fact of life in the decades ahead. Defense against the corroding effects of inflation will be absolutely essential, making it necessary for a more exacting personal financial plan.

Our intention in this chapter is to provide a few initial guideposts based on the observations made in the first two chapters. In addition, 14 profiles (in addition to the Stonestons), are presented, all of whom have different financial opportunities and requirements. We believe that you can identify with one or more of the individuals or families presented in the profiles and then apply some of the financial recommendations developed to your own financial planning process.

Initial Guideposts

Before we discuss specific investment strategies in the next section of this book, it is important to confront you with some guideposts for defending against inflation.

1. Keep committed expenses as low as possible.
2. Make your money work harder and remember the power of compounding.

3. Scrutinize and manage your tax dollars to make sure your after-tax dollars are as high as you can legally make them.

4. Quantify the financial consequences of major life events—children, education, new career, retirement—and plan financially for these events with specific objectives and determination to make your plan work.

5. Learn about personal financial planning by doing it, not by reading about it, or having it done by others.

Let us examine each of these initial guideposts in some detail.

Keep Committed Expenses Low

Too frequently, many people earning a significant income have little left for the acquisition of assets that can act as inflation hedges. Too often, an open display of affluence seems to be the goal of the successful person. This person is the "conspicuous consumptive." He not only has one car, but two or three; his sailing sloop sits idle most of the year; TV sets are in everyone's room; and he is a member of a country club, a tennis club, and a diner's club. As one rises on the economic scale, the definition of necessities becomes very broad. It embraces luxury travel, a wardrobe for every occasion, lavish entertainment, and a sumptous home. Some of it may be unavoidable as one climbs upward in the economic-social strata, but a good deal of it stems from the social pressure to spend.

The more you can muster the determination and willpower to separate the true demand for goods and services from the simulated counterpart— the social pressure to spend—the more you will have to make your money earn more and to stay ahead of the inflationary pace.

Spending habits have to be re-evaluated in order to keep committed expenses reasonable. Shop for goods and services that will provide for the longest period of time, given the price tag. Fads, fashions, and foibles should be given secondary consideration. If you stock up to avoid price increases, you should know your wants for a longer time frame than when you shop in an impulsive, fashion-responsive manner.

Make Your Money Work Harder

In inflationary periods, you must strive to put your money to work to stay ahead of the inflation rate. In other words, it is not enough that your assets merely appreciate while you are holding them; they must appreciate *more than* the inflation rate. As we will see in the discussion of investment opportunities, interest rates on various savings and short-term investments vary significantly. Rates of return on various stocks differ considerably, and real estate opportunities should be considered by some. Putting your money in a savings account that pays a 6 percent compound interest rate is preferable to holding cash in a checking account, but you have to find ways to make your money work even harder if you are going to stay ahead of an inflation rate of 7–8 percent or more.

To illustrate the difference between a few percentage points in rates of interest, let's examine the consequences of a few alternatives. With the expenditure of little time or effort, you can, at the present time, place your idle cash in an account at a savings and loan association that will provide a 6 percent compound rate of return. Left 10 years, $10,000 in cash assets would accumulate to $17,910 or an increase of $7,910. Of course, this return will be reduced by your marginal tax rate and would, therefore, provide less after-tax dollars.

If you took a little more time, you could find some longer-term saving certificate plans which currently provide a rate of return close to 8 percent. Left 10 years, $10,000 in cash assets would accumulate to $21,590—or an increase of $11,590.

If you were able to find an investment which provides a 10 percent compound rate of return, the $10,000 in assets would accumulate to $25,940 in 10 years—an increase of $15,940. Table 3–1 shows accumulated amounts over 10 years on an investment of $10,000.

From the table, you can see that there are significant differences between the amounts accumulated for the various rates of return. These differences

TABLE 3-1

Rate (%)	Accumulated Amount	5%	6%	7%	8%	9%	10%
5	$16,290	–	–	–	–	–	–
6	17,910	$1,620	–	–	–	–	–
7	19,670	3,380	$1,760	–	–	–	–
8	21,590	5,300	3,680	$1,920	–	–	–
9	23,670	7,380	5,760	4,000	$2,080	–	–
10	25,940	9,650	8,030	6,270	4,350	$2,270	–

NOTES:
At 5%, the $10,000 will be $16,290 in 10 years—that is, $1,620 less than it would be at 6%; $3,380 less than it would be at 7%; $5,300 less than it would be at 8%, etc.

At 8%, the $10,000 will be $21,590 in 10 years—$2,080 less than it would be at 9%; and $4,350 less than at 10%.

are even more significant when the number of dollars you have to invest increases. For example, if you had $50,000 to invest and were able to get a return of 6 percent, the accumulated amount in 10 years would be $89,550 (5 times $17,910 using the table). However, an investment returning 10 percent would accumulate to $129,700 in 10 years (5 times $25,940 using the table)—a difference of $40,150. Another way of using the table is to find the desired percentage—in this case 6 percent—at the top of the table and read down to the percentage being compared—in this case 10 percent. The difference for a $10,000 investment is $8,030 which, when multiplied by 5 ($50,000/$10,000), equals $40,150.

Preservation of asset values is a very important guidepost to personal financial planning, particularly in times of rapid change. In bad times, you can borrow against your assets; in inflationary times, your assets grow in value as prices rise and provide collateral for borrowing. This would permit you to obtain control of more assets that will also rise in value as prices rise.

Manage Tax Dollars

One of the largest annual expenditures made by people earning more than $25,000 is for taxes. In 1939, a married couple with two children earning a salary of $25,000 paid out about $1,700 in income taxes. Today, the same income situation will require $4,380 in taxes.

With such a tax system, after-tax dollars are the only ones that accumulate capital. To make those after-tax dollars as large as is legally possible is one of the most significant challenges and opportunities in developing a successful financial plan. You have to manage your tax dollars just like any other investment. You have to generally understand tax regulations and forms and realize the need for tax planning. The proper time for annual how-to-slash-your-income-taxes planning is in the late summer and early fall *before* the year ends. This is when you can take advantage of what the tax laws allow in minimizing income and maximizing expenses.

Section IV of this book covers income tax planning and provides sufficient coverage to enable you to give closer scrutiny to the dollars you pay out to the government.

A Lifetime Plan

No matter what your age or financial circumstances, you can and should develop a lifetime or a rest-of-your-life plan. The reason for such planning is to provide a way to compare your financial objectives with the means for achieving them. A plan is also a guide for present actions; as such, it is not a guide for all future actions, but a plan that needs periodic challenge and revision as the future becomes more certain.

We strongly recommend developing plans for multi-year periods related to major life events. These multi-year plans should not be in great detail, primarily because some events are far in the future and cannot be estimated precisely enough to develop meaningful detailed financial analyses. We suggest that you first develop your thoughts about time periods where major life events will possibly take place. For example, with most people, the major time periods are:

1. Period before marriage.

2. Period before children are born.

3. Period before children are in school.

4. Period before children are in college (if college education is planned for the children).

5. Period after children require no support and before retirement.

6. Period during retirement.

For each of the above periods applicable to you, we suggest that you estimate total income, total committed expenditures, and major discretionary expenditures. In the next, immediate period, develop detailed year-by-year plans as discussed for Bill and Sally Stoneston in the last chapter. Obviously, Bill and Sally are planning for the period before children are in college and for the period after two of their children will require little or no support. Bill is also contemplating partial retirement, and this is a major event which requires some financial planning.

Learn by Doing

Despite the plethora of academic treatises and financial advisors, the statistics on the extent of personal financial planning present a rather dismal record. We firmly believe that there is really no substitute for involvement in the personal financial planning process. *You* have to formulate your objectives; *you* have to assess your earnings capacity, your spending habits, and your major life events. You may need assistance in getting information on investment opportunities, tax planning, estate planning, and so forth. However, remember the best advice generally follows the right questions. You have to be involved to formulate the right questions. So if you have not tried to complete the worksheets we discussed in Chapters

1 and 2, get yourself in gear and get going. Remember that while you are waiting, others are creating.

Profiles of Financial Fiction

The profiles we are about to present are fictitious people whose resemblance to real people is not so much coincidental as it is disguised. The profiles present the financial situation of people ranging in age from 25 to 68, in all periods of life—unmarried to married with grown children, and in different financial circumstances. The profiles are designed so that you can identify with one or more of the people and can say "I have that problem, too." You can then be motivated to examine the opportunities available and the recommendations suggested in later chapters.

Before presenting each of the 15 profiles in detail, we have prepared a summary (*see* Table 3–2) of the people to acquaint you with their financial situation.

Linda Hanson, Entrepreneur

Linda Hanson is a 25-year-old owner and manager of a fast-growing, fashion-conscious apparel shop for women with youthful tastes. Having started in the business 7 years ago, she has worked hard to develop the business, often putting in "90-hour" weeks. When she does have time to play, she plays hard, often taking spur-of-the-moment vacations to far-away places. But with her $25,000 income from her shop and no family responsibilities, Linda is capable of spending hard.

Her shop is situated in the heart of the district adjacent to a large university. She has developed a reputation for quality clothing and abilities to predict the changing consumer tastes and to buy appropriately. In recent years she has been able to earn in excess of her salary and her equity in the shop has grown to $20,000.

She is firmly convinced that she can successfully manage the shop up to a sales level of $400,000 from its current volume of $280,000. Such a volume should allow her to enjoy an annual salary of $35,000, with earnings after salary of $5,000–10,000 per year. Her goal in the next five years is to increase the volume of her present store, train another young woman to manage it, and open an adjacent store selling soaps, fragrances, and cosmetics.

TABLE 3-2
SUMMARY OF PROFILES

	Age	Occupation	Marital Status	Income	Committed Expenses	Net Worth	Insurance Coverage
Linda Hanson	25	Owner of women's apparel shop	Single	$25,000 *	$23,000	$42,500	None
Bob and Joanna Hart	26 25	Marketing Consultant Systems Analyst	Married, no children	31,500 *	18,400	27,000	$25,000 17,000
Ken and Carole Cast	28 26	Professor	Married, son—1½	26,000 *	18,000	47,000	60,000
John and Jane Herman	32 31	Marketing Exec.	Married, Daughter—10 Son—8	30,000 *	25,800	60,000	50,000
Bart and Dorothy Boney	36 35	Orthopedic Surg.	Married, Daughters—10, 7 Sons—5, 1	40,000 *	29,500	57,200	140,000
Dick and Ellen Peterson	37 35	Aerospace Engin. Part-time Acct.	Married, Daughter—16 Sons—11, 8	20,000 * 5,000 *	15,000	40,700	45,000
Gordon and Hortense Piet	42 40	M.D.—Internist	Married, Sons—11, 6 Daughter—8	48,000 *	45,000	68,000	150,000

43

TABLE 3-2—Continued
SUMMARY OF PROFILES

	Age	Occupation	Marital Status	Income	Committed Expenses	Net Worth	Insurance Coverage
Robin and Ann Enderson	42 43	Gov't. Admin. Bank Teller	Married, Sons—17, 16	26,000 * 7,000 *	22,700	76,000	10,000
Paige Wynn	48	Part-time Trustee	Divorced, custody of daughters—18, 15 Son—8	30,000 *	28,000	261,000	100,000
Pete and Mary Jones	55 51	Controls construction corp.	Married, 2 married children	35,000 *	35,000	500,000	50,000
Frank and Sue Richards	59 59	M.D.—Obstetrician	Married, 2 married children	21,000 *	29,000	250,000	30,000
Jack and Elaine Martin	52 50	V.P. of Large Corp.	Married, 3 married children	90,000 *	80,000	615,000	200,000
Ivy Smith	60	Investor	Widow	23,000	16,000	210,000	5,000
Joe and Peggy Lund	68 64	Retired—Investor	Married, 3 adult children	43,000	35,000	500,000	33,000

* From sources other than capital assets—salary, self-employment income, etc.

44

While Linda's income prospects are good, her committed expenses are high as well. She spends about $23,000, including taxes, as follows:

- $350 per month for a somewhat luxurious two-bedroom apartment which she uses for entertaining and a place to relax. She also spends about $2,500 a year on furnishings for the apartment—including antiques and paintings—which she estimates are worth approximately $20,000.
- $1,500 a year for clothes.
- $1,500 for food—with a lot of dining out and expensive meals at home. This doesn't include her many business lunches and dinners.
- $500 for use of a private tennis club near her apartment.
- $7,500 for income taxes.
- $3,000 for vacations. Because of the nature of her business and her exhaustive work schedule, she takes expensive spur-of-the-moment vacations. In January, for example, right after the Christmas rush, she went to Mexico for 5 days.
- $2,500 for transportation and miscellaneous expenditures. She leases an imported sports car for which she is paying $150 per month.

Linda has no insurance program. Her net worth, other than her furnishings of $20,000, includes approximately $1,000 of marketable securities, $1,500 in a passbook savings account in a commercial bank, and her equity in the shop.

The Hustling Harts

Bob and Joanna Hart, 26 and 25, are a hard-working, success-seeking, ambitious, college-educated couple whose achievement-oriented values have been shaped by blue-collar parents. Unlike their parents, however, they have also been influenced by the zero-population movement and have agreed to wait to have children for a few years.

Joanna majored in computer sciences in an undergraduate program and has worked for four years as a systems analyst-programmer in the computer center of a major metropolitan bank. In the last year, she was promoted to a supervisory position in the center and is regarded as one of the most promising managers at her level. She is earning $17,000 a year. She believes she will rise to executive ranks in the bank but is concerned with her lack of managerial education. She believes her career chances would be enhanced by an MBA degree. With her technical background, supervisory experience, and management education, she would be in a fine career position.

Bob also is ambitious and is pursuing his MBA degree at night to further his potential as a corporate executive. He currently is a marketing consultant for a specialty steel manufacturer and earns $14,500 at his present job. He is not sure about staying with his present employer and appears to be interested in becoming an operating executive in a smaller company. His technical skills are not as marketable as Joanna's—he majored in drama in undergraduate school.

The Hart's committed expenses of $18,400 include:

Housing		
Mortgage and real estate taxes	$2,800	
Insurance	150	
Remodeling	1,200	
Utilities	350	$4,500
Auto expenses	900	
Food	1,900	
Clothing	1,700	
Recreation and entertainment	700	
Life insurance	500	
Medical and dental	300	
Miscellaneous	500	
Income taxes and FICA	7,400	
	$18,400	

Last year other expenditures included:

New automobile	$2,800
Furniture	2,700
Vacations	800
Stereo	400
Gifts and contributions	1,200
Education	1,000
	$8,900

Their insurance program includes a $25,000 whole-life policy on Bob; Joanna is covered by a group policy at the bank which is tied to the amount of her salary—about $17,000. The prospects for increased income for the Harts are good. Both are interested in getting additional education to enhance their careers. They do not plan to have children for another five years and, thus, have the possibility of increasing their net worth.

Their current net worth is about $27,000 with approximately $16,700 represented by equity in the house ($8,000) and furnishings for the house

($8,700). They have two cars, required for commuting purposes, worth a total of $3,000; they own $5,000 of a blue-chip security; they have $1,500 in a savings account; and $800 is the cash surrender value on Bob's life insurance policy.

Although their primary goals in the next few years are related to education and career development, they also have a few other plans:

- A trip to Japan estimated to cost $3,000.
- A reflex lens camera and accessories estimated to cost about $1,000.

The Packing Professor

Ken and Carole Cast are married with a one-and-a-half-year-old son. Ken is a 28-year-old Ph.D. who is an assistant professor in a major business school on the West Coast. Their lifestyle includes a lot of outdoor activities that do not demand a lot of monetary expenditures to provide satisfaction. Typically, their weekends are spent in cross-country skiing or hiking, and summers include an extended number of backpack trips into the mountain ranges that are close to the metropolitan area in which they live.

Ken's income from the university is about $16,000; in addition, he earns about $10,000 from a variety of consulting assignments and executive development programs which Ken's specialty in finance and marketing enable him to perform. Ken's income prospects are somewhat tied to the university, and the expectations are that the increases will be related to cost of living adjustments. He is currently writing a book with one of his colleagues, and perhaps the book will generate some additional income.

Because Ken and Carole have a somewhat modest lifestyle without lavish entertainment and expensive vacations, they have been able to keep their committed expenses to about $18,000, which include:

Housing	$5,000
Auto expenses	900
Food	2,400
Clothing	1,500
Recreation and entertainment	300
Life insurance	300
Medical and dental	500
Gifts, contributions, etc.	1,100
Income taxes	6,000
	$18,000

The Cast's net worth is approximately $47,000, which consists of: $9,000 equity in their house; $7,000 in furnishings; $5,000 in two cars— an old convertible and a late model Volvo station wagon; $10,000 in widely-traded securities; $10,000 in a savings account in a savings and loan association; $6,000 in death benefits in a retirement program available to university professors. The program includes a matching contribution of approximately $1,200 per year from the university, with another $1,200 being a salary deduction.

The Cast's insurance program includes a $10,000 whole-life policy on Ken and $50,000 of group term coverage provided through the university. Although the Casts do not have many specific objectives other than exploring new trails in the mountains and developing professionally, they have discussed the possibility of having another child soon and of purchasing additional furniture for their house.

The Young Executive

See John run. See him run fast. See his wife Jane. Not a primary school reader but the model of a corporate comer. John Herman is a 32-year-old marketing executive with a freight forwarding company. An economics undergraduate degree coupled with an MBA has enabled John to rise rapidly in the company. He expects to receive three significant raises in his rise to the top management of the company. His wife, Jane, is 31 years old, a member of Junior League, and active in several other civic organizations. The Hermans have two children—a girl aged 10 and a boy aged 8.

John's current salary is $30,000, and he expects his raises to increase his salary to $45,000 (in current dollars) by the time he reaches 45. He also expects annual raises approximately equal to increases in the cost of living. The Herman's basic committed expenses are approximately $26,000 and include:

Housing (mortgage payments, property taxes, fuel and utilities)	$ 7,200
Transportation	1,600
Food	2,500
Clothing	2,500
Entertainment (including club dues)	2,000
Medical and dental	800
Contributions	1,200
Life insurance	1,000
Income taxes and FICA	7,000
	$25,800

In addition, the Hermans regularly take a winter ski vacation ($2,000) and are purchasing a summer home with monthly payments (including taxes and insurance) of $300 per month ($3,600). Furnishings for both homes require about $3,000 each year.

The Herman's net worth is approximately $60,000: $20,000 equity in a $60,000 home; $6,000 equity in a recently purchased $40,000 summer beach property; $20,000 in furnishings for the beach home and primary residence. John also has $10,500 in a company-sponsored stock program; $2,000 in a regular savings account in a commercial bank, and $1,500 cash surrender value in life insurance. John has a $50,000 whole life insurance policy on his life.

The Herman's goals include the following:

- Put both the children through 4 years of college.
- Retire at age 55, with an annual income of $21,000.
- Sell their personal residence after retirement and move to their beach property.

The Sailing Surgeon

Bart Boney, orthopedic surgeon, 36, avid sailor and skier, is a man on the move in many ways. His wife, Dorothy, 35, is a trim mother of four active children—two daughters, 10 and 7, and two sons, 5 and 1. Dr. Bart is one of four orthopedic surgeons in an incorporated professional practice and currently derives a salary of $40,000 from the practice.

Because of the Boney's love of sailing and other water sports, they recently moved to a run-down lakefront home which they purchased for $60,000 but which required over $30,000 to remodel. To finance the purchase of the house and property, Bart secured a $40,000 long-term mortgage and a 5-year note for $24,000. Therefore, one of the Boneys' short-term financial goals is to pay off the note. The annual payment on the note is about $5,800. In addition, they would like to make some landscaping improvements to the house, build a new dock, and make additional purchases for furnishings. They estimate that they would like to spend $10,000–15,000 per year during the next three years for these desires in addition to the payments on the note.

Dr. Boney's income prospects appear rather good since orthopedic surgeons are in great demand in his part of the country, where outdoor recreational opportunities result in a significant number of injuries over and above the normal injuries requiring orthopedic surgery. The Boney's basic committed expenses are about $29,500 and include:

Housing (mortage, property taxes, fuel, utilities)	$ 7,000
Transportation	2,200
Food	3,000
Clothing	4,000
Education (including private Catholic schools for the older children)	900
Recreation and entertainment	1,500
Gifts and contributions	1,400
Medical and dental	1,200
Insurance	800
Federal income taxes	7,500
	$29,500

The Boney's net worth is approximately $57,200. The major asset of course is the remodeled lakefront home with a market value of approximately $90,000, of which $26,000 represents the Boneys' equity. They have $12,000 in furnishings and another $900 equity in automobiles, which include a brand new Toyota and an older model station wagon. The remainder of the net worth is represented by $10,000 in regular savings accounts; $2,300 equity in some raw land which Dr. Boney purchased years ago; $800 cash surrender value of life insurance; $1,400 in silver coins. Dr. Boney also has a $3,800 interest in the profit-sharing and retirement program of the surgical practice. Dr. Boney currently has $140,000 of life insurance, of which only $10,000 is whole life. In addition, his beneficiary would receive an additional $80,000 if he dies of accidental causes.

In addition, the Boneys plan to repay the note and make additional improvements to their home. They plan to provide 4 years of college education for each of the children. Given Dr. Boney's hectic pace, more recently he has given some consideration as to how his family might live if he were to die. He feels that they would need approximately $20,000 a year to continue in a style somewhat related to their current standard of living.

The Anxious Aerospace Engineer

Dick Peterson is a 37-year-old aerospace engineer with three children—ages 16, 11, and 8. One of Dick's concerns is that he does not believe that his income prospects are very great in the topsy-turvy aerospace industry. He is also worried about job security. However, because he enjoys the life style that is available in the Pacific Northwest, he is not interested in seeking employment outside the region. Preferably, he would like to find employment in a company that would utilize his engineering knowledge and his interest in the outdoors.

Dick is currently earning $20,000, and his wife, who works part time, earns $5,000. The Petersons' net worth is $40,700, represented by $18,000 equity in the house; $7,400 in furniture and personal property; and $3,300 in the market value of two automobiles. In addition, they have a $6,900 equity in some land in the nearby mountains; $4,700 in regular savings accounts; and 100 shares in a speculative over-the-counter security with a current market value of $400.

The Petersons have been able to keep their committed expenses, including income and social security taxes, at about the $15,000 level. Their life insurance consists of $35,000 in a group insurance policy with Dick's employer and $10,000 of whole life insurance. Dick is not interested in acquiring any more insurance.

The Petersons' financial goals are not too specific, except that Dick is interested in finding employment that is a little more stable and perhaps combines his interest in the outdoors with his engineering skills. They are interested in educating their children but believe that their children can help defray most of their educational costs by working and saving before and during college. They would like to build a chalet on the land that they have in the mountains, which would allow them to spend more time pursuing their outdoor way of life.

Conspicuous Consumption

Dr. Gordon Piet, 42, is fortunate because his practice income as an internist is higher than the average—about $48,000 before income taxes. Unfortunately, he splurges so much that most of his monthly income is needed to pay loans. Trying to please his wife and children, Dr. Piet has made massive expenditures for a large home, expensive vacations, luxurious furnishings, and lavish parties. In doing so, he has accumulated a staggering amount of commitments which drain away $3,750 per month, leaving only $250 for living expenses for a family of five—his wife and 3 children, ages 11, 8, and 6.

Dr. Piet came from a poor family and worked his way through medical school. He has apparently adopted the attitude that he can spend freely because he is making a lot of money and is going to make a lot more.

To begin with, he purchased a $82,000 residence near his country club with mortgage payments and related insurance and property tax expenditures amounting to $750 per month or $9,000 per year. He pays for income tax payments due, home furnishings, vacations, and country club living by taking out loans. He currently has several loans amounting to $35,000 and is supposed to be paying them off at the rate of $1,100 a month. Actually, he is paying only the interest on some loans. His insurance program is mostly expensive permanent insurance for which it pays a monthly premium of $250, or $3,000 per year for $150,000 of coverage. In addition, he is making payments of $400 per month on installment loans on medical equipment and lease payments on late model large automobiles. Income tax payments of $1,200 per month and church contribution of $50 per month bring the total to the staggering amount $3,750 or $45,000 per year!

Unfortunately many of his past and present expenditures have not resulted in any marketable or income-producing assets. The Piets' net worth is largely related to personal assets—$20,000 equity in the house and $30,000 furnishings. The only other assets the Piets have are $8,000 of over-the-counter "promising" securities and $10,000 cash value of life insurance. Dr. Piet is in good health and, oddly enough, in good spirits. Income prospects are bright.

Dreams of Your Own Business

Forty-two-year-old Robin Enderson, married with two boys ages 17 and 16, is contemplating starting his own business and leaving a position as an administrator in a state agency where he has spent some 18 years. His income currently is $26,000, and his wife, Ann, earns approximately $7,000 from her job in a local bank. Their net worth includes $50,000 equity in a house with a market value of $70,000; a piece of raw land worth approximately $25,000; and $1,000 worth of savings. Mrs. Enderson expects a share in an inheritance of $50,000 of property from her parents, but she feels the inheritance may be a long way off since her parents are still in good health.

When he reaches 50, Robin will be entitled to a pension of approximately $10,000 a year for the rest of his life. However, if he leaves before age 50, his benefits will be very little. The Endersons' committed expenses are running approximately $22,700. Mr. Enderson has a $10,000 whole life insurance policy on his life.

Last spring, Robin decided he would like to chuck his career as an administrator and start his own business. He thinks he has reached the top of the agency career ladder and no longer finds his job a challenge. He has done considerable thinking about his financial situation. He knows that his expenses will continue to run at the current level, if not higher, for a number of years. The boys will soon start college. He could reduce his expenses by buying a smaller house or renting, but they have lived in the home for 11 years. It represents the place where they raised the boys and is in a comfortable suburb near Robin's work.

He frequently thinks of the challenge of starting and succeeding at something new, but he knows the risks of starting a small business, the responsibilities for the boys' education, and the pains of moving.

Divorce—Financial Opportunities and Problems

Paige Wynn is an energetic, financially astute divorcee with three children —two girls, 18 and 15, and a son 8. Paige, 48, was recently divorced and received a substantial settlement from her successful lawyer husband. In the divorce settlement, she received a large, beautifully landscaped residence with a fair market value of $96,000; $35,000 in savings accounts in savings and loan associations, earning 5½%; $80,000 in marketable securities with a yield of about 2 percent; a late model station wagon worth $5,000; and household furnishings worth about $45,000. Paige also receives $600 per month ($200 per child) for the children's support, which will continue until age 19 for each child. In addition, she receives $1,500 a month in alimony which will continue until her death or until she remarries.

Paige received her degree in economics, and her father was the founder and chairman of a successful manufacturing business. Her father created a substantial living trust for which she is the trustee. As trustee, she receives $400 a month—the amount the bank said it would charge for such a service. Her father also pays the premiums on a $100,000 life insurance policy on her life. Educational trust funds have also been set up by her former husband, and these funds will be used for college financing.

Paige's income prospects are not too bright since she does not wish to work while the two youngest children are still at home. In addition, she has not worked professionally for some time, and the prospects of finding challenging work are not very encouraging.

Her committed expenses are about $28,000 and consist of:

Housing-related expenses	
Property taxes	$ 3,000
Part-time housekeeper	1,500
Gardener	1,200
Utilities and fuel	1,600
Insurance	2,500
Automobile expenses	1,300
Food	2,400
Clothing	3,000
Education and recreation	1,900
Medical and dental	2,800
Gifts and contributions	900
Federal income taxes	7,500
Miscellaneous	400
	$28,000

Her goals include the raising of the children and securing a college education for each of her children. She is also interested in obtaining more return from her investments since she is concerned about rising expenses, with a somewhat fixed income from her trustee's duties and alimony, and the loss of child care payments as the children reach 19.

The All-American Businessman

Pete Jones grew up in the Golden Era of big bands in the late 30s and early 40s. He and his girlfriend were avid fans of Glenn Miller at a time when the Dodgers played in Ebbets Field, the Giants in the Polo Grounds, and the Yankees in Yankee Stadium.

Pete put in World War II in the Navy Seabees, returned home to marry his high school sweetheart, and start his career. He used his construction experience from the Navy to start a small contracting business, which has prospered and expanded over the years.

We find Pete now at the age of 55 with two married children in their twenties, for whom he has no financial obligations.

Pete now has a net worth of about $500,000, his assets being approximately as follows:

Controlling 51% interest in construction corporation	$225,000
Cash	25,000
Listed stocks and bonds	100,000
Rental real estate	50,000
Life insurance (face value)	50,000
Home and furnishings	50,000
	$500,000

Pete has a business associate who has owned 35 percent of the construction corporation for many years. About 15 years ago, Pete gave his children 14 percent of the construction corporation stock. Of a total insurance of $50,000 on Pete's life, $30,000 is payable to his wife Mary and $20,000 to his children.

Pete now has an income of about $45,000 a year, including a salary of $35,000 from the construction corporation, about $5,000 in dividend and interest income from his securities, and $5,000 rental income. His and Mary's committed expenses run about $35,000 a year, including $12,000 income taxes, so they have about $10,000 available for discretionary expenditures.

Pete's son and son-in-law are both well-established key members of his business, and he is very interested in transferring a larger interest in the business to his children. He is interested in the possibility of making gifts, both to accomplish this transfer to help his children somewhat financially and to reduce the impact of estate taxes in the event of his death. His primary concern, however, is to retain control over the business and assure that he and his wife will be adequately provided for.

The Old Time Baby Doctor

Dr. Frank Richards is an obstetrician practicing as an individual. He is 59 years of age and because he has unfortunately suffered two heart attacks, he is unable to obtain additional insurance. His wife, Sue, is about the same age and in good health. Frank and Sue have two married children—a son who is trained in obstetrics and is just completing his tour of duty in the armed services, and a daughter. The son and daughter each have two children. Frank and Sue have no financial responsibility to either of their children.

Frank and Sue have assets of about $250,000, including the following:

Cash	$ 8,000
Marketable securities	30,000
Practice accounts receivable	20,000
Rental real estate	130,000
Life insurance on Frank (face value)	30,000
Home	26,000
Personal effects	6,000
	$250,000

Frank's life insurance has a present cash value of about $10,000.

Frank and Sue have a current income of $29,000 a year, including about $21,000 from his practice, $7,000 from the rental property, and $1,000 dividends and interest on the securities. Their committed expenses, including $5,000 income taxes, are just about equal to their $29,000 income, so they have little if any in the way of discretionary expenditures. Frank figures that Sue's financial needs after his death would require an income of about $12,000 a year. He assumes that because of his physical condition, he will predecease Sue, and his interests are therefore to provide this $12,000 a year to his wife, and save estate taxes if that is feasible.

Executive Suite

Jack Martin has spent all of his adult life as an employee of Supreme Machine Tool Corporation, a large company whose stock is listed on the New York Stock Exchange. At the age of 52, he is now a Vice President of the company, with an annual salary of $90,000 a year. He and his wife, Elaine, have three children, all of whom are in their twenties and married, and five grandchildren. Jack and Elaine have no financial responsibilities toward their children. They do, however, give Jack's mother, Thelma, who is 77 years old, $3,000 a year to help with her support.

Jack and Elaine have a net worth of $615,000, composed of the following assets:

Checking account		$ 3,000
Savings accounts		40,000
Listed stocks and mutual funds		100,000
Unimproved investment real estate		25,000
Life insurance (permanent)		50,000
Supreme stock acquired by exercise of options	$200,000	
Less bank loan	100,000	
Net		100,000
Options for 2,000 shares of Supreme stock at $19.00 per share, present market value $25.00 per share		12,000
Present value of pension plan account		60,000
Deferred compensation $150,000 payable over ten years following death, retirement, or termination of employment (discounted value)		105,000
Home	$175,000	
Less mortgage	60,000	
		115,000
Automobiles and other personal property		5,000
		$615,000

In addition to these assets, Jack has group insurance through Supreme totaling $200,000, composed of $150,000 group life insurance and $50,-000 travel accident insurance.

Jack and Elaine have income of $102,000 a year, made up of his

$90,000 salary plus $12,000 of dividends and interest from bank accounts and securities. Their committed expenses, including $40,000 income tax, are about $80,000 a year, so they have about $22,000 a year of discretionary expenditures. Jack does not really expect to progress further in the corporate hierarchy, but does expect slight increases in salary— more or less cost of living increases, until his retirement.

Jack's first goal is to be sure he takes care of himself and his wife financially. After that, he is thinking of assuring some liquidity for his estate in the event of his death. Finally, if these two goals can be accomplished, he would be interested in doing something for his children and possibly grandchildren.

The Well-Off Widow

Ivy Smith is a widow aged 60 with three married children and several grandchildren. She has no financial responsibility for any of her children.

Ivy has assets of $210,000, detailed as follows:

Savings accounts	$ 65,000
Listed securities	45,000
Rental real estate	65,000
Life insurance (face value)	5,000
Home	25,000
Personal effects	5,000
	$210,000

Ivy and her late husband, John, were long time residents of a community property estate. When John died last year, he left his community one-half of the rental real estate in a trust, with the income to go to Ivy during her lifetime, and the property to go to their three children on her death. She therefore has $23,000 of current income, made up of $18,600 rental income, one-half of which comes from the trust, $1,500 dividends, and $2,900 interest on savings accounts. Her committed expenses, including $5,000 income taxes, are about $16,000 a year, so she has about $7,000 a year discretionary expenditures.

Ivy's objectives are to be able to handle any prolonged illness, to reduce death taxes to the extent possible, and to do something for her children and grandchildren.

The Retired Executive

Joe and Peggy Lund are 68 and 64 years of age, respectively. They have three grown children, two of whom are married, and three grandchildren 1–7 years of age. Joe and Peggy have no financial responsibility for any of their children. Joe retired at the age of 60 and has been drawing a pension of $24,000 a year, which is payable to him for life. Joe and Peggy are getting Social Security benefits of about $4,000 a year, and dividends and interest of $15,000 a year, so they have total income of $43,000. Their committed expenses, including $10,000 income taxes, are about $35,000 a year, so they have $8,000 available for discretionary expenditures.

Joe and Peggy have accumulated assets of about $500,000, including the following:

Checking account		$ 5,000
Savings accounts		40,000
Listed securities		245,000
Special situation securities		45,000
Unimproved investment real estate		50,000
Self-employed retirement plan		25,000
Home	$85,000	
Less mortgage	25,000	60,000
Summer home		30,000
		$500,000

Peggy was self-employed for some years and built up the self-employed retirement plan to the amount of $25,000. She plans to start drawing on this when she is 70, when presumably she and Joe might be in a lower income tax bracket. In addition to the assets listed above, Joe has $33,000 of insurance on his life, which is pretty well paid up.

Joe's objectives are first to take care of his wife and himself. He is particularly concerned about the possibility of his dying and his $24,000 a year pension disappearing with him. His second objective is to reduce death taxes and finally, if there is anything left over, to help his children and grandchildren.

INVESTMENT OPPORTUNITIES

Now that we have talked about gathering some information about financial planning, and now that you are up to your ears in financial records and worksheets, we would like you to think about working the plan that you have formulated for the next period of your life.

As was suggested in Chapter 1, personal financial planning may be defined as the *accumulation* and *utilization* of financial resources to obtain the maximum utility for the individual and the family during the lifetime of the planner, and the effective *distribution* of resources after death.

As this definition suggests, financial planning has both long-term and short-term objectives. Short-term objectives for most people relate to financial requirements such as buying a home, financing childrens' education, purchasing a second home, and saving for extended travel. But the long term has to be considered as well in order to provide for the needs of your family if and when the planner becomes disabled, retires, or dies. One of the real challenges in personal financial planning is to mesh both short- and long-term objectives. You must not neglect one for the other; you must actively plan for both the present and the future.

Many of you have started on your investment program.

In its broadest sense the word "investing" includes every way in which you store up assets for future years. Many of you have an investment in your social security coverage or in a retirement program your employer makes available to you, or in a self employment retirement trust. Your savings account is a form of investment; you are very likely to have an investment in the form of your life insurance; and your house is an investment. All these forms of investment have a significant bearing on the program in a narrower sense—security holdings, mutual funds, investment partnerships, etc. In addition the factors of age, family responsibilities, income expectations, and income and estate taxes also have a bearing on your personal financial planning and investment program.

Because of these many factors, it is hard to generalize about the best set of investment objectives. However, most investment counselors would agree that there are several "firsts" involved in formulating and implementing an investment plan.

Financial Security—The Four Firsts

A definition of financial security would include these four elements: (1) an annual income, usually secured by a job; (2) a place to live; (3) a savings account—a reserve fund which can be used in case of emergency; and (4) life insurance—a source of future income if the planner should die.

The first two, an annual income and a place to live, have far-reaching implications on long-term financial planning. Income obviously is a big factor in providing sufficient resources for accumulating assets and establishing a standard of living. However, the larger the income does not necessarily mean the larger the resources accumulated or the estate developed. Unfortunately, as we suggested before, an income level sets in motion complicated problems of living up to ones career or income position. Many people of significant income have committed expenses sometimes as great if not more than their income, and they never seem to accumulate a significant net worth— like Piet and his conspicuous consumption.

Sometimes income is not the most important aspect of one's life. There is a significant trade-off between working and leisure time. With increasing frequency, particularly in mid-career, executives are "dropping out" of large organizations, primarily because they feel that they have insufficient time to spend with their family or to enjoy aspects of life which are non-job related. Some of these trade-offs are examined more fully in the last section of this book when we discuss the integration of life planning and financial planning.

A house is also something that we typically associate with security, and unfortunately it sometimes prevents the accumulation of financial resources which provide other satisfactions to the individual. For example, take the successful young businessman—a guy, maybe 30 years old with an income in excess of $30,000, and with every reason to believe that his income will go much higher in the future. He buys a $100,000 home, primarily because he says he "needs" to take care of the needs of his family, wife, and three children. The house obviously is large and, although he can afford the initial purchase price, the question really is, can he afford to maintain the standard of living which this house requires? The house is typically in a section of town where neighbours put pressure on him to spend for social reasons. His wife may need to hire domestic help; they probably will have to entertain, and to entertain in a fairly luxurious style; they will require expensive landscaping and furnishings within the house. The satisfaction of all these tastes will soon appear to be necessities, and he will work harder and earn more money to meet them. However, will he accumulate any financial resources?

The third element, a savings account, presents less of a problem as to conflict between short- and long-term objectives. Investment planning suggests that you not invest any money which you might need on short notice in other kinds of investments except a savings account. You should have sufficient reserves—money in the bank or its equivalent—before you start your investment program. The amount of savings depends on what your needs are likely to be. Some suggest, as a rule of thumb, an amount equal to 6 months salary. This amount obviously should be adjusted to fit your individual needs for ready cash. You might need more than the suggested figure, or less. In the chapter on savings accounts and short-term money market investments, a more precise way is suggested for looking at the amount of ready cash necessary—cash forecasting.

The fourth element is life insurance protection for one's family in the event of death of the family income earner. The question of what is adequate insurance, or how much insurance should be carried before starting an investment program, is difficult to answer. The key to determining how much insurance is necessary depends on the individual involved and the family involved, and each situation must be considered separately. The next chapter deals with some basic facts about life insurance with which everyone should be familiar, and suggests an analytical process which can be used to determine how much and what kind of protection is needed at various stages of a lifetime.

In the discussion of how much life insurance one should have, the importance of social security is stressed as death insurance, as protection against complete disability, and as a minimum retirement income. Recent legislation has increased the value of social security, and social security benefits should be analyzed in a discussion of an individual's insurance or retirement program.

Phases of an Investment Lifetime

As was suggested in Chapter 3, financial planning should be related to several time periods during a lifetime. These periods include: the period before marriage; the period after marriage but before children are born; the period before children are in school; the period before children are in college; the period after the children require no financial support; and retirement.

Obviously no individual or family is likely to fit precisely into a specific pattern; in fact standard prescriptions are almost impossible at any stage because of the large number of variable factors, including health, stability of employment, prospects of increased income, or inheritance. Keeping in mind, therefore, that circumstances alter many cases, the following suggestions are only a rough guideline to the considerations pertinent at various stages for people who wish to develop their own financial plan and who are interested in the various investment alternatives best for the particular periods during his lifetime.

Period Before Marriage

Broadly, this is the period from the first paycheck to the time when family responsibilities and expenses begin to mount. This is a period of little or no financial responsibilities except your own financial plan; there is little need for insurance for the protection of other people.

In today's environment many young people start at substantial salaries, and if they keep their committed costs at a relatively low level, they will be able to accumulate a significant amount for an investment program of a long-term nature. You can probably take higher risks in investment programs during this period because if losses occur you will have time to make them up. Time is obviously on your side. In addition, even if the amount that you save to invest is small, the potential growth of capital over a long period—40 to 50 years—is substantial because of the compounding power. At this stage an investment program should have long-term growth objectives because income from investments is usually not a factor during this period.

Period Before Children

As some of the profiles showed, it is not unusual that many young married couples decide not to have children for some period of time. With both the man and the woman working, the opportunity is great to have substantial com-

bined income. Again, the opportunity for building a significant net worth is available before the responsibilities of
children come along. Insurance is still not a big factor because there still is not a heavy need for protection of other
people, particularly if both people are working and the
survivor is able to continue working after the death of the
spouse.

If the couple keeps their committed expenses to a reasonable level, a significant amount may be available for
an investment program. Of course, there is tremendous
pressure to spend in the early years of marriage—to buy a
house or rent a nice apartment, to provide furnishings, to
have two cars (particularly if both are working), and to
purchase "convenience" appliances because of the limited
amount of time available for housework. Careful budgeting
should be started during this period in order to make sure
that some amount is available for investment during this
period.

Period Before Children Are in College

From the time parenthood becomes self-evident to the
time the youngest are self supporting is a period when certain financial considerations are very important. Protection
of the widow and children in case the husband should die
becomes the first and most compelling aspect of financial
planning and one that increases with the size of the family.
Therefore, insurance needs should be analyzed carefully
during this period to determine how long insurance will be
needed and what is the most economical way of obtaining it.
It is also a time for living, a time when spending money
may be the best way to use it. There is obviously a need for
additional clothing, food, and housing, and the basic committed expenses increase significantly. There is the need for
travel and vacations, and significant educational expenditures may be made if private schools or special educational
programs are elected.

It is a period when income may increase significantly,

and tax planning becomes a critical aspect of the financial planning process. It is also a time after the children get into elementary school when the spouse of the primary earner can think about doing something other than housework. This may mean supplemental income for the family, or significant educational expenditures for the spouse to prepare for a career of some significance.

As the children reach junior high school age, there should be some consideration as to how college expenses are going to be financed. There are a variety of ways this can be done, some of which have tax advantages. No matter how you finance these expenses, there will be a significant amount of money required as the children begin to approach college age. College costs have roughly doubled in the past 15 years, and what they will be when your children are ready to enter college, is anybody's guess, but they probably will be higher.

Period After the Children Have Completed Their Education and No Longer Require Support

The period folowing the completion of the children's education is usually a period when the earning power of the planner is likely to be at its highest. For example, a recent American Dental Association survey showed that dentists earn their highest income between ages 45 and 49; American Bar Association figures indicate that an attorney's peak earnings usually occur at about the same time. But the figures also show that after the earnings peak is reached, earnings either stay relatively stable or begin to decline somewhat. So this is the period when the preparation for a satisfactory retirement income ought to be made. Since the children have grown and no longer require financial support, committed expenses should decline, and significant amounts should be generated for investment in income-producing assets.

Needs for life insurance protection should be reviewed again, taking into consideration all the available resources the family may now possess. With the children grown and financially independent, less insurance may be required. Funds saved by reducing or eliminating unnecessary payments for insurance premiums can be used to help build the retirement account more rapidly. This is a period when estate planning should be undertaken, since one has to face up to the eventuality of dying.

Investment policy can still be aimed at building up capital, but risk is a much more important factor than in the earlier years. Time is no longer running strongly in the planner's favor. Counseling is essential at this point to determine the extent of possible estate problems as related to the planner's asset picture.

Retirement

A comfortable income during retirement is, of course, the primary goal of much financial planning and investment decision making. Financial independence in the retirement period results from planning and self-discipline in the periods previously discussed. For most people it requires an early start and an understanding of the kinds of investments most suitable at different stages, an intelligent compromise between too much and too little protection for dependents, and a great deal of determination.

Investment Alternatives

An investment program has to be related to the major periods during a planner's lifetime. Unfortunately, investment literature has little in the way of prescription for individuals as to how to allocate portions of their non-consumed wealth to specific investment opportunities within various asset categories. Recently, one author tried to analyze how four investment attributes—liquidity, income, appreciation, and safety—change over a lifetime and how asset holdings might change. Exhibit 11 shows the suggested holdings of various assets at age levels which correspond somewhat to the lifetime periods discussed above.

Although Exhibit 11 provides some guidance as to how individuals should allocate investment funds, there is hardly the *right* way or the *only* way for each of us. There are a number of ways by which people can succeed in implementing a financial plan. The various investment opportunities of which you should be aware are presented in this section and Section III. Topics discussed include insurance, savings and short-term money market investments, securities—stocks and bonds, investment trusts and mutual funds, real estate, investment partnerships, pension and profit-sharing programs, owning your own business, and some less traditional types of investments including gold and silver. In Section IV, tax planning and estate planning are discussed. All these opportunities are presented, primarily because you should be aware of what each of these opportunities provide in the way of benefits and risks. It is not the intention to give detailed treatment of each investment opportunity primarily because several sources are already available on each type of investment. (In Chapter 17, we provide additional sources of information.) How-

		Asset		
	EXHIBIT 11			
	HOLDINGS AT VARIOUS AGE LEVELS			
Age	Savings Account, %	Corporate Bonds, %	Common Stock, %	Real Estate, %
25	45.0	29.0	19.0	7.0
35	19.0	16.5	32.0	32.5
45	13.0	17.0	33.0	37.0
55	20.0	23.0	28.0	29.0
65	34.0	42.0	14.0	10.0
Average Holding	26.2	25.5	25.2	23.1

SOURCE: Keith Smith, "The Major Asset Mix Problem of the Individual Investor," *Journal of Contemporary Business*, Winter 1974, p. 59.

ever, we do want to provide sufficient information to enable you to formulate your own investment objectives, to avoid some investment pitfalls, and to analyze and evaluate the quality of information and advice provided by financial and investment counselors.

In Section V, an investment program for each of the profiles introduced in Chapter 3 is suggested. You should then determine what investment alternatives are best for you to pursue, drawing upon some of the suggestions that we have made in the book and the profiles.

Chapter 4

LIFE INSURANCE

The only intelligent reason for purchasing insurance is that the purchaser faces an already existing risk of economic loss. The risk arises out of the possibility of premature death resulting in economic loss to those who may be dependent upon the insured for all or part of their monetary income. The one who faces this risk finds that the insurance mechanism may be used to transfer to the insured group through the insurer the risk of the loss arising from his death. In effect, the insurer says, "You pay me a reasonable fee (the premium), and I'll assume this risk; if your death occurs while the insurance is in force, I'll pay the stipulated amount (face value of the policy) to your beneficiaries so that they will not suffer the loss that would otherwise be theirs." [1]

This chapter examines some basic principles of life insurance, the types of policies, and ways to determine how much insurance you need.

Understanding Life Insurance

Although there are a wide variety of insurance policies, the underlying principles are basically simple. With a knowledge of how insurance works, you can readily assess the different policies and their use for protection and investment purposes.

---

[1] From *Life and Health Insurance Handbook,* 3d ed., Davis W. Gregg and Vane B. Lucas, eds. (Homewood, Ill.: Richard D. Irwin, Inc., 1973), p. 29.

Obviously the cost of pure protection increases as one grows older because the probability of death is greater. For instance, mortality tables show that out of every 100,000 people aged 40 at the start of this year, about 353 will not be living by December 31. Out of the same number of people in the 70-year bracket, 4,979 will not survive the year. In order to pay $1,000 each to the beneficiaries of those who die this year, $353,000 per 100,000 lives insured is required for the 40-year-old group—$4,979,-000 for the 70-year-olds. Ignoring the insurance companies' cost of doing business and simply dividing by the number insured, this works out to a rate of $3.53 per $1,000 of pure insurance for the 40-year-old group and $49.79 per $1,000 for the older group. Table 4-1 provides the cost of $1,000 pure insurance protection at various ages.

TABLE 4-1

Age	*Rate per $1,000*
20	$ 1.79
25	1.93
30	2.13
35	2.51
40	3.53
45	5.35
50	8.32
55	13.00
60	20.34
65	31.75
70	49.79
75	73.37

SOURCE: Data from Commissioners 1958 Standard Ordinary Mortality Table.

Because the death rate increases rapidly with age, the cost of annual insurance would necessarily rise steadily to the point where the premiums become prohibitive during the last several years of a normal lifetime. Therefore, insurance company mathematicians devised a way, many years ago, to make it possible for you to pay a level premium every year. The amount of the premium is established when the policy is purchased, and the premium remains constant thereafter. To accomplish this, the insurance companies have developed the concept of a "reserve fund," built up over the years by requiring you to pay more than the actual cost of insuring your life during the earlier years of your policy. In the process of making a level premium possible, the insurance companies have caused their policy holders to build up savings accounts within the insurance policy. This savings or reserve is the cash value stated in the policy.

Straight Life

To understand the effects and significance of the savings element, let us examine the way one policy works—the straight life policy, the best-known insurance policy (sometimes called ordinary or whole life insurance). The name means that the premium amount will remain level from the first year you pay until you die, cancel the policy, or attain the age of 100. The face amount, the amount the insurance company is obligated to pay your beneficiary, or you at age 100, remains the same.

After about two years of paying premiums on a straight life policy, your policy has a cash surrender value, which is the amount the company will pay to you if you cancel the policy. The cash surrender value exists because, as is explained earlier, the amount you are paying in the earlier years of the policy exceeds the costs of the company to insure your life. The remainder is held and managed for you by the insurance company to provide the reserve required by the terms of your policy. At the same time, the amount of pure insurance on your life is decreasing. The pure insurance on your life, at any time, is the difference between the face amount of your policy and the cash surrender value. Therefore, you should remember that straight life policies involve an increasing amount of investment or savings and a decreasing amount of term insurance. Figure 4-1 depicts this relationship.

By varying the relative proportions of pure insurance and the savings aspect, life insurance companies have been able to develop many different policies. All of them, other than term, represent some combination of increasing savings account and decreasing term insurance. Other things

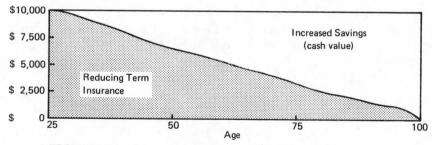

FIGURE 4-1   Insurance and Savings in Straight Life Insurance

being equal, the higher the premium, the faster the cash value will increase, and the faster the protection element will decrease.

Types of Policies

No matter how many combinations may exist, basically, there are four different types of policies: (1) term insurance; (2) straight life; (3) limited payment life; and (4) endowment.

Term

Term insurance is a lot like fire insurance. It protects you for a limited period of time. If, as you hope, you are still living at the end of that time, your protection ceases just as a fire insurance policy expires. If the policy is renewed or another term policy is issued to replace it, a higher premium is charged because the policy holder is older and his chances of dying are greater than in the previous period.

Term policies are ideal for providing a large amount of level protection for a limited time at the lowest premium outlay. Of course at the end of the period, when the insurance is discontinued, the policy has no cash value. Term insurance may be renewable or convertible or both. Renewable term policies include an option permitting the insured to renew the contract for specified number of periods—5, 10, 15, or 20 years—or to a certain age, such as 60, 65, or 70, without further medical examination. Term policies may allow you to convert the full amount of insurance to a Straight Life, Limited Payment Life, or Endowment policy without medical re-examination at any time while the insurance is in force.

Term policies have several advantages. As we mentioned, term is the lowest cost policy for pure protection. Normally, the needs of individuals change over a lifetime, and term insurance can be used to provide for temporary needs such as a college education or a period when the mortgage is being paid on the house. The flexibility of renewable term insurance and its low premium suggest its use in all well-planned life insurance programs.

Straight Life

The straight life policy is the most common type of insurance policy. The policy holder agrees to pay, during his lifetime, a specified premium each year for an amount (face value) which the company will pay at the death of the insured. The amount of the premium depends primarily on the age at which insurance is obtained and is based on the mortality experience of the age groups in which the insured belongs. Table 4-2 shows the premiums per $1,000 of insurance for 5-year renewable term and straight life policies published by a large company.

Since most straight life policies have a savings element or cash surrender value after the first few years, you can stop paying premiums at any time, take the cash value, and terminate the policy. Another alternative is to borrow from the cash surrender value in order to pay future premiums. Your insurance coverage, however, will be reduced by the amount you have borrowed until the loan is repaid. You may repay your policy loan at any time, but you are never required to do so. In recent years, the cost of borrowing against the cash value of insurance policies has been substantially lower than the cost of borrowing at a bank—the cost being between 4.6% and 6%.

Another alternative to the policyholder is to convert the contract to paid up straight life insurance for an amount less than the original face amount. A fourth alternative is to have the original face amount continued as term insurance for a specified period, the length of which depends on the amount of the cash value and the face amount of the original policy.[2] A fifth alternative is the minimum deposit plan which allows the insured to use part of his or her annual dividends to buy additional term insurance instead of taking the cash. This additional term insurance is priced lower than regular term insurance.

Limited Payment Life

These policies are similar to straight life in that level premiums are paid, but the premiums are limited to a specific period of years—20 or 30 years —or until a specified age is reached—60 or 65. The insured still remains insured for life. Premiums for limited payment life are larger than for straight life because you are buying the same lifetime protection with only a limited number of premiums.

Endowment Insurance

Endowment policies combine a systematic savings program with life insurance protection. The only real justification for endowment insurance is that it provides a convenient method of savings for those individuals otherwise not inclined to save. You pay a fixed premium for a specified period of time—10, 20, 30, or up to a certain age. The period of time is called

---

[2] William Kirby. *Life Insurance from the Buyer's Point of View*. American Institute for Economic Research, July 1974.

TABLE 4-2

Age Nearest Birthday	Annual Costs per $1,000 of insurance	
	5-year Renewable Term	Straight Life
20	$ 4.44	$13.09
21	4.47	13.44
22	4.48	13.78
23	4.52	14.15
24	4.57	14.53
25	4.60	14.93
26	4.65	15.35
27	4.71	15.78
28	4.79	16.25
29	4.86	16.72
30	4.95	17.23
31	5.05	17.77
32	5.19	18.33
33	5.35	18.92
34	5.55	19.54
35	5.79	20.19
36	6.06	20.88
37	6.40	21.60
38	6.76	22.36
39	7.17	23.16
40	7.61	24.01
41	8.09	24.91
42	8.63	25.84
43	9.19	26.82
44	9.82	27.88
45	10.52	28.98
46	11.30	30.15
47	12.16	31.39
48	13.11	32.71
49	14.17	34.10
50	15.34	35.59
51	16.61	37.17
52	17.92	38.85
53	19.28	40.63
54	20.80	42.55
55	22.49	44.57
56	21.28	43.95
57	22.91	45.92
58	24.70	48.00
59	26.63	50.21
60	28.76	52.55

the "endowment period." The face amount is payable to you at the end of the period if you are still alive. If you die before the maturity date, the insurance of course is paid to your beneficiary.

Endowment policy cash values have to accumulate more rapidly than other forms of whole life policies because the cash value has to equal the face amount of the policy at the end of the endowment period. Endowment insurance is a systematic way of "forcing" you to save towards specific goals such as the children's education or your own retirement.

Special Types of Policies

Some policies combine the features of straight life or limited payment life with reducing term for a level premium. This policy presumably relates to the notion that at certain periods of life—when children are young—insurance requirements may be greatest, reducing as the children grow older and as the insured's income increases. For example, an insurance company brochure heralds its family income policy by saying: "While designed to provide a specific program of cash and income benefits upon death, each $1,000 face amount of family income insurance combines $1,000 of permanent ordinary life insurance with a large amount of term insurance that reduces gradually over the family income period. For example, a $10,000 20-year family income policy combines $10,000 of ordinary life and $35,480 of 20-year reducing term insurance, providing a total of $45,480 initial insurance protection."

Group Insurance

Group insurance is issued to a large number of persons who must have a common employer or other restricted association such as the American Institute of Certified Public Accountants. All the members of the group are insured under the terms of a single policy without medical examination.

Group insurance is fundamentally term insurance on a year-to-year basis. The premiums for group insurance are usually lower than term insurance purchased on an individual basis. For example, the University of Washington recently offered a new group policy to its employees with the monthly premium cost of 21¢ per thousand dollars of insurance. Assuming an average age of the faculty and employees to be 40, the average cost for 5-year renewable term policy at age 40 purchased individually from a reliable low cost insurer would be about 2½ times the group cost. The reasons for the lower premiums on group policies are because of the low acquisition costs to the insurer—medical examinations are eliminated and commissions are much lower on group policies. Also, collection costs of the insurer are less since the employer usually collects (through salary deduction) and pays the premium.

Planning the Life Insurance Program

The question of "how much life insurance is enough?" requires some analysis to answer. An analysis of the requirements of your dependents is necessary in order to provide your dependents the support they would receive if you were alive. The analysis should take into consideration the specific needs—not only how much but when—of your dependents and the amount and liquidity of your assets to meet the needs.

Needs can normally be classified into four categories:

- Immediate cash requirements after death, including estate taxes
- Mortgage requirements
- Educational requirements
- Continuing income requirements

Immediate Cash Requirements

Many expenses that come into existence at your death simply do not exist when you are living. For example, there are funeral and burial expenses; there may be significant medical expenses related to illness before death; there may be major debts owed at death. If you have a significant estate, you may have substantial estate taxes to pay. If your estate is $100,000 or less, estate taxes will not be a problem for your dependents; if your estate is greater than $100,000, your estate taxes can be a significant factor in your estate settlement. Estate planning becomes an important aspect of your financial planning, a topic which is covered in some detail in Chapter 15.

Immediately after death, there should also be an emergency fund to handle the readjustment period during which your dependents recover from the emotional shock of your death and to financially plan for a standard of living different from the level enjoyed when your income was available.

Since most of us usually do a poor job of planning for death, our dependents may not have enough assets or not enough assets of a liquid nature to take care of immediate cash requirements. It is little wonder then that some suggest that the initial use of life insurance is to provide the cash required immediately after death.

Mortgage

In this age of buying expensive homes and financing the purchase with a large mortgage, many breadwinners die leaving their family with a substantial mortgage. From the point of view of cost alone, it makes little economic difference whether the mortgage is paid off immediately or is covered by additional income provided for your survivors. From a psychological point of view, it may be very desirable to have funds available through insurance to leave your home clear of debt.

Educational Requirements

Educational expenses, like the mortgage, could be paid from income provided by insurance, but your children may find it reassuring to have a specific fund set aside for educational purposes. The amount of the fund depends on several factors—type of college, length of education, children's ability to generate money for educational purposes, and availability of scholarships. A minimum amount of $5,000 should be set aside; some suggest as much as $20,000 per child for the more expensive universities.

Continuing Income Requirements

Immediate cash requirements, a mortgage fund, and an educational fund are usually satisfied by a specific cash sum. Income for the family has to be satisfied by a flow of income related to certain periods of the lifetime of your widow and children.

The calculation of the income required is complicated because it raises fundamental questions about how well the family should be provided for. Most of us would like to provide our family with the same standard of living to which it is accustomed. To maintain the same standard of living, however, should not require the same level of expenditure. With one of the family deceased, some expenses will be reduced and some may be even eliminated. All the deceased's spending on clothes, transportation, and food will disappear. Life insurance premiums will be eliminated. Income taxes will be less; mortgage payments may be eliminated if a special mortgage fund has been set up.

Some suggest that a widow with children will need about two-thirds of the family's gross income. A more accurate way of determining the requirements is to start with the amount of your committed expenses

(Chapter 2) and adjust the amount for expenses which can be reduced or eliminated. For example, we indicated that the Stoneston's committed expenses were $26,000 before income taxes. This amount could be reduced by $3,360 if a mortgage fund is set up—by $2,100 for life insurance premiums. In addition food, clothing, and transportation expenditures could be reduced. The Stoneston's committed expenses could be reduced to approximately $19,000 before taxes after Bill Stoneston's death. Taxes would only be paid on income from invested assets and from earnings of Sally if she decided to work. We estimate total expenses to be $2,000 per month, or $24,000 if Bill were to die.

For some families, some of the expenses may be met by income from assets that have accumulated during the lifetime of the deceased. In addition, some income may be generated by the widow after her spouse's death. (This is assuming the wife outlives the husband.) It may well be that the wife has been working and has a capability to earn or continue to earn a substantial income after her spouse's death.

Determining Insurance Needs

Basically, there are eight steps involved in determining your insurance needs. These are as follows:

1. Estimate your immediate cash requirements.

2. Determine the liquid assets available if you were to die in the near future.

3. Estimate your mortgage requirements and educational requirements.

4. Determine assets available to handle requirements for mortgage payments and educational purposes.

5. Calculate your dependents' income requirements during these four periods:

   a. the period during which *more than one child* is less than 18 and dependent upon your spouse.

   b. The period in which *only one child* is less than 18 and dependent upon your spouse.

   c. After your *youngest child* reaches 18 and until your spouse reaches 60.

   d. After *your spouse* reaches 60 and until his or her death.

6. Determine the income available:

   a. From your spouse's earnings.

   b. From assets available, if any, after provision for immediate cash requirements, mortgage and educational funds.

   c. From social security benefits.

7. Determine the amount of insurance necessary to provide the difference between the income required and income available.

8. Determine the type of insurance policies you need to provide flexibility and to minimize your premium outlay.

And remember, insurance needs go up and down as income and responsibilities go up and down. Without children, insurance requirements are not great. Children and a mortgage mean increased responsibilities and insurance protection. As children reach college age, insurance needs normally reach a maximum. As the children become financially independent, the need for insurance declines. At retirement, insurance again is no real factor except for liquidity for estate settlement purposes.

Because of the changing need for protection, we strongly recommend that you go through the eight steps outlined above at least every 5 years, and buy insurance policies that provide for changing needs. This is discussed later in the chapter.

To illustrate what's involved in performing these eight steps, let's go back to the Stoneston family and assume that Bill Stoneston has been invited to perform the somewhat ticklish assignment of evaluating the competence of the president of "You Bet Your Life Insurance Co." In his assignment he discovers a staggering amount of fictitious insurance policies generated to inflate the earnings picture of "You Bet" to keep Wall Street touting the glamorous earnings picture of the company. Well, Bill is so astounded and so grieved by such corporate machinations that he suffers a heart attack and dies. Would his wife Sally and the three children be in good hands with the present insurance policies or not? Let's see.

Step 1—Estimate Your Immediate Cash Needs

Cash is immediately required for funeral expenses, payment of current bills including medical bills, an emergency fund, and estate taxes. Death costs obviously will vary depending upon whether you want your ashes spread at sea (about $350) or buried with a Viking Ship and other accessories for your life in the hereafter (a custom for rich Nordic families in the Middle Ages). *The Widows Study,* published in 1970 by the Life Insurance Agency Management Association, indicated an average for death costs to be about $1,500. The Stonestons estimate was $3,000.

Because of the size of the estate, estate taxes will be approximately $45,000 for the Stonestons. Sally would like an emergency fund of $20,000 available to handle unforeseen financial requirements and to have financial peace of mind until the readjustment period is over.

Current bills, per Exhibit 12, will amount to $10,000—$15,600 less the borrowings on the cash value of life insurance policies. The borrowings will reduce the face amount proceeds from the insurance company to the named beneficiaries.

EXHIBIT 12
Stoneston—Present Net Worth as of 12/31

	Estimated Current Value
I. Assets	
Liquid:	
Cash (checking and regular savings accounts)	$ 1,700
Term savings accounts	3,300
Short term investments—Treasury bills, Certificates of deposit, etc.	15,000
Marketable securities	33,300
Accounts receivable	–
Cash value of life insurance	6,500
	$ 59,800
Not So Liquid:	
Real estate	$111,000
Investment partnerships—Real estate	54,000
Special situations—Stoneston & Associates	35,000
—Other	16,400
	$216,400
Retirement Funds:	
Keogh self-employment trust	$ 27,100
Personal:	
Residence	$ 95,000
Furnishings	36,000
Automobile	3,000
Boats	2,000
	$136,000
Other: Thomas Brown trust	$ 65,000
	$504,300
II. Liabilities	
Short-Term Obligations:	
Current bills	$ 1,500
Borrowing on cash surrender value of life insurance	5,600
Automobile	2,000
Other notes and contract payable	–
Personal loans	–
Accrued taxes	6,500
	$ 15,600
Long-Term Obligations:	
Mortgages on real estate investments	$ 42,000
Mortgage on personal residence	33,000
	$ 75,000
Total Liabilities	$ 90,600
Assets − Liabilities = Net Worth	$413,700

Thus, immediate cash requirements will be:

Funeral	$ 3,000
Estate taxes	$45,000
Current bills	$10,000
Emergency fund	$20,000
	$78,000

Step 2—Determine the Liquid Assets Available

As Exhibit 12 indicates, the Stonestons' liquid assets amount to $59,800. However, only $53,300 is available since the cash surrender value of the life insurance would no longer be available if Bill dies. Of course the face amount of the policies would be available.

In addition to the $53,300, the proceeds from the Thomas Brown Trust and from the self-employment trust would be available, making a total of $145,400 of cash for immediate requirements.

Obviously, each individual's case is different, but the step of determining the assets immediately available begins with your net worth statement where you have classified assets by their liquidity. The "not-so-liquid" assets normally require some time to convert to cash. Assets of a personal nature normally include the house, furnishings, and automobiles, which will be used by the deceased's dependents some time after his death. They may eventually be converted to cash—i.e., sale of the house—but at least not until some readjustment period has taken place.

Step 3 and Step 4—Estimate Your Mortgage and Educational Requirements and Assets Available

The Stonestons currently have three mortgage loans on the following properties:

Personal residence	$33,000
Summer cabin	24,000
Rental property (occupied by Bill Stoneston's parents)	18,000
	$75,000

The Stonestons planned to have the mortgage on the personal residence paid if Bill died. They also planned to have Bill's parents move into the house with Sally and the children if Bill died. The net equity in the house rented to his parents is $8,000 ($26,000 fair market value less mortgage of $18,000). They also planned to have the mortgage on the summer home paid if Bill died.

As to education for the three children, the Stonestons estimated $5,000 per year for six years (assuming some graduate work) for each child, or $90,000. Two factors make the calculations of total funds required for education a little more complicated. One factor is Social Security benefits; the other factor is that these funds are not needed immediately. So we have to calculate the amount that must be set aside *now* in order to have the funds later. Since the amount you set aside today can earn interest between now (the time of death) and the time it is needed, it is obvious that the amount that must be set aside now is going to be less than the sum of the payments to be made in the future. You may calculate the amounts that must be set aside by using a technique called *present value analysis*.

Let's calculate the present value, or the amount the Stonestons must set aside today for educational purposes. First, Social Security benefits: although Social Security benefits are paid to eligible students between 18 and 22, determination of the exact amount is too complex for our treatment here. For calculation purposes, you may assume that the Social Security program will pay at least $1,200 per year for each of the two youngest children while attending college. Based on this assumption, the Stonestons will need the following amounts for each child:

Paige	age 14	$30,000
Michael	age 13	$30,000–$4,800 or $25,200
Amy-Ann	age 3	$30,000–$4,800 or $25,200

Using present value factors, we can determine the present value, or the amount the Stonestons have to set aside today, to have the funds available for each child. Using the factors in Table 4-3, we can calculate the amount presently needed. For Paige, the Stonestons do not need the funds for 4 years, so we go to Colume 3 of the Table in the 4th year and find 0.82. The present amount required is $30,000 x 0.82 or $24,600, which will earn 5 percent per year for 4 years and thus grow to the $30,000 required when Paige enters college.

Similarly, the present amount required to have $25,200 for Michael 5 years from now is $25,200 x 0.78 or $19,565. For Amy-Ann, the present amount will be $25,200 x 0.48 or $12,096. The total educational funds to be presently set aside are $56,352 or $56,400 rounded to the nearest $100.

TABLE 4-3

PRESENT-VALUE FACTORS AT 5% INTEREST

Column 1 Number of Periods (Years)	Column 2 Series Factors (See Footnote)	Column 3 Sum Factors (See Footnote)
1	1.00	0.95
2	1.95	0.91
3	2.86	0.86
4	3.72	0.82
5	4.55	0.78
6	5.33	0.75
7	6.08	0.71
8	6.79	0.68
9	7.46	0.64
10	8.11	0.61
11	8.72	0.58
12	9.31	0.56
13	9.86	0.53
14	10.39	0.51
15	10.90	0.48
16	11.38	0.46
17	11.84	0.44
18	12.27	0.42
19	12.69	0.40
20	13.09	0.38
21	13.46	0.36
22	13.82	0.34
23	14.16	0.33
24	14.49	0.31
25	14.80	0.30
26	15.09	0.28
27	15.38	0.27
28	15.64	0.26
29	15.90	0.24
30	16.14	0.23
31	16.37	0.22
32	16.59	0.21
33	16.80	0.20
34	17.00	0.19
35	17.19	0.18
36	17.37	0.17
37	17.55	0.16
38	17.71	0.16
39	17.87	0.15
40	18.02	0.14

NOTE: Column 2 relates to the present value of a series of payments to be made at beginning of period; Column 3 relates to a single sum needed at a future time. Please see the text and examples therein on how to use these factors.

Exhibit 13 shows Steps 1 through 4 and an analysis of what assets can be used to fund the requirements we have discussed to this point.

Exhibit 13 shows that $67,400 is available for income requirements or other purposes. In addition, Sally and the children have $136,000, represented by the house, furnishings, an automobile, and a boat. Also, the cabin and waterfront property has a value of $85,000. After such an analysis, Sally and the children may decide to eventually sell the waterfront property or move into a smaller residence or both. But for our discussion, let's assume that they decide to continue to live in their house and keep the waterfront property—possibly renting the property for all but the summer months to cover property taxes and maintenance.

EXHIBIT 13			
Step		*Requirements*	*Sources*
1. Immediate cash requirements		$78,000	
2. Cash immediately available:			
Liquid assets	$53,300		
Self-employed retirement trust	27,100		
Thomas Brown Trust	65,000		$145,000
NET, after immediate cash requirements			67,400
3. Mortgage requirements:			
Personal residence	33,000		
Summer cabin	24,000	57,000	
Educational requirements		56,500	(113,400)
NET, before use of not-so-liquid assets			($ 46,000)
4. Assets available, other than personal, which can eventually be converted into cash:			
Net equity in house rented	8,000		
Investment partnerships	54,000		
Special situations	51,400		113,400
NET, available for income requirements			$ 67,400

Step 5—Calculate your Dependents' Income Requirements

As mentioned previously, we suggest that you consider your dependents' income requirements during the following time periods, which are related to Social Security benefit periods:

- The period during which more than one child is less than 18 and dependent upon your spouse
- The period in which only one child is less than 18 and dependent upon your spouse
- After the youngest child reaches 18 and until your spouse reaches 60
- After your spouse reaches 60 and until her death.

To determine income requirements during the first period above, we suggest that you start with your current committed expenses and adjust them for the expenses that will be eliminated or reduced after your death. For example, the Stonestons' committed expenses of $26,000 would be reduced by $3,360 if the mortgage fund were set up; by $2,100 for the life insurance premiums they are currently paying; and by $1,800 to $2,000 for Bill's food, clothing, and transportation costs. They estimate committed expenses to be about $24,000, including income taxes, after Bill's death— about $2,000 per month. This level of committed expenses, in current dollars, would continue until the children no longer require financial support. After the children have grown or after the youngest has reached age 18, Sally believes her income requirements would drop to about $18,000 in current dollars—about $1,500 per month—and continue at that level until her death.

Step 6—Determine the Income Available

Basically, there are three primary sources of income available to meet your dependents' income requirements:

1. Earnings generated by your spouse working after your death.
2. Income from assets available after provision for immediate cash requirements and for mortgage and educational requirements.
3. Payments from Social Security benefits.

For many, payments from Social Security furnish much of the income protection. For a widow with two or more children, benefits can go as high as $707.90 per month. These payments continue until the youngest child reaches 18, or until age 22 if the child is a full-time student. In her later years, a widow gets a Social Security pension—as much as $404.50 a month if she waits until she is 65 and about $290 if she takes the benefits at age 60.

Step 7—Determine the Insurance You Need

Based on the calculations you have made in Steps 1 through 6, you can turn to Worksheet 7 in Appendix A and determine the insurance you need. To assist you in completing this Worksheet, we will complete such a worksheet for the Stonestons. Exhibit 14 is the completed worksheet. A few explanatory notes are helpful.

To convert income needs to insurance needs, you have to calculate the amount of money necessary today—called present value—to provide an income series for years in the future—called an annuity, in financial calculations. Thus the $55,255 on line 1 in Exhibit 14 represents the present

---

EXHIBIT 14

INSURANCE ANALYSIS

Time Period	Widow's Age From	To	Number of Years
1. Period during which *more than one child* is less than 18 and dependent upon your spouse.	37	42	5
2. Period in which *only one child* is less than 18 and dependent upon your spouse.	43	52	10
3. Period after your youngest child reaches 18 and until your spouse reaches 60.	53	59	7
4. Period after your spouse reaches 60 and until his or her death.	60	death	?

value of an annuity at 5 percent of $12,144 for 5 years. In other words, it will take $55,255 invested at 5 percent today to allow monthly payments of $1,012 to be made for the next 5 years. This calculation is made easy by referring to Table 4-3 again. Using the table, we find the multiplier (column 2) for 5 years (4.55) and multiply it by the annual income needed ($12,144) to arrive at the present sum needed ($55,255).

To compute the amount of insurance needed as shown on line 2 of Exhibit 14, $59,210, it is necessary to not only use the "present value of an annuity" concept but also the concept of "discounted cash flow." On line 2, we indicate that $9,360 (the annuity) is needed for 10 years. We first use the multiplier for 10 years—8.11—in Table 4-3, and multiply it by $9,360 to arrive at $75,910. However, the $75,910 of insurance needed for annual

| | Income Analysis | | | | |
| | Monthly | | | Yearly | |
Income Required	Less Social [1] Security Available	Less Widow's Earnings	Balance Needed	Amount Needed	Insurance Required
$2,000	$708	$280 [2]	$1,012	$12,144	$55,255
1,667	607	280	780	9,360	59,210
1,500	–	280	1,220	14,640	40,945
1,500	289	280	931	11,172	61,458
		Total Income Requirements			$211,817
		Additional Cash Required (from Steps 1 to 4)			–0–
		Total Insurance Needed			$216,868

[1] In 1974, the benefits for a widowed mother and one child were $606.80; family maximum $707.90; check with your local social security office for current benefits.
In 1974, the full benefits for a widow at age 65 were $404.50; reduced benefits begin at age 60 for widows and the reduction factor is 19/40 of 1% for each month of entitlement age 60–65. For example, the reduction factor would be 19/40 × 36 months or 0.171; thus the retirement benefits would be 0.829 of full benefits at age 62. At age 60, the benefits will be 0.715 of full benefits.
[2] $67,400 assets available (see Exhibit 13) at 5% or annual earnings of $3,370.

payments of $9,360 is not needed until 5 years from now. So we have to determine the amount required today—the present value—to be invested at 5 percent, which will accumulate to $75,910 in 5 years. To determine this amount, we have to use a discount factor in Column 3 of Table 4-1. The discount factor is 0.78. Thus multiplying $75,910 by 0.78, we determine that $59,210 of insurance is needed today to enable a stream of monthly payments of $780 to be made for 10 years, but 5 years from now.

To compute the insurance shown on line 3 of Exhibit 14—$40,945—we multiply $14,640 by 6.08 and then by 0.46, since payments are not required for 16 years. To compute the insurance shown on line 4 of Exhibit 14— $61,458—we multiply the annual income requirement by 16.67, or what a lifetime annuity will cost, and then discount that amount by the factor of 0.33 for the 23 years between now and when Sally Stoneston is 60 years old.

This analysis suggests that the Stoneston's insurance requirements are approximately $217,000. In the net worth analysis of the Stonestons, in Chapter 1, we determined the insurance coverage on Bill Stoneston to be approximately $270,000 ($275,900 as shown in Exhibit 3, Chapter 1, less amount borrowed of $5,600 on cash value of policies).

This analysis suggests that the Stoneston's could possibly reduce their insurance coverage. The Stonestons have at least two alternatives *if* they wish to reduce their insurance coverage. One, they can continue to borrow on the increasing cash value of the policies, thereby reducing the insurance coverage by the amount of the borrowing. The Stonestons are currently paying 5 percent on the amount they have already borrowed on the cash value of the policies. They certainly can find alternative investments yielding greater than a 5 percent return. Two, they could reduce the amount of group coverage by $50,000 and thus save the premium on that amount.

Step 8—Determine the Type of Insurance You Need

Insurance needs generally increase with the birth of each child and reach a maximum after the last child is born. Once the children are grown and become financially independent, insurance needs decrease significantly.

To demonstrate the changing need for protection, we have used the insurance worksheets for analyzing the insurance needs of some of the people presented in the profiles in Chapter 3. The people we have selected are:

Bob and Joanna Hart; 26 and 25; both working; mortgage $18,000; net worth other than personal, $7,300; no children *insurance needs approximately $22,000.*

Bart and Dorothy Boney; 36 and 35; mortgage $64,000; net worth other than personal, $17,500; 4 children under 11; *insurance needs approximately $330,000.*

Robin and Ann Ederson; 42 and 43; mortgage $20,000; net worth other than personal, $26,000; 2 children approaching college; *insurance needs approximately $147,000.*

Pete and Mary Jones; both 55; mortgage paid off; net worth other than personal, $400,000; children grown; *insurance needs approximately $70,000.*

Joe and Peggy Lund; 68 and 64, retired; pension $24,000; net worth other than personal $410,000; children grown; *insurance needs approximately $60,000.*

Because of the changing need for protection, it is important to have insurance policies that enable you to change your insurance protection. One approach is to have a base of Straight Life, or permanent type insurance, equal to the amount necessary to take care of your spouse's income requirements after the children are grown. For example, for the Stonestons, the permanent type of insurance might be about $97,000—the amount necessary to provide for Sally from age 53 until her death.

To take care of insurance needs above this base of permanent insurance, we suggest the use of renewable term insurance for a period of at least 20 years or until age 60. Whenever a term policy is renewed, the amount of insurance can be changed in proportion to your different insurance needs. We strongly recommend that before you decide to renew your insurance, you again go through a computation to determine your insurance needs to adjust for factors such as the family's standard of living, inflation, additional dependents, assets, spouse's earning capacity, etc.

Selecting the Right Insurance Company

Currently, there are approximately 1,800 life insurance companies in the United States. To select the right one for you requires evaluation of three important factors: [3]

1. Financial strength and integrity of the company;
2. Service; and
3. Cost of the policy you are considering.

---

[3] *How to Select the Right Life Insurance Company.* (Des Moines, Iowa: Bankers Life Company, 1971).

Financial Strength and Integrity

Life insurance involves a long-term financial guarantee, and you should be concerned about the company's ability to fulfill its obligations to you whenever it is called upon to do so—tomorrow or 50 years from now.

To obtain information on the financial strength and integrity of insurance companies, we suggest that you obtain a copy of *Best's Insurance Reports.* This hefty volume is available in the reference room of most metropolitan public libraries. This volume contains a report on each life insurance company in the United States, as well as many in Canada. It shows detailed financial information about the company, an analysis of company investments, a brief history of the company and its growth, and a description of the company's method of operation. Exhibit 15 shows a considerably abridged version of the 1974 A.M. Best Rating for The Bankers Life Company.

Best's recommendation is given to those companies which, in the opinion of Best's, meet sufficiently high standards of financial strength and stability. In the 1974 edition of *Best's Insurance Reports,* there were 492 companies recommended, 135 of whom received its highest recommendation in both overall company results and safety margins.

Service

If you are not willing to plan and maintain your own insurance program, you will probably rely on the local representatives of the company you select to provide the insurance you require. You should seek an agent who has competence and integrity. Ask your friends or associates for recommendations from companies that have financial strength and stability. Talk to several agents and find out about their experience and approach to determining your needs. Obtain a proposal and a sample policy and study their provisions thoroughly at your leisure. Make sure you understand *what* insurance policy you are buying and *why* before you sign the application.

Cost

There are significant differences between companies in the cost of life insurance. To assist you in determining the net cost of a policy for comparative purposes, a method known as the "interest-adjusted" method has been adopted by the life insurance industry. As its name implies, the method applies an interest factor to the yearly premiums, dividends, and cash value increases.

The net costs of selected companies has been prepared by several independent sources recently. The Pennsylvania Insurance Department published *A Shopper's Guide to Life Insurance* in 1962. This guide shows which of the largest companies have the lowest cost and which have the highest cost for straight life insurance. Part of the summary in the guide states:

> "—It pays to shop for life insurance (as well as other kinds of insurance). Costs may vary over 170 percent.
>
> —You can't tell which is the best buy on straight life insurance by looking at premiums alone. A policy with the lowest premium may actually be the highest cost policy.
>
> —Use the "average yearly cost" figures in this guide in deciding which are the lowest cost policies."

A recent study published by the American Institute for Economic Research, *Life Insurance From the Buyers' Point of View,*[4] included ratings of selected companies (*see* Exhibit 16).

---

[4] Available from the American Institute for Economic Research, Great Barrington, Mass. 01230, for only $1.

EXHIBIT 15

WHY IS THE RATING OF THE A. M. BEST COMPANY IMPORTANT . . . TO YOU?

- Insurance companies attaining a Best's recommendation have established a record which attests to their soundness, permanency, and financial stability. Best's rating, however, is not a recommendation of the specific policy provisions, rates or claims practices of the insurance company.

- Best's analysis of the financial condition and operating performance of an insurance company is dependent upon such vital factors as:

  - Sound underwriting
  - Controlled expenses
  - Adequate reserves
  - Sound investments

- The information provided is an accurate digest of the complete report in the 1974 edition of Best's Insurance Reports which is compiled independently by the A. M. Best Company and without remuneration.

HISTORY

The company was incorporated under the laws of Iowa on June 30, 1879, as an assessment association, under the name of The Bankers Life Association. On October 26, 1911, the association was transformed into a legal reserve mutual life insurance company and the name was changed to "Bankers Life Company," which continues as the company's legal name. In 1969, the articles of incorporation were amended so that the company could use the name, The Bankers Life, at its discretion and where permitted as its style and mark.

BANKERS LIFE COMPANY
711 High Street
Des Moines, Iowa 50307

Assets	Year Ending Dec. 31, 1973
*Total bonds	$1,018,177,845
*Total stocks	166,865,743
Mortgage loans	1,059,432,375
Real estate	65,372,234
Policy loans	144,446,249
Cash	7,211,909
Life & annty. prems. due	96,398,752
Acc. & health prems. due	6,424,099
Accrued invest. income	28,582,844
Other assets	5,570,208
Separate account bus.	83,121,310
Admitted Assets	$2,681,603,568

Liabilities	
Net policy reserves	$2,262,464,838
Policy claims	34,014,308
Dividend accumulations	84,211,543
Div. res. to 12/31/74	58,336,703
Comm. taxes expenses	20,709,830
Securities val. reserve	1,491,683
Special group res.	12,457,060
Other liabilities	31,144,879
Separate account bus.	83,121,310
Total Liabilities	$2,587,952,154
Special surplus funds	9,512,189
Unassigned surplus	84,139,225
Total	$2,681,603,568

*Securities are reported on the basis prescribed by The National Association of Insurance Commissioners.

MANAGEMENT

The company is purely mutual and it has long been most ably managed by highly capable and experienced insurance executives. In all respects it enjoys excellent standing and it has recognized the interests of its policyholders, who control its affairs. It has shown healthy growth and presently ranks among the largest fifteen mutual life companies measured by both assets and insurance in force.

OPERATIONS

It is one of the few life companies that operates on a nationwide basis being licensed in all states, the District of Columbia, Puerto Rico and the Canadian Provinces of Manitoba, Ontario, and Quebec. Operations are conducted on the branch office system and it is currently represented by more than 1,350 soliciting agents. A complete portfolio of ordinary insurance is written, standard and sub-standard, with provision for disability and double indemnity benefits, annuities, accident and sickness, group life and group accident, sickness, hospitalization and surgical benefits, all on the annual dividend plan. The maximum retention by the company is $600,000.

It commenced the writing of group insurance in 1941, and in 1942 introduced a new series of group permanent insurance policies, combining the flexibility obtainable under a group contract with the advantages of individual policies written under a pension trust. In 1967, it introduced a variable annuity for group money purchase pension and profit sharing plans. In 1968, it organized BLC Equity Services Corporation as a wholly owned subsidiary to market and service group H. R. 10 variable annuity transactions. This subsidiary company markets two mutual funds, the BLC Growth Fund, Inc. and BLC Income Fund, Inc.

In early 1974, the company formed BLC Insurance Company as a subsidiary of BLC Financial, a wholly owned subsidiary of Bankers Life Company. The new property/liability affiliate will begin offering automobile and homeowners coverage to employers for inclusion in their employee benefit programs by 1975. This will enable the employee to have available these types of coverage on a payroll deduction basis, in much the same way that group life and health is now offered.

OPERATING COMMENTS

Net Yield: The return on assets as reflected by the net yield before Federal income taxes in 1973 was 6.49% a very good rate of return. Over-all net investment income provides ample margins (192.2%) to cover contractual interest required to maintain policy reserves.

Expenses: In operations a very important item is expenses, which have been kept very low.

Mortality: Careful selection and underwriting of business has produced a very favorable mortality experience.

Lapses: Policy lapses and surrenders have been low.

Net Cost: Net cost to policyholders is remarkably low.

POLICYHOLDERS' RECOMMENDATION

The results achieved by the company have been most favorable. In our opinion it has most substantial over-all margins for contingencies. Upon the foregoing analysis of its present position we recommend this company.

OFFICERS

Chairman of the board and chief executive officer, Harold G. Allen; president, R. N. Houser; executive vice president, J. R. Taylor; senior vice presidents, M. D. Cramer, H. F. Dean, W. G. Schneider; senior vice president and secretary, R. E. Cassell; senior vice president and chief actuary, C. L. Trowbridge; vice president and general counsel, H. T. Bailey; financial vice president, R. W. Ehrle; agency vice president, R. E. Freeman; vice president – mortgages, G. E. Rickert; vice president – marketing services, G. D. Reifsnider; vice presidents, D.F. Carter, C. G. Conover, J. H. Elken, J. G. Helkenn, G. D. Hurd, D. L. Krieg, R. E. Larson, A. R. Roberts, D. L. Schroeder, J. T. Watson.

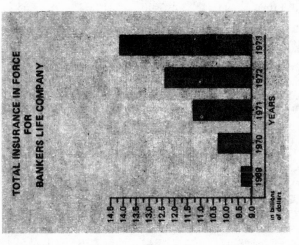

TOTAL INSURANCE IN FORCE
FOR
BANKERS LIFE COMPANY

YEARS

in billions of dollars

FINANCIAL SUMMARY

Benefits Paid in 1973	$ 331,565,698
Total Premium Income 1973	$ 553,229,622
Admitted Assets On 12/31/73	$ 2,681,603,568
Insurance Issued in 1973	$ 2,110,407,880
Total Insurance In Force 1973	$14,226,829,883

SOURCE: A. M. Best Company, Morristown, N.J.

EXHIBIT 16

Selected Companies in the order of 20-Year Net Cost per $1,000 Face Amount, Continuous Premium Paying Policies, Age 35	20-yr. Payments Accum. at 3½%	20-yr. Surrender Value	20-yr. Net Cost
Northwestern Mut. (W. L. PU @ 90)	$444.15	$371.82	$72.33
Mass. Mutual (Conv. Life)	452.23	374.93	77.30
Phoenix Mutual (Ord. Life)	497.00	413.32	83.68
Bankers Life Co. (Pref. Whole Life)	446.80	362.00	84.80
Guardian Life (Mod. 3)	468.73	382.25	86.48
Mass. Mutual (Mod. 3 Life)	456.56	367.63	88.93
State Mutual of Amer. (Pref. Prot.)	432.89	342.00	90.74
Central Life Assurance (Wh. Life)	472.86	381.85	91.01
John Hancock Mutual (Pref. 25)	482.98	389.27	93.71
Conn. Mutual Life (Wh. Life)	435.81	342.07	93.74
Guardian Life (Ord. Life Std.)	483.60	389.59	94.01
National Life of Vt. (Wh. Life)	490.98	394.71	96.27
Mutual Benefit Life (Ord. Life)	447.52	350.98	96.54
Bankers L. (Iowa) (Spec. Wh. L.)	442.80	344.00	98.80
Central Life Assur. (Spec. Wh. Life)	460.38	361.35	99.03
Central Life Assur. (Gra. Prem. L.)	457.54	358.04	99.05
Conn. Mutual Life (Gra. Prem. L.)	457.49	357.88	99.61
New York Life (Whole Life)	459.03	358.00	101.03
Equitable Life of U.S. (Exec. Pol.)	483.44	382.20	101.24
National Life of Vt. (Ord. Life)	496.16	394.71	101.45
Mutual Bene. (Ord. L. Inc. Prem.)	396.47	294.87	101.60
Dominion Life (Whole Life)	436.74	335.00	101.74
Penn Mutual (Whole Life)	463.77	361.00	102.77
State Farm Life (Exec. Prot.)	427.76	324.86	102.90
General American (Economaster)	481.44	378.50	102.94
Indianapolis Life (Ord. Life)	441.35	337.00	104.35
Lincoln Nat'l Life (Graded-10 Life)	429.12	324.00	105.12
Indianapolis Life (Bus. Mens')	439.17	334.00	105.17
State Farm Life (Whole Life)	467.73	360.91	106.82
Sun Life Assurance (Whole Life)	462.01	352.54	109.47
Provident Mut. (Prot. 25,000 Basis)	449.68	340.00	109.68
State Mutual of Amer. (Wh. Life)	452.71	342.07	110.64
Amer. United (Exec. Special)	471.67	360.27	111.40
Lincoln National (Ord. Life)	468.44	356.93	111.51
National Life of Vt. (Gra. Prem.)	482.91	371.37	111.54
Confederation Life (Whole Life)	455.39	343.00	112.39
Equitable of Iowa (Ord. Life)	474.51	362.02	112.49
Provident Mutual (Whole Life)	474.34	361.00	113.34
Penn Mutual (Mod-3 Life)	445.76	331.00	114.76
Monarch Life (End. @ 90)	504.02	389.00	115.02
Mutual Trust (Ord. Life)	476.67	360.18	116.49
Canada Life (Pref. Life)	474.10	357.00	117.10
Nationwide (Exec. Equity)	479.27	361.36	117.91

94

EXHIBIT 16 —Continued Selected Companies in the order of 20-Year Net Cost per $1,000 Face Amount, Continuous Premium Paying Policies, Age 35	20-yr. Payments Accum. at 3½%	20-yr. Surrender Value	20-yr. Net Cost
Nat'l Life of Vt. P.E.P. (PU @ 95)	512.84	394.80	118.04
Pan American (Whole Life)	443.25	325.00	118.25
Mutual of N.Y. (MONY Provider)	461.19	338.00	123.19
State Farm Life (Mod-5)	456.94	333.43	123.51
Security Benefit (Sec. Pref. Wh. L.)	495.90	372.00	123.90
Ohio State (Paid up @ 97)	508.10	383.25	124.85
Ohio National (Exec. Prot.)	456.13	327.68	128.45
Crown Life (Select Ord. Life)	452.62	321.00	131.62
Bankers Life (Flex. Ord. L.)	495.26	362.00	133.26
Security Mutual Life (Exec. Spec.)	525.00	391.16	133.84
Mutual of N. Y. (Whole Life)	551.33	417.00	134.33
Columbus Mutual (Pref. Life)	494.69	357.00	137.69
Amer. Gen. (Wh. Life Par)	514.37	375.02	139.35
John Hancock (Mod-3)	523.93	384.20	139.73
Columbus Mutual (Exec. PU @ 95)	496.91	357.00	139.91
Prudential of Amer. (Exec. Wh. L.)	528.19	388.00	140.19
John Hancock (Mod-5)	499.20	357.81	141.39
Farm Bureau Life (Ord. Life)	491.59	350.00	141.59
Prudential of Amer. (Mod-3)	524.07	382.00	142.07
Metropolitan Life (Pref. Wh. L.)	528.01	385.00	143.01
Ohio National (Pref. Wh. L.)	503.92	360.18	143.74
Ohio Nat'l (Wh. Life PU @ 98)	504.17	360.18	143.99
Crown L. (Exec. Spec. End @ 80)	504.90	355.00	149.90
* Aetna Life (Whole Life)	494.36	342.00	152.36
Mutual of N.Y. (Exec. Equity)	597.93	421.00	176.93

* Nonparticipating

Chapter 5

SAVINGS ACCOUNTS AND SHORT-TERM MONEY MARKET INVESTMENTS

In the discussion of net worth, we indicated that many people maintain some of their net worth in very liquid assets. These assets include cash and special types of short-term investments that can be conveniently converted into cash. Such assets are normally relatively free from risk and include cash and checking accounts, savings accounts, short-term money market investments such as U.S. Treasury bills, bankers' acceptances, and commercial paper.

Bank Accounts

Checking and regular savings accounts in commercial banks are perhaps the most liquid form of asset other than cash.

In addition to providing liquidity, bank accounts in the right number and of the right kind can be a great help in keeping your finances in order and telling you where you stand. At a minimum, we suggest that you have three accounts. First, there should be a "funnel" account in which all incoming money is deposited, whether it comes from salary, income from a professional practice, investments, gifts, royalties, or etc. By funneling all your income into this account, you are not likely to overlook any income when it comes to year-end income analysis and preparation of your tax return. Such an account also enables you to readily obtain income for pre-year-end tax planning that we will discuss in Chapter 14.

The second account is the family checking account, and deposits to this account are made by transfers from the funnel account. Normally, both you and your spouse should be signatories on each of the accounts, but the one who handles the financial records should be the one who makes transfers from the funnel account to the family checking account. The amount of the transfer may be a lump sum monthly amount that is necessary to handle estimated short-range expense items, or it may be an amount based on a cash forecast. We will discuss cash forecasts and how a cash forecasting system may be used to predict cash needs and amounts available for discretionary purposes.

Since funds in a checking account do not earn any interest, the amounts maintained in such an account should not be great, preferably only enough to meet near-term objectives and to avoid bank service charges. Many commercial banks provide "free" checking accounts if you maintain a minimum balance in your checking account—$200 or $300. If your balance falls below this amount, a service charge, non-tax deductible, is made by your bank on your account. Even though the charge is not large in absolute terms, it is large in percentage terms. For example, a $1 monthly charge against your account if your balance drops below $200 but stays above $100 for each month is $12 per year or 12 percent per year.

The third account is the general savings account in which a very small amount, say $1,000 or $2,000, should be maintained to provide a short-term supply of money in case anything has been overlooked by your cash estimating system. This general savings account held jointly with your spouse might best be maintained in the bank in which you have the funnel checking account and the family checking account. In our own case, we have a "single statement account" in which the savings account used for general savings is combined with family checking.

The general savings account should be kept to a minimum, because a savings account maintained in a commercial bank has relatively low interest rates compared to other kinds of savings or short-term money market investments. Such investment opportunities are discussed later in this chapter.

In addition to these three basic accounts—the funnel account, family checking account, and general savings account—you may wish to consider additional accounts that provide a source of record keeping and convenience for you or your tax advisor at tax preparation time. For example, these special purpose accounts may include a separate savings account for your spouse, so that if you died suddenly the special account could be used for meeting current expenses after your demise. Some people set up an income tax savings account in which a certain amount is put away each month from the funnel account to make income tax payments. Another might be a real estate checking account which helps you keep tabs on deductible expenditures on income-producing property, information useful in preparing specific schedules on your individual tax return.

Need for Liquidity

There are several important reasons why one should hold liquid assets in commercial bank accounts. *First,* it may be convenient to do so. For example, you may find you have $500 left over at the end of the month in your checking account. Obviously this is a blessed event and your initial reaction may be to reconcile your bank account. However, if you really have the $500, you may wish to keep it there since you know that next month's expenditures will soon be coming up. *Second,* you may wish to keep liquid assets as a reserve against unforeseen situations such as a delay in the receipt of income or an unexpected expense. These higher-than-usual demands for cash can be met without having to liquidate part of your investment position. Unfortunately, it often happens that when part of the long-term investment portfolio has to be liquidated, the portfolio is in a negative (short-term hopefully) position. You are then forced to accept an unnecessary capital loss, not to mention the commission on the sale of stock.

Third, liquid assets act as funds that can be used to take advantage of opportunities which occur with the short-term volatility of some investment media. *Fourth,* there is the income aspect of a savings account in a commercial bank. Although the interest on a regular account in a commercial bank is relatively modest, it is much better than the rate you obtain when the money is tucked in your drawers.

To obtain the greatest return from your liquid assets and to make your cash work for you, we strongly recommend the use of a cash forecast.

Cash Forecast

A cash forecast is very simply a way of conveniently recording the estimates of the amounts and timing of cash receipts and cash expenditures (committed and discretionary). It is the only way of *accurately* determining the amount of liquid assets you should have, and *what* cash is available for other purposes and *when.* It is also useful to prevent crises that come about when cash shortages occur—crises related to everything from borrowing at unfavorable interest rates to selling assets in unfavorable market conditions.

To show you what a cash forecast looks like and how you can prepare one, let's again drop in on the Stonestons. Exhibit 17 is a cash forecast for the next year for the Stonestons. The amounts shown in the "total" column in Exhibit 17 are based on the "Income and Expenditures Analysis" projection which the Stonestons prepared previously (*see* Exhibit 9 in Chapter 2). The cash forecast is prepared to show the timing of the receipt of the total estimated income of $44,700 during the year and the timing of the total estimated expenditures of $78,700 (committed $53,900 and discretionary $24,800) during the year. More importantly, the cash forecast shows the timing of the cash available or cash required during the year. The total cash required is $34,000 ($78,700 minus $44,700). The Stonestons have significant estimated cash requirements in January, May, June, July,

EXHIBIT 17

CASH FORECAST

	Total [1]	Jan.	Feb.	Mar.	Apr.
Income:					
1. Own business	30,000	3,000	3,000	3,000	3,000
2. Royalties	14,700	2,500		2,000	2,500
3. Total	44,700	5,500	3,000	5,000	5,500
Committed Expenditures:					
4. Other than insurance, taxes, interest and installment pay.	23,800	2,000	2,000	2,000	2,000
5. Insurance	2,100	300		150	300
6. Taxes	7,000	1,700			1,900
7. Interest	500				
8. Real estate investments	10,500	870	870	870	870
9. Investment partnerships	7,500	5,000			
10. Self-employment trust	2,500			600	
11. Total	53,900	9,870	2,870	3,620	5,070
12. Excess (deficiency)	(9,200)	(4,370)	130	1,380	430
Discretionary expenditures:					
13. Somewhat	4,800	200	200	200	1,000
14. Extended travel	20,000				
15. Total	24,800	200	200	200	1,000
Cash available or					
16. Cash (required)	(34,000)	(4,570)	(70)	1,180	(570)
17. Cumulative requirements	(34,000)	(4,570)	(4,640)	(3,460)	(4,030)

[1] *See* Exhibit 9, Chapter 2.

and August. In only two months—March and October—is excess cash available.

What this cash forecast suggests is the need for a build-up of liquid reserves in savings accounts and/or short-term investments during the first 3 or 4 months of the year to have funds available for the heavy cash drain to fund the travel to Europe. Presumably, the Stonestons' liquid assets of $59,800 shown in their net worth statement (Exhibit 2 in Chapter 1) can be used for the cash required.

The amount of detail and the period covered in the forecast is a matter of individual preference. One approach is to prepare a cash forecast in the level of detail shown in Exhibit 17 for twelve months in advance. For the

May	June	July	Aug.	Sept.	Oct.	Nov.	Dec.
3,000	3,000			3,000	3,000	3,000	3,000
		2,500		2,700	2,500		
3,000	3,000	2,500		5,700	5,500	3,000	3,000
2,000	1,800	2,000	2,000	2,000	2,000	2,000	2,000
	150	500	100	150	300		150
	1,700			1,700			
	250						250
870	870	870	870	870	870	900	900
	2,500						
	600			600			700
2,870	7,870	3,370	2,970	5,320	3,170	2,900	4,000
130	(4,870)	(870)	(2,970)	380	2,330	100	(1,000)
200	200	200	700	500	200	200	1,000
6,000	4,000	4,000	6,000				
6,200	4,200	4,200	6,700	500	200	200	1,000
(6,070)	(9,070)	(5,070)	(9,670)	(120)	2,130	(700)	(2,000)
(10,100)	(10,170)	(24,240)	(33,910)	(34,030)	(31,900)	(32,000)	(34,000)

three months immediately ahead, you may wish to provide more detail about committed expenses in order to control your expenditures and to *work* your plan. Some people enjoy paying meticulous attention to their monthly cash budget; others are not so enamored with such detailed cash planning. However, no matter what your inclination about detailed cash forecasting may be, remember your forecast will only be realized if you control your expenditures. Have some method in mind to figure out how much you have spent and to control your expenditures month by month. One simple way to provide such control is to transfer each month from the funnel account to the family checking account only the amount you plan for normal committed expenses. For example, the Stonestons would transfer $2,000 at the beginning of each month. In addition, they would transfer an amount to cover the other expenditures—insurance, taxes, investments—as these expenditures were required. Thus, they would basically have to manage $2,000 (line 4 of Exhibit 17) each month and make sure they lived within that total budget.

In the final analysis, the best reason for a cash forecast is to prevent surprises. A well-prepared forecast takes into account how much and when cash is required. Timing is most important because if you know when cash is required, you have time to arrange for it—through selling of assets at a favorable point or through the arrangement of borrowing on favorable terms.

Analysis Alternatives

The cash forecast, like other planning models, can be used to assess the cash consequences of different alternatives. To show the use of a cash forecast in analyzing alternatives, assume that the Stonestons decide not to go on an extended trip to Europe during the year but instead:

• Bill Stoneston grinds away at his consulting practice for all but two weeks of the year; hence income is up about $20,000; taxes are also up $9,000 to $16,000 because of the increased income.

• Instead of extended travel, they decide to take two one-week vacations.

• Sally plans to spend $1,000 on furnishings, increasing the somewhat discretionary expenditures to $5,800.

The revised cash forecast is shown in Exhibit 18. The revised cash forecast shows income up $20,000; committed expenditures up to $62,900, reflecting the increase in taxes of $9,000; discretionary expenses down

$14,000, with the total cash required decreasing $25,000 ($20,000 — $9,000 + $14,000) to $9,000. The revision also demonstrates the effect of taxation on additional income and how decisions can affect the level of discretionary expenditures.

Determining the Right Liquid Investment

As earnings grow and your finances become more complex, you will find that there is a need to maintain some liquidity—beyond the checking and regular savings account suggested above. Choosing the right kind of savings institution and short-term money market investments is largely dependent upon the rate of return that can be obtained in various short-term investment media and the liquidity preference of the individual investor.

The pattern and range of interest rates differ from one savings institution to another, so it will probably pay to shop around to determine where your savings will earn the most. Basically, there are three kinds of savings institutions open to you, and we will briefly discuss each of these at this point.

Commercial Banks

Commercial banks typically pay a lower passbook savings rate than savings and loan associations and mutual savings banks. The only reason one would choose to have liquid assets in a passbook savings account would be convenience. A commercial bank usually provides all the services you need under one roof. It has been suggested before that you can maintain your various checking accounts there, arrange loans, conduct your estate planning business, rent a safe deposit box, and also use the services of the bank to invest in money market investments.

Savings and Loan Associations

Interest rates on savings and loan association passbook accounts that permit you to withdraw your money at any time are generally higher than those offered by commercial banks. Still higher rates may be obtained in such associations on accounts that require you to leave your money on deposit for some fixed period ranging from three months to several years.

	EXHIBIT 18 CASH FORECAST				
	Total	Jan.	Feb.	Mar.	Apr.
Income:					
Own business	50,000	3,000	3,000	6,500	3,000
Royalties	14,700	2,500		2,000	2,500
Total income	64,700	5,500	3,000	8,500	5,500
Committed Expenditures:					
Basic	23,800	2,000	2,000	2,000	2,000
Insurance	2,100	300		150	300
Taxes	16,000	1,700			4,900
Interest	500				
Real estate investments	10,500	870	870	870	870
Investment partnerships	7,500	5,000			
Self-employment trust	2,500			600	
Total	62,900	9,870	2,870	3,620	8,070
Excess (deficiency)	1,800	(4,370)	130	4,880	(2,570)
Discretionary expenditures:					
Somewhat	5,800	200	200	1,000	1,200
Vacation	5,000			2,500	
Total	10,800	200	200	3,500	1,200
Cash available or Cash (required)	(9,000)	(4,570)	(70)	1,380	(3,770)
Cumulative requirements		(4,570)	(4,640)	3,260	(7,030)

Mutual Savings Banks

Mutual savings banks located on the East Coast and Pacific Northwest offer passbook interest rates substantially above those of commercial banks and roughly comparable to those of savings and loan associations.

Exhibit 19 provides a comparative chart on the yields of various savings accounts available on May 15, 1974. Regardless of what savings institution you choose, make sure your savings are government insured. A commercial bank or mutual savings bank should be a member of the Federal Deposit Insurance Corporation (FDIC). A savings and loan association should be protected by the Federal Savings and Loan Insurance Corporation (FSLIC). The FDIC and FSLIC provide insurance on each account up to $40,000; in the event of a bank failure, the deposit would be paid by the FDIC or

May	June	July	Aug.	Sept.	Oct.	Nov.	Dec.
3,000	6,500	3,000	3,000	6,500	3,000	3,000	6,500
	2,500			2,700	2,500		
3,000	6,500	5,500	3,000	9,200	5,500	3,000	6,500
2,000	1,800	2,000	2,000	2,000	2,000	2,000	2,000
	150	500	100	150	300		150
	4,700			4,700			
	250						250
870	870	870	870	870	870	900	900
	2,500						
	600			600			700
2,870	10,870	3,370	2,970	8,320	3,170	2,700	4,000
130	(4,370)	2,130	30	880	2,330	100	2,500
200	220	200	700	500	200	200	1,000
			2,500				
200	200	200	3,200	500	200	200	1,000
(70)	(4,570)	1,930	(3,170)	380	2,130	(100)	1,500
(7,100)	(11,670)	(9,740)	(12,910)	(12,530)	(10,400)	(10,500)	(9,000)

FSLIC. However, funds may not be paid immediately. If you have over $40,000 to keep in savings accounts, you should take steps to keep every cent insured. The insurance limit applies to all money you have in *one* institution, including your checking account balances. When your checking and savings deposits exceed $40,000, take some of the money to another bank or savings institution. Any number of accounts in your name can be fully insured if spread around in different banks or savings and loan associations. If you are married, you can insure up to $120,000 in the same institution by opening two individual accounts and a joint account. Trust accounts for each of your children are also fully protected.[1]

---

[1] "When Banks Run Out of Money," *Money,* September 1974.

EXHIBIT 19

Medium of Savings on Investment	Yield (%)	Minimum Investment	Risk *	Special Considerations
SAVINGS ACCOUNTS At Savings and Loan Associations and Mutual Savings Banks:				
Passbook account	5.25	no minimum	1	Interest is paid from day of deposit to day of withdrawal.
3–12 month savings certificate	5.75	$100–$500	1	Penalties for early withdrawal: three months' interest is forfeited and rate is reduced to passbook rate:
1–2½ year savings certificate	6.50	$100–$500	(applies	
2½–4 year savings certificate	6.75	$100–$500	to all)	
4 year savings certificate	7.50	$1,000		
At Commercial Banks:				
Passbook account	5.00	no minimum	1	Interest is paid from day of deposit to day of withdrawal.
3–12 month savings certificate	5.50	$500	1	Penalties for early withdrawal: three months' interest is forfeited and rate is reduced to passbook rate.
1–2½ year savings certificate	6.00	$500	(applies	
2½–4 year savings certificate	6.50	$500	to all)	
4 year savings certificate	7.25	$1,000		

* Risk: See legend in Exhibit 4.

SOURCE: "How Much Can You Get for *Your Money*," *Investing*, July 1974, pp. 6–7.

Money Market Investments

The financial market is divided into three interrelated parts: the stock market, the bond market, and the money market. The stock market means trading in corporate equity securities that are issued and outstanding. The bond market covers trading in debt issues of relatively long-term maturities. The money market generally encompasses activity in short-term (usually less than two years), high-grade debt instruments that carry a minimum element of risk so that they may be readily turned into cash without material loss.

When the world of finance is operating as it has done historically, long-term interest rates are higher than short-term rates. Those who lend their money for a longer period naturally demand a more generous compensation. But in recent years, it has been a "new ball game," and lending money for 30 days has brought a higher return than lending it for 30 years. In making investments in the short-term money market media, one should be guided by safety and liquidity.

US. Treasury Bills

Those with at least $10,000 (purchases above that minimum must be in $5,000 increments) will not find greater safety, liquidity, or choice of maturities than that available from U.S. Treasury bills. Technically, these bills do not pay interest, they sell on a discount basis, and the Treasury pays face value (or par) at maturity. The difference between your cost and face value if you hold to maturity, or the sale price if you sell before maturity, is your return. You can buy Treasury bills through your broker or commercial bank, although the service fee may run as high as $30. To avoid the fee, some investors buy directly from the Federal Reserve Bank through periodic auctions.

At the auctions any individual is free to participate along with all the institutional investors by submitting written bids specifying what he or she is willing to pay for the bills. One does not have to be present at the auctions but can participate simply by sending a signed and dated letter specifying: (1) the amount desired (you can buy T bills in increments of $5,000 above a $10,000 minimum); (2) the maturity desired (you can get a choice of 3, 6, or 12 months); (3) delivery instructions (you can pick the bills up in person within 6 days after the issue date or have them mailed to you); and (4) mailing address for the discount check.

The small investor typically mails in a form for non-competitive tender, which is simply an agreement to pay the average price of the bids that are accepted. The forms can be completed in less than a minute and, as has been suggested before, the securities can be picked up at the Federal Reserve Bank or received in the mail. There is no fee or commission for an investor buying bills at the FRB, so this is a rather painless way to make a substantial interest rate investment over and above the savings certificate rates. Treasury bills are always in bearer form; that is, they are negotiable and must be safeguarded like cash.

Government-Agency Issues

Federal agency financing has expanded rapidly in recent years—from just over $1 billion in 1945 to more than $80 billion in 1973. This enormous appetite for borrowed funds has made federal credit agencies a major taker of funds raised in securities markets. In 1973, for example, the agencies were by far the single largest borrower, accounting for more than 30% of the net increase in all securities in the U.S.[2]

Some two dozen agencies issue securities. While some carry a minimum purchase requirement of up to $25,000, others—like the Federal Land Bank issues—can be purchased in denominations as low as $1,000. The following are some recent specifics on government agency obligations which can be purchased for $5,000 or less:

• Federal Land Bank issues are sold quarterly with a minimum $1,000 purchase required. Maturities as short as 18 months are offered. Interest is exempt from state and local taxes.

• Federal National Mortgage Association issues are sold quarterly, with a $1,000 purchase required. These securities mature in a minimum of 18 months. Interest is not exempt from state and local taxes.

• Banks for cooperative obligations are sold every month with a minimum $5,000 purchase required. These issues are offered in maturities as short as 6 months. Interest is exempt from state and local taxes.

• Federal Intermediate Credit Bank issues are offered every month, a minimum $5,000 purchase required. The shortest maturity available is 9 months. Interest is exempt from state and local taxation.

• Export-Import Bank securities appear at irregular intervals and are sold in $5,000 minimum denominations. The maturity periods vary, and interest is subject to state and local taxes.

The government agency issues have recently been paying interest rates far in excess of what can be earned at a savings bank. For example, in

---

[2] *The Morgan Guaranty Survey*. (New York: Morgan Guaranty Bank, August 1974), p. 3.

August 1974, a bank for cooperatives issue, sold in minimum $5,000 denominations, paid 9.85 percent on funds committed for six months. The maximum a savings bank could pay at the time was 5.3/4 percent for the identical period.

Another type of government issue is the municipal paper issued by state and city agencies to raise working capital while they are waiting to collect tax receipts or to float new long-term bonds. Although many notes are not guaranteed, municipal obligations are generally regarded second in safety only to federal government and agency issues. Maturities are one year or less, and there is an active market in the notes, making a wide range of maturities available. While most big municipalities only issue notes in $25,000 denominations, many smaller ones make $5,000 and $10,000 denominations available.

The biggest attraction of municipal paper is its generous, tax-exempt yield. In the summer of 1974 many high-rated issues were yielding 7–8 percent—the equivalent of say 11.3 to 12.9 percent for someone in the 38 percent tax bracket. Since the interest is also exempt from city and state income taxes within the state where the notes are issued, the tax savings can be even greater than first appears. Example: If you are a New York City resident whose federal tax bracket is 38 percent, you are likely to find yourself in a 50 percent or higher tax bracket when you count your city and state income taxes. That means that a New York municipal note yielding 7 percent will be producing a handsome 14 percent pre-tax equivalent.

Greater Return, More Risk

The corporate world also offers possibilities for short-term investment by the individual investor. Commercial banks offer banker's acceptances, which are drafts drawn on a bank usually by an exporter or importer with a maturity date corresponding to the delivery of the goods being financed. The bank can then sell the obligation to another customer or to a firm that makes a market in such instruments. Banker's acceptances were used originally to finance international trade, but today the bankers are apt to convert any loan into an acceptance. Like treasury bills, they are sold at a discount and redeemed at face value. Usually, the minimum investment is $25,000, but we have found them in a minimum of $5,000; we have also found that there is no transaction fee for the placement of the investment by a commercial bank with whom you are a customer.

If you are playing the short-term game with $100,000 or more, you can consider negotiable certificates of deposit (CD's), which are sold by commercial banks. The major concern is safety. In a period of tight money crises that has been witnessed recently, some have feared the reliability of certain banks and recommend buying CD's only from the largest banks.

Another short-term instrument is. commercial paper. Commercial paper is a direct but unsecured obligation of a corporation, often a finance company, and it comes in maturities ranging from 5–270 days. The quality of commercial paper is rated by the financial services but it is not registered with the Securities and Exchange Commission. The standard minimum investment for paper bought through a dealer is $100,000, although some offer smaller denominations. We have found that you may arrange with a commercial bank who pools accounts for purchase of commercial paper to invest for a much smaller amount such as $5,000. One must be cautious about the issuer since commercial papers are unsecured IOU's of the issuer. When Penn Central declared bankruptcy, it defaulted on $85 million of commercial paper.

Exhibit 20 summarizes the yields and other factors of various short-term money market investments.

Other Short-Term Investments

Recently, investors have been offered a new way to get in on the short-term money market. There are now mutual funds that help small investors take advantage of short-term rates without having to worry about minimum denominations, the problems involved in keeping their money invested steadily, or other direct investment problems.

The strategy followed by all of these funds is to hold money market securities that mature within a few months or weeks. In the summer of 1974, because of the lofty interest rates, most of the funds earned between 10 and 12 percent on their diversified portfolios. The funds retain 1 percent of their gross yield as a management fee and to cover interest expenses. Income and capital gains, if any, are accrued daily and distributed monthly, either as additional shares or cash. Most funds allow investors to get in and out as often as they like without paying a sales charge or redemption fee.

Exhibit 21 shows a list of some money-management funds and some basic information about them.

Another recent money market development has been what is termed "floating-rate" notes, sold in denominations of $1,000 with a minimum initial purchase of five notes ($5,000). In July 1974, for example, Citicorp, the parent of the First National City Bank, sold an initial offering of $560 million of such notes. These notes guaranteed investors at least a 9.7 percent return through May 1975, a yield higher than the bank's posted rate for similar maturity deposits of $100,000 or more. Interest is payable semi-annually at a rate one percentage point above the average weekly rates

EXHIBIT 20[1]

Investment Medium	Yield*	Minimum Investment	Risk†	Special Considerations
CERTIFICATES OF DEPOSIT				
3 month	11.15	$100,000	1, 2, 3, 4 (applies to all)	Issued only by commercial banks; an active secondary market exists.
6 month	10.75	$100,000		
one year	9.75	$100,000		
BANKER'S ACCEPTANCES				
1–270 days	10.75	usually $25,000	1, 2, 3, 4	Bought from a bank or dealer; money is used to finance short-term, self-liquidating transactions—usually involving import-export trade, difficult to find denominations and maturities one wants.
COMMERCIAL PAPER				
30–89 days	9.25	varies but usually $25,000	1, 2, 3, 4 (applies to both)	Promissory note issued by a corporation and bought from commercial banks, some brokers, some corporations directly and other dealers. Buyer must normally hold until maturity, may get higher rate on larger sums. Since these IOU's are unsecured, one must be cautious about issuer; when Penn Central declared bankruptcy, it defaulted on $85 million of commercial paper.
90–270 days	9.00			
U.S. TREASURY ISSUES				
3-month Treasury bill	7.92	$10,000	1, 2 (applies to all)	All Treasury issues are guaranteed by the full faith and credit of the United States Government.
6-month Treasury bill	8.15	$10,000		
1-year Treasury bill	8.20	$10,000		
2-year Treasury note	8.13	$1,000		
4-year Treasury note	8.25	$1,000		
6-year Treasury note	8.01	$1,000		
8-year Treasury bond	7.54	$1,000		
10-year Treasury bond	7.40	$1,000		
20-year Treasury bond	7.98	$1,000		

EXHIBIT 20 [1]—Continued

Investment Medium	Yield *	Minimum Investment	Risk †	Special Considerations
U.S. Savings Bond, Series E	5.50 compounded semiannually	$18.75	1	Matures in 5 years and 10 months; can be redeemed at any time after 2 months for value stated in Treasury chart.
U.S. Savings Bond, Series H	5.50 compounded semiannually for first 5 years; 6.00 for remaining 5 years.	$500	1	Matures in 10 years; can be redeemed at par on written notice after 6 months of issue date.
OTHER U.S. GOVERNMENT AND AGENCY ISSUES (Federal Home Loan Banks, Federal Land Banks, etc.)				
6-9 month	9.00	$1,000 (many issues are in $5,000, $10,000 or $25,000 denominations)	1,2 (applies to all)	Though some agency issues are not backed by the full faith and credit of the United States Government, it is widely believed that Congress would not permit a U.S. agency to default.
1 year	8.57			
2 year	8.58			
4 year	8.50			
6 year	8.40			
8 year	8.40			
10 year	8.34			
RECENT TAX-EXEMPT ISSUES				
1-year municipal note	5.75*	Although many issues are available in $1,000 units, more often the denomination is $5,000.	1, 2, 3, 4 (applies to all)	There's a thin market for many tax-exempts, and the seller of an odd lot may not get a good price.
5-year municipal note	5.25*			
10-year municipal bond	5.35*			
20-year municipal bond	5.74*			

	Yield	Denomination	Risk†	Remarks
U.S. Project note (2–12 month maturity)	5.30	$1,000	1, 2, 4	Issued by Department of Housing and Urban Development; guaranteed by the full faith and credit of the United States Government; also usually exempt from state taxes.
RECENT LONG-TERM CORPORATE BONDS				
AAA electric utility	9.07	Almost all issues are in $1,000 denominations.	1, 2, 3, 4 (applies to all)	Note the difference between the yields on similarly rated electric utility and industrial bonds. The spread is now at record levels as the earnings ability of electric utility companies is in question.
AAA industrial	8.40			
AA electric utility	9.22			
AA industrial	8.47			
A electric utility	9.68			
A industrial	8.74			
RECENT STRAIGHT PREFERRED STOCK ISSUES				
AAA	8.60	Varies with stock price and policy of brokerage houses.	1, 2, 3, 4 (applies to all)	More than 90% of new preferred stock is bought by corporations; for them, the dividend on preferreds is 85% free of federal tax.
AA	8.80			
A	9.30			
BBB	9.70			

* These yields are for prime-rated issues; higher yields available on lesser-rated issues.
† RISK:
¹ Inflation. Even an 8 or 9 per cent yield may not keep pace with inflation, and the lender may get his principal back in dollars eroded in buying power.
² Changes in interest rates. If interest rates rise still higher, securities sold before they reach maturity will probably be worth less than when bought.
³ Credit of the issuer. While the federal government should be able to pay interest on and then repay its loans, a corporation, or even a municipality, may not. This brings up another risk: If rating services suspect the credit of the issuer and downgrade the rating of its securities, the value of the securities will probably fall.
⁴ The market itself. If you decide to sell your security before maturity, you may find you have to take a discount from the presumed market value because there isn't sufficient demand for the type or size of security you are offering.

SOURCE: "How Much Can You Get for Your Money," *Investing,* July, 1974, pp. 6–7.

EXHIBIT 21

Fund	Minimum Investment	Commission
American General Reserve Fund c/o Channing Company PO Box 1411 Houston, Texas 77041	$5,000	1 percent
Anchor Reserve Fund Westminster at Parker Elizabeth, NJ 07207	$100	8.75 percent
J. B. Cabot Short Term Fund 104 South Central Avenue Valley Stream, NY 11580	$5,000	none
Capital Liquidity Figueroa at Fifth Street Los Angeles, CA 90017	$3,000	none
Capital Preservation Fund 495 Hamilton Avenue Palo Alto, CA 94301	$1,000	none
Daily Income Fund 230 Park Avenue New York, NY 10017	$5,000 *	none
Dreyfus Liquid Assets 757 Fifth Avenue New York, NY 10022	$5,000	none
Fidelity Daily Income Trust PO Box 193 Boston, MA 02101	$5,000	none
Holding Trust 382 Miracle Mile Coral Gables, FL 33134	$1,000	none
Money Market Management 421 Seventh Avenue Pittsburgh, PA 15219	$1,000	none
Oppenheimer Monetary Bridge One New York Plaza New York, NY 10004	$1,000	none
The Reserve Fund 1301 Avenue of the Americas New York, NY 10019	$5,000 *	none
Scudder Managed Reserves 10 Post Office Square Boston, MA 02109	$1,000	none

* $1,000, if forwarded by a stockbroker.

SOURCE: "Cash Management Funds Balloon," Christian Science Monitor, August 26, 1974, p. 5.

for 3-month Treasury bills. In addition, holders of these notes are guaranteed a redemption at face value two years after their issue. These floating rate notes are not bank deposits; they are uninsured, unsecured debt obligations of the Citicorp. The notes are traded on the New York Stock Exchange.

Chapter 6

STOCKS AND BONDS

When long-range type of investment is to be considered, most individuals think first of securities—that is, stocks and bonds. Listed or other publicly-traded securities may be liquid in the sense they can be sold at any time, but the possible sacrifice of having to sell them at a particularly bad time must be considered. Therefore, they should be considered as longer term invest-ments because it may be necessary to hold them for some years for a satis-factory result.

Basic Differences Between Stocks and Bonds

Essentially, stockholders are owners of the business, while bondholders are creditors.

As owners of the business, stockholders are entitled to a share of the earnings of their corporation. Small stockholders of large publicly-held corporations are really only entitled to: (1) such dividends as may be declared by the directors of the corporation; (2) any appreciation in the value of the stock; and (3) the possibility of receiving assets in any liquida-tion of the corporation. The small stockholders can only hope that increased earnings of the corporation will result in increases in dividends and the price of the stock. This may or may not happen, as we shall see later in the discussion of timing.

Bondholders, as creditors, are entitled to the prescribed interest payable on their bonds plus repayment of their principal amount on maturity. This means that bondholders do not participate in the growth of the corporation.

117

On the other hand, they have considerably more security. For example, in the difficulties of Consolidated Edison in 1974, the bondholders certainly came out ahead of those owning stock. There seemed no doubt that the company would be able to continue its payments of interest on bonds, and the redemption of its bonds on maturity, even though it had ceased to pay dividends on its common stock for the first time since the 1880s.

Bondholders are ahead of stockholders, both as to receipt of income and to repayment in the event of liquidation of the corporation. It is possible for bondholders to expect some increase in value of their bonds because of either changes in the money market or changes in the market's evaluation of the issuer of the bonds.

Theoretically, there is some inflation hedge available to owners of stocks, and certainly none to owners of bonds. What you think the rate of inflation will be in the future is something you must decide for yourself. If you contemplated an inflation rate of 25 percent, bonds would certainly be no good.

Stocks

There are an infinite variety of corporate stocks available to the prospective purchaser. There are probably 5,000 actively-traded stocks, and another 50,000 with some degree of public trading. There are all kinds and sizes of businesses, with all degrees of geographical coverage.

There are cyclical and non-cyclical stocks. Cyclical stocks are those such as the steels, machine tools, metals, etc. Non-cyclical companies are those selling products that are consumed quickly and are replenished even when wallets are flat. Examples are foods, shoes, soaps, soft drinks, tobacco, medical, dental, and hospital supplies.

It seems to have become impossible to define high risk and low risk stocks. Utilities used to be considered "widows and orphans stocks." Recently, with high interest rates, inflation in costs, and the difficulty of getting regulatory commissions to increase rates, the Dow Jones utility average has been at its lowest level since 1954. Of course, the passing of its common stock dividend early in 1974 by Consolidated Edison has had a marked effect on the whole utility market.

It is useful to have some kind of yardstick to compare your results in stocks with some published index. One method of doing this is to divide the current market value of your stock portfolio by the current amount of the selective index. This will give you a personal "unit." You can then make a comparison at any later date by dividing your personal "unit" into the later current market value of your portfolio.

Assume that you started this computation when your total portfolio had a market value of $50,000, and you used as your published comparison the Dow Jones Industrial Index which was stated at 1,000 at that time. Dividing 50,000 by 1,000 would give you a personal unit of 50. If, at a later date, your portfolio had a current market value of $60,000, dividing by your unit of 50 would give you a result of 1,200. If the Dow Jones Industrials at this later date were less than 1,200, you would have been out-performing the market as measured by this average. If, on the other hand, the DJI were over 1,200, you would have been falling behind. If you invest more funds in your portfolio, or withdraw some funds by selling securities, it will be necessary for you to establish a new base unit by dividing the DJI quotation at a date after the change into your then total market value of your portfolio.

Bonds

The types of bonds generally owned by investors may be divided by issuer into U. S. Government, municipal, and corporate.

The first thing to consider in the purchase of bonds is the degree of risk the investor wishes to assume. He can say there is no risk in purchasing U. S. Government bonds, as to receiving the par value of the bonds at maturity. There may still be a possible decline in market value of the bonds, because of changes in the money market during the period the bonds are held. If longer term bonds, such as those maturing in year 2000 or later, are purchased, it is unlikely that the investor will hold them to maturity. As a result, these money market fluctuations may be quite significant.

Municipal bonds come in all kinds. Merely because they are issued by a government body does not by any means indicate they are 100 percent pure. There is a big difference between general obligation bonds, backed by all of the assets and revenue-raising capabilities of the state or city, and revenue bonds, secured only by the revenues of a particular project, such as a road or bridge. Chesapeake Bay Bridge bonds have been selling at 40–50 percent of face value because of the uncertainty as to payments of both interest and face value at maturity.

Corporate bonds also come in all degrees of risk. Quality ratings of corporate bonds are published by Standard & Poor's and Moody's. The highest ratings by both services are AAA, defined as high-grade and gilt-edge. An A rating is described as the highest medium-grade bond. Any bond rated below A, which gets into combinations of B, C, and D is doubtful as an investment, although it may be a good speculation. These speculative bonds may have substantial price changes because of the investors' opinions as to the corporation continuing to meet interest payments and pay off the principal on maturity. For example, Western Union 10¾ s ('97) fluctuated from 56 to 98¾ in the first half of 1974. At their low, these bonds were yielding 19 percent.

In choosing between various A or better-rated bonds, similar yields can be found from both high coupon bonds selling at about par, or maturity value, and low coupon bonds selling at substantial discounts from par. Yield is a combination of the current interest return and the capital gain to be realized when the bonds are redeemed at maturity. For example, when New York Telephone 9 percent bonds due May 1, 2014 were selling at 96, Standard Oil Co. of California 5¾ percent bonds due August 1, 1992 were selling at 73. Yet the yield of 9.38 percent on the New York Telephone bonds was only slightly more than the 8.76 percent yield on the Standard Oil Co. of California bonds. Which was the better buy? Like everything else, it depends. One big factor to consider is that the New York Telephones could be "called" by the company at 108 in 1979 or later. This means there is no guarantee you will be receiving that 9 percent interest for 20 or 30 years.

If interest rates should drop sharply by 1979, so New York Telephone could sell new bonds at a 6 percent interest rate, they would obviously do this and call in their 9 percent bonds. The return on the Standard Oil of California bonds is more "guaranteed," regardless of what happens to the money market. The other factor to consider is that the capital-gain portion of the yield is more lightly taxed and, therefore, more valuable than the current interest portion. The so-called "deep discount" bonds such as the Standard Oil of California have some favorable characteristics.

On the subject of yields, as with any investment, the lower the risk, the lower the yield. For that reason, U. S. Government bonds tend to yield somewhat less than corporate bonds. An exception comes about in the case of municipal bonds because of their tax exemption. For this reason, a municipal bond will yield 2–3 percent less a year than a corporate bond of comparable quality. Whether or not this lower yield is desirable depends on your individual tax bracket, a subject that is discussed in Chapter 14.

Convertible debt instruments, either bonds or debentures, are a field of their own. At the right time, an investment in convertibles may give you some of the income features of bonds with at least some hedge against inflation in the form of participation in a greatly increased stock price. As with any other investment, you pay something for the conversion feature by accepting a lower rate of interest income than you would receive on a comparable nonconvertible debt instrument. Economically, you accomplish the same result with a convertible as you would if the same company were offering a straight nonconvertible debt instrument. At the same time you would be buying a warrant giving you the right to acquire a share of its stock at a certain price for a certain period of time.

Exotics

Short-selling, warrants, options (puts and calls) are technical subjects. An option to sell stock is a put; an option to buy stock is a call—you can call for the stock. Since none of them produce any income, they are all pure gambles as to whether the price of the security will go up or down, rather than the traditional "buying a piece of America" which is often advanced as a reason for buying a common stock. Another way of looking at this comparison, however, is that if a stock is bought solely or mainly for price appreciation, you might as well buy a warrant or a call if the numbers work out better. Contrariwise, if you are that sure the security is going down, a short sale or a put may be the course to follow. Some investors have done very well in recent years by selling short high price-earnings multiple stocks on the theory that sooner or later these would come down closer to the P/E ratio of seven of the Dow Jones Industrials.

The interest in options increased in 1973 to permit the opening of the Chicago Board Options Exchange, which trades in call options on 32 widely-held stocks, such as American Telephone & Telegraph, Ford, IBM, and Xerox. More recently, the American Exchange has started trading in options. The number of shares covered by options traded in a recent week was more than 20 percent of the shares traded on the entire New York Stock Exchange.

A call option has considerable appeal to a buyer. The stock is going to go up in price, go down, or stay unchanged. If the price goes up, the buyer sells the option at a profit or exercises the call and sells the stock at a profit. He has controlled a certain amount of stock with a small capital investment. If the stock goes down, he loses the amount he paid for the option, but probably loses considerably less than if he had purchased the stock outright. If the price of the stock remains unchanged for the option period, the buyer loses the option price.

As an example, Texaco closed recently at 24¼. On this same day, you could have purchased a call option at 3⅛ giving you the right to buy Texaco at 25 for the next eight months. Assume Texaco went to 40 in the next eight months, and you closed out your investment. If you bought 100 shares of stock, you would make $1,575—if you put about the same amount into a call option on 800 shares, you would make $9,500. The mathematics, ignoring commissions and any other expenses, would look like this:

| | Stock | Call option | |
		Sell call	Sell stock
Sales price of stock at 40	$4,000		$32,000
Sales price of call at 15 *		$12,000	
Less—			
Cost of stock at 24¼	2,425		
Cost of option at 3⅛		2,500	2,500
Cost of stock at 25			20,000
Profit	$1,575	$ 9,500	$ 9,500

* When the stock is selling at 15 points above the call price, the call should sell for at least 15. If it does not, you can of course exercise the call, acquire the stock at 25 and sell it at 40.

Of course, if Texaco does not go to 25 or higher in the next eight months, you will lose the $2,500 you paid for the call option. If you had bought the 100 shares of stock, you would at least have the current value of the stock.

Statistically, history favors the seller of the call option. He is bound to get the selling price of the option, or "premium," and all he can lose is some appreciation he might have realized by holding the stock and not selling any option.

Probably no more than a fraction of your security portfolio should be invested in options, because of their speculative nature and the complete lack of dividend income.

Importance of Dividends

In the 1960s, the heyday of the growth stocks, dividends were pooh-poohed. The theories advanced were that any dividends were nothing compared to the increases you were going to get in the value of the stock; it was better to leave the earnings in the Company and let it invest them for further growth. If you got dividends, they were going to be all taxed away from you anyway.

Now the experts seldom push that growth stock theory. One formula advanced for successful selection of common stocks says you should never buy anything with less than 4.5 percent yield. The basis of this formula is that this yield puts a "floor" under the price of the stock. If you buy a stock at a 4.5 percent yield, and the price of the stock drops 50 percent, you then, of course, have a 9 percent yield. Somewhere along the line, this yield itself is going to be enough to stabilize the price of the stock. On the other hand, a growth stock paying no dividends can fall forever without any restraining influence of any yield computations. The other plus of the reasonable dividend is that it is nice to have some income while you are waiting for the price of your stock to go up, or perhaps come back, if it drops immediately after you buy it.

A study has been made of 540 stocks listed on the New York Stock Exchange continuously from 1946 to 1965.[1] The 540 stocks were divided into five groups, ranging from the 108 stocks paying the highest dividends to the 108 stocks paying the lowest dividends. It was found that over this twenty-year period the total return from investment, including both dividends and price appreciation, ranged downward exactly in the order of the five groups. Group one, the highest dividend payers, had a total annual return of about 16 percent, while group five, the lowest dividend payers, had an annual return of 12–13 percent. Note that this was true in a period that was probably the best possible to select for the growth stock. The 16 percent annual return on the best dividend payers included about 7 percent in dividends and 9 percent in price appreciation, while the 12 percent for the lowest dividend payers included only 2 percent in dividends and 10 percent in price appreciation. So the question can be asked, "Yes, but what about taxes?" Well, let's look at it for an individual in the 50 percent bracket—one a married person reaches at $44,000 taxable income.

	High Dividend Payers (%)		Low Dividend Payers (%)	
	Before taxes	*After taxes*	*Before taxes*	*After taxes*
Dividends	7.0	3.50	2.0	1.0
Price appreciation (capital gains)	9.0	6.75	10.0	7.5
Total annual return	16.0%	10.25%	12.0%	8.5%

So even with a fairly high tax rate, the high dividend payers came out after taxes with a substantially better return. The mathematics are such

---

[1] Richard W. McEually, "Investing For Dividends," *Trusts and Estates,* August 1974, p. 512.

that even at the top individual rate of 70 percent, the high dividend payers still looked better.

This concept is true even over the "long pull." If you had purchased $10,000 of stocks in 1871, when stock market history really started in this country, you would have an appreciation in price of about $200,000 now. However, you would have had about the same amount of dividends, so that these would have been equally significant.

Even in the bull markets of 1926–1929 and 1949–1968, the greatest bull markets in the last hundred years, dividends were highly important. Dividends in 1929, for example, were on the average 50 percent higher than in 1926. On stocks purchased in 1949 and held to 1968, the average dividend return for the 19 years would have been $2.70 on each dollar invested in 1949. By 1968, your average annual yield would have been 20 percent on your 1949 cost. When you think about it, increases in dividends *lead* to bull markets. There generally has to be a reason for stocks increasing in price, and increases in yields are the principal reason.

Don't conclude from this discussion that you can be successful by just going out and buying *any* stock yielding 4.5 percent or more. There are many stocks around with high yields at the moment, because the opinion of the market is that these yields will not continue. So what you are looking for is a substantial "well-protected" yield, with indications it will continue. One method of trying to ensure the continuity is to look at the rating of the stock. Stocks are rated, much like bonds. Standard & Poor's ratings are designed to indicate the relative stability and growth of earnings and the relative stability and growth of dividends. The ratings for common stocks are as follows:

A+	Highest	B+	Average	C Lowest
A	High	B	Below average	
A—	Above average	B—	Low	

Certainly if you are looking for a well-protected yield, you should not go below B+, and probably not below A—.

Your Individuality

In thinking about security investments, consider first your own situation— your needs and your desires. Also consider your temperament—the old Wall Street adage is "do you want to eat well or sleep well?" If you make a lot of money, you may run considerable risk. But if you want to sleep well and avoid all worries, be sure you know how to go about it. Investing all of your money in U. S. Government bonds may give you the headache of being much more subject to inflation than if you made alternative investments.

Some individuals wish to build up a large estate to will to their children or others. Others may want to take it easy, and be free from care, not being very concerned about what they may leave, if anything, on their demise.

Some variables to consider are age, family status, your net worth, and your top income tax bracket. A $50,000 portfolio of securities is not likely to be composed of the same items in the same percentages as a $3 million portfolio. Certainly what is a right investment for a 35-year-old bachelor is not likely to be the choice for an 80-year-old widow. If the four factors to be considered in an investment are liquidity, income, appreciation, and safety, the bachelor and the widow might assign percentage weights as follows: [2]

	35-Year-Old Bachelor	*80-Year-Old Widow*
Liquidity	15%	0%
Income	0	60
Appreciation	60	0
Safety	25	40
	100%	100%

These evaluations would lead the bachelor to have perhaps two-thirds of his assets in common stocks and real estate, with the other third in bonds and savings accounts. The widow, on the other hand, might have three-quarters invested in savings accounts and bonds, and one-quarter in common stock and real estate.

Flexibility

Many years ago a man with a modest business adopted the practice of investing any available funds in Union Carbide stock. He followed this practice for a number of years, and his net worth increased substantially

---

[2] Keith Smith, "The Major Asset Mix Problem of the Individual Investor," *Journal of Contemporary Business,* Winter, 1974, p. 58.

with the fortunes of Union Carbide. Aided by numerous stock splits and stock dividends, he was able to leave $2 million in market value of his one stock to his family at his death, without ever having really had a substantial income. This story has been duplicated in the past by holders of IBM and employees of various other corporations.

Looking into the future, it now seems more difficult to duplicate this performance. One investment counselor has described the modern situation as "incredibly difficult to hold and find stocks for long-run investment." [3] Another author has described one of the most important factors in stock prices, price/earnings multiples, as being established politically—"by the actions of the President of the United States, Leonid Brezhnev, Chairman Mao, the Arabs, or the devil, depending on which market expert you care to believe."

Diversification is more important now than ever, and you probably need a minimum $50,000 investment to get that diversification. The Rowe Price New Era Fund, made up of natural resource stocks, did a lot better than the stock market as a whole in the 1971–74 era. The 15 issues particularly recommended in 1971 were up an average of 51% by May 1974. Still, five of these issues were down by percentages of 12–70 percent. As a result, a vice president of the Fund recommended that the individual put no more than 30 percent of his funds in natural resource stocks, and spread that investment over at least four groups of natural resource companies.

Nevertheless, some selection can help. The natural resource stocks did better than the market as a whole in recent years. This is shown by the results of one portfolio, recommended in mid-1973, for the first year ending in mid-1974. The market value, expressed as a percentage of the original 1973 investment, compared as follows with some generally used averages.

Recommended portfolio	115.7%
Dow Jones Industrials	85.3
New York Stock Exchange Composite	76.7
Standard & Poor's 425 Industrials	77.5

The portfolio did better because it leaned heavily to natural resource stocks. The breakdown of the portfolio was as follows:

---

[3] Baird Brittingham, quoted in "The Times Are Out of Joint," *Forbes,* November 15, 1973.

	Percentage of 1974 *Market Value to* *1973 Investment*
5 Oil stocks	70.4–95.4%
4 Gold stocks	133.3–238.4
4 Industrial stocks	77.4–106.2
2 Forest product stocks	107.3–111.9
1 Mutual fund (Rowe Price New Era)	92.9

Note the wide variations in results, not only as to groups, but as to individual stocks in the groups. All of the golds did well, but the top performer of the four was about 80 percent better than the bottom stock of the group. Maybe the answer is some degree of specialization by industry, based on research, but then a fairly wide diversification as to individual stocks in each industry.

A sum of $100,000 invested in high grade corporate bonds would have produced in income the amounts shown below in the various years.

1925	$5,600
1950	2,900
1965	4,400
1974	8,500

The low returns in 1950 and 1965 have been cited as the principal reason the laws of most states were changed to permit investing trust bonds in common stocks in order to increase the income of the investments. Certainly this philosophy is dubious in the 1970s, with bonds yielding 8 percent or better, while the average stock yields 3–5 percent and appreciation in value has certainly not been present in the immediate past.

The point of these stories and figures is flexibility. Do not become irrevocably committed to any course of action over a long period of years, as what seems so good at the moment may be exactly the wrong thing to do or the wrong security to own at some time in the not-too-distant future.

Timing

The economic law of supply and demand still determines stock prices. The real question determining whether the price of the stock is going to increase or decrease is the relationship of those who wish to buy the stock to those who wish to sell. This is what makes investing in stock so difficult for the investor who cannot predict psychological or other intangible factors. No statistical measures can account for fluctuations like those in the prices of Pacific Northwest over-the-counter industrial stocks during the period 1969–1974. During this five-year period, while the earnings of this group of stocks were about doubling, the average market price of this group was down about 70 percent.

The financial analyst who presented the statistics on these Pacific Northwest stocks remarked that one could almost throw darts at the board and make money in the stocks from the base of 1974 prices. However, the article was headed "Some OTC Sleepers." A sleeper has generally been defined as a stock with values not recognized in its market price, such as undervalued assets, superior prospects, low price earnings ratio, etc. The problem is that finding a sleeper does not do the investor any good unless the sleeper sometime awakens. Unless the investing public, or enough of them, come to the conclusion this particular stock is a sleeper, and create enough demand to bid up its price, these unrecognized values continue to be unrecognized and the stock does nothing from a price viewpoint. For example, for the last 16 years one of the international oil stocks has been described by various investment writers as an undervalued situation, with greater earnings, dividends, and potential per dollar of market value than comparable companies in its group. A small investor who purchased some of the stock 16 years ago has read every few months of the "sleeping" qualities of this stock, but it has never awakened in these 16 years.

The timing problem for the average investor is one of trying to ensure that he is not buying at a peak. A stock is most often going to come to his attention when it has had some reason for performance. This well may have created some interest in and demand for the stock, and therefore run the price up considerably. A real trick, if it can be accomplished, is to find a stock with potential for which there is not a very substantial demand and hope your sleeper will awaken; demand will increase as other investors realize the virtues of the security you have selected. The professionals in Wall Street used to say admiringly of one very successful investor, "he always buys his straw hats in September."

One solution to the timing problem is known as dollar averaging. Under this method, the individual invests a fixed amount each month or other period of time in whatever security he selects. The result is that the individual buys more shares at lower prices and, contrariwise, fewer shares at higher prices. Caution must be exercised to follow through religiously on this method and not quit because things look dismal. That is exactly the time when the most benefit can be deemed from dollar averaging, because the greatest number of shares will be acquired when the price is at its lowest and the prospects are the least hopeful.

Assume you are going to invest $100 per month in a security. In Situations A and B your first five purchases are as follows:

	A		B	
Month	Price	Shares Purchased	Price	Shares Purchased
1	10	10.0	10	10.0
2	8	12.5	11	9.1
3	6	16.7	12	8.3
4	5	20.0	13	7.7
5	8	12.5	14	7.2
		71.7		42.3
Price end of fifth month	$10		$15	

In which situation do you do better? In A, the price is back where you started after five months. In B, the price has steadily advanced each month, and after five months is 50 percent higher than the starting point. So B must be better? Don't be fooled! Here's how your results actually compare.

	A	B
Total shares purchased	71.7	42.3
Market value—		
Per share	$ 10	$ 15
Total	$717	$634.50
Cost	500	500
Appreciation in value	$217	$134.50

Dollar averaging is probably only feasible if a mutual fund or monthly purchase plan for a stock is used. This is because of the high percentage of brokerage fees in relation to purchase price in the case of ordinary small orders. The mutual fund is the only answer because diversification is so necessary. Otherwise, you may be dollar averaging down on a stock that never comes back during your lifetime.

Studies of dollar averaging have been made which conclude that even if an individual had started this method at the market peak in 1929, which was not reached again for 25 years, he would still have done well. These studies, however, do not turn out nearly as well since 1965—the start of a period when all the old laws seemed to have been repealed anyway.

Over long periods of time, the average annual return from common stocks, including both dividends and appreciation in value, has been 8–9 percent a year. The result has been that stocks have done poorly when high-grade bonds yield 8 percent or more, as they did in 1970 and 1974. The Dow Jones Industrial index dropped from 985 to 631 in 1969–1970 and from 1051 to 578 in 1973–1974. This is understandable. If one can secure an 8 percent or better return, with very little risk, why take the chance of whether or not the common stock will increase in value? If enough people adopt this attitude, the demand for bonds goes up, the demand for stocks goes down, and therefore, the prices of stocks go down.

This 8–9 percent long-range annual return on common stocks has been a good inflation hedge—again over long periods. In the period 1958–1970, for example, there was an average annual inflation of 2.6 percent, and an annual average increase of 5.5 percent in the DJI. But looking at a shorter period of time, for the years 1966–1970, average annual inflation was 4.3 percent, and the DJI went down an average 3.5 percent a year. In the mid-1970s, with the inflation as it is, one hesitates to say that stocks are any kind of adequate inflation hedge.

Chapter 7

INVESTMENT COMPANIES (MUTUAL FUNDS)

Investing today, from the viewpoint of most investors, is a much more complex problem than it was in the past. Many individuals just don't have the time to gain knowledge about the complexities involved or sufficient funds to provide the diversification that is important in any investment program. For many individuals, then, the solution to their investment problem may be the investment company. An investment company may be defined as a commercial enterprise that has obtained money from institutions and individuals for the primary purpose of investing the money in various securities to achieve certain financial objectives. By pooling the funds of many investors they provide greater diversification, presumably better management, and a continuous supervision of investments.

Since investment companies' portfolios normally include common stocks, these investment companies may provide an opportunity to partially protect against inflation and the depreciation of the dollar over a long term. Although there are two major categories of investment companies—the closed-end investment companies and the open-end companies—most people have been attracted to invest in open-end companies, commonly referred to as mutual funds. Therefore, most of this discussion centers on this kind of investment company.

What Is a Mutual Fund?

A mutual fund is an open-end investment company, namely because the company continuously offers new shares to the public at a price determined by the net asset value of the portfolio securities. As additional funds are received from investors, open-end companies or mutual funds issue new shares and invest the funds received from the purchasers. The selection, purchase, and sale of individual securities by the mutual funds is under the continuous supervision of professional investment managers. Thus, mutual funds seek to do for the individual what he might do for himself if he had the time, the inclination, the background, the experience, and sufficient resources to spread his investment among many businesses.

The growth of open-end companies has been especially rapid in the past decade. Total assets of the open-end companies (about $47 billion in 1973) now exceed those of the closed-end funds by about eight-fold.[1]

Most people attracted to investment companies are interested in the diversification and the convenience that these companies provide. For example, one share of a mutual fund may represent part ownership in a large number of other companies even though that share may represent an investment of only a few dollars. Generally, a mutual fund stands ready to sell new shares on demand and is ready, under normal circumstances, to buy back its shares at current net asset value. The asset value will vary from time to time, depending on the underlying portfolio securities held by the mutual fund so that liquidation value could be either more or less than the investor's cost. By purchasing a share in a mutual fund, an investor secures an interest in a number of companies that might run from a dozen to over a hundred. While the investment skill and management of the various mutual funds will vary, the mutual fund does offer investment *diversification*. Investment in a number of companies substantially reduces the risk involved when you invest in only a few companies; and typically an investor with a limited amount of funds (usually less than $50,000) can only invest in a few companies or in securities.

Mutual funds also offer *convenience*. Payers of dividends and interest file information returns with the Internal Revenue Service giving the names and tax numbers of the recipients. Under IRS automated data processing system, these information returns are cross-checked against tax returns filed by recipients of dividends and interest. An investor holding a diversified list of stocks in many companies might innocently overlook some dividends in reporting his income. When one receives dividends from a mutual fund, payment is made by only one company—the mutual fund—even though

---

[1] American Institute for Economic Research, *Investment Trusts and Funds*, p. 8.

indirectly the investor is receiving income from the many different companies in the portfolio of the mutual fund.

Mutual funds also offer other advantages.

• *Liquidity*—Normally a mutual fund stands ready to redeem its shares at net asset value, and therefore liquidity is secured.

• *Automatic reinvestment*—Most mutual funds offer shareholders plans for the automatic reinvestment of investment income, dividends, and capital gains distribution.

• *Continuity of income*—Income is also an advantage of the mutual fund. Typically, continuity of income is somewhat assured since dividends and interest come from a diversified number of companies. Therefore, the shareholder can expect to receive some income under virtually any business condition. In 1973 mutual funds shareholders received $1.3 billion in investment income dividends, bringing the total of such payments since the first U.S. mutual fund was formed in 1924 to $15.9 billion.[2]

• *Flexibility*—A mutual fund provides many aspects of flexibility. You can invest almost any amount at almost any time; you can select from literally hundreds of mutual funds whose investment aims hopefully coincide with yours. Moreover, investment management provided by the mutual funds promises advantages when used with tax-motivated investment programs for family members such as a child. By using a custodian account permitted in all 50 states, a child can become a stockholder. Investment return which might be heavily taxed to a grandparent or a parent can be shifted to a custodian account for a child. Investment income so shifted might be free from all tax or taxed at a lower rate. To avoid the possibility of adverse estate tax consequences, a grandfather or a father setting up a custodian account should not name himself as a custodian. He should name another adult family member as a custodian—i.e., the child's mother. If such custodians are inexperienced in investment matters, investment problems which otherwise might develop can be avoided by investment in mutual funds.

Mutual funds are attractive also to those who are setting up self-employed retirement programs. Many mutual funds now allow Keogh plan programs to be developed. In such cases a self-employed individual uses a bank as a custodian of the Keogh account. There is a small annual maintenance fee for such accounts, but that is the only thing that is necessary.

Some funds even offer free estate planning services, such as the review of your will to provide recommendations regarding an investment program that is consistent with your will. You can also get group life insurance with some voluntary accumulation plans that are provided by mutual funds. The accumulation plan allows for the acquisition of mutual fund shares on a

---

[2] *Mutual Fund Fact Book,* p. 13.

periodic payment basis. One of the reasons for the popularity of these accumulation plans is that they offer individuals an opportunity to build an investment program with relatively small purchases, usually out of current income. A widely recognized benefit occurring from regular, periodic investments is dollar cost averaging which is discussed in the previous chapter.

Types of Mutual Funds

Mutual fund shares do not provide a complete solution to the investor's problem. Each individual must decide how much of his saving should be placed in such shares and how much in other investment media. In addition, he must decide whether he can do a better and less expensive job by investing directly in securities. And finally, he must select those mutual funds that are best suited to his particular circumstances from among the large number of various types of investment companies. Unfortunately, the selection of the type of mutual fund is a very perplexing kind of problem. In early 1973 there were over 580 actively sold mutual funds in the United States, varying in age, size, purpose, and policy. Many have existed for more than 40 years. Many have offered their shares within the past year. Several measure their size in billions of dollars, while a considerably higher number have yet to reach their first million. So no matter what investment preference you have, you probably can find a fund to provide it. As John Springer in his book *The Mutual Fund Trap* has indicated, mutual funds by and large fall into five basic categories.

Balanced Funds

The objective of the balanced fund is to minimize investment risk so far as this is possible without unduly sacrificing possibilities for long-term growth and current income. Balanced funds have sought to achieve these goals by investing some money in common stocks and some in bonds and preferred stocks. Balanced funds seek to maintain certain levels of speculative and conservative common stocks and different classes of fixed income securities.

Income Funds

Income funds strive for good dividend and interest income through investments in bonds and preferred stocks. In recent years the income funds, along with the balanced funds, have performed better than capital gain and growth funds, as you might imagine, since income from securities has substantially increased as the stock market prices have remained low or have decreased.

Diversified Common Stock Funds

These funds assume that the best way to make your money grow is by placing your bets on the growth of the economy. Such funds keep most of their assets in common stock at all times. Most emphasize long-term capital growth. Some also try to provide a fair dividend return.

Growth Stock Funds

These funds are sometimes called capital gains funds. Typically, most buyers of such funds are not interested in dividends, but are more interested in investments in growth companies who put earnings to work to produce more growth and presumably stock value appreciation. The growth funds usually have the objective to maximize capital gain. A recent report indicated that one or more characteristics served to identify a fund whose apparent objective is maximum capital gain.[3] These characteristics are:

1. A clear-cut statement in the prospectus that capital appreciation is the sole objective and that higher-than-average risks will be taken in an effort to achieve it.

2. The choice of non-diversified, rather than diversified, investment company status.

3. Provision for the use of borrowed money to provide capital leverage.

4. Use of short-selling and/or puts and calls to increase possible profits or to provide a "hedged" position.

5. High rate of intended or actual portfolio turnover.

6. Extremely low or non-existent yield from investment income.

7. Investment in stocks of relatively small, little-known companies.

8. Substantial investment in "letter stock"—i.e., private placement of unregistered securities which cannot be sold publicly until registered.

9. Reliance upon technical approaches to the timing of purchases and sales of stocks.

10. Provision for additional compensation to management based on performance.

11. Concentration of investment in a limited list of holdings, especially if the fund is relatively large.

---

[3] *Investment Companies* (New York: Wiesenberger Financial Services, Inc., 1973).

For example, two funds that would probably be categorized as growth or capital gain funds would be the Rowe Price New Era Fund and International Investors Inc. The Rowe Price New Era Fund was set up specifically for shareholders who believe in the inevitability of inflation. The fund's prospectus suggests:

"The Fund's basic purpose is to increase shareholders' invested capital at a rate sufficient to at least offset long-term erosion of the purchasing power of the dollar. The Fund pursues this goal through investment in companies which primarily own and/or develop real estate and natural resources which are expected to offset higher business costs through the ability to adjust prices or control operating expenses."

As of December 31, 1973, the prospectus indicates that 54.6 percent of the fund's common stock holdings were held in natural resource investments, real estate, energy sources, forest products, precious metals, and non-ferrous metals.

International Investors Inc. states its primary investment objective as "capital appreciation based on the long-term economic and productive development of the Free World outside the United States. . . . The company's present policy is to concentrate its investments in the gold mining industry." As of December 31, 1973, the fund's investment portfolio indicated 85.1 percent of the holdings in gold mining stocks or gold mining related securities.

Bond Funds

These funds are investment trusts where the objective is loaning money to industries, utilities, states, cities, or other public bodies. One type of bond fund would be one which principally holds municipal bonds. Their attraction lies in the fact that interest received is exempt from federal taxes, and usually from taxes in the state of issuance. The higher your normal tax bracket, the more attractive these bonds become.

The above five classifications relate primarily to the type of investment objective of the fund. Another way to classify funds is to relate to the fund's method of selling and promotion.

Load and No-load Funds

Load funds are ones which charge a commission or a "load" of about 8.5 percent which is deducted immediately from the sum invested. This load is used to finance the heavy outlay made for staff sales and sales promotions.

While all funds assess their shareholders an annual management fee, a number of the funds charge no commission to new investors; these are called "no-load" funds. These funds are not promoted by any salesmen, and must be discovered by the investor himself through advertisements in financial publications or word-of-mouth. In addition, they may be obtained by writing to Investment Company Institute, 1775 "K" Street, N.W., Washington, D.C. 20006. Wiesenberger's *Investment Companies* also provides comprehensive information about mutual funds of all types. This book is available in many public libraries and most brokers' offices.

Given the fact that load funds charge a pretty hefty commission, why invest in load funds given the availability of no-load funds? The answer can only be performance. However, a recent study comparing the 5- and 10-year performance in leading load and no-load funds came up with this striking conclusion:

"Regardless of investment objective, the no-load funds on average did better than the load funds in both periods of time. A partial explanation is that no-loads tend to be significantly smaller. This gives them more maneuverability than the loads." [4]

Load and no-load funds can be found with all the five investment objectives discussed previously.

Closed-end Investment Companies

Under definitions provided by the Investment Company Act, an investment company is considered closed-end when it does not stand ready to redeem its shares at asset value or the approximate value. Beyond this distinction, it is very difficult to provide an all-inclusive description of a closed-end investment company. Closed-end investment companies may have broadly diversified portfolios and be comparable in many respects to mutual funds. For example, it may be heavily invested in a few special situations. It may concentrate entirely on foreign securities. It may concentrate on a specific industry or group of industries. Closed-end investment companies may have a dual-purpose fund with separate classes of shares for investors with differing income and capital growth requirements. In addition, closed-end investment companies may be small business investment companies or real estate investment trusts.

---

[4] T. Dale Rhodabarger, ed., *Personal Money Management For Physicians* (Oradell, N.J.: Medical Economics Company, 1973), p. 99.

As we have indicated, the number of mutual funds far exceeds the number of closed-end investment companies, but in the last two years there has been a revival in the founding of new closed-end investment companies. Between late 1969 and early 1973, thirty new closed-end funds with varying investment policies were offered to the public.

One important characteristic of closed-end companies is the relationship between the purchase and sale price and the net asset value of the shares. The net asset value is determined by adding the market value of all the securities held in the company's portfolio plus cash and notes receivable, subtracting dividends payable or other liabilities including any bonds or preferred stocks issued by the company, and then dividing the remaining sum by the number of shares outstanding. The prices of closed-end company securities depend on the supply and demand for such securities on the open market; therefore, shares may be sold below or above their net asset value. The difference is a "discount" or a "premium," depending on whether the selling price is below or above the net asset value. The premiums or discounts on any specific issue may fluctuate widely even within a single year. The chart in Exhibit 22 illustrates how the average discount of 10 diversified, closed-end companies changed, from month to month, from 1966 through 1972.

Another important characteristic of a closed-end company is that the capitalization is relatively fixed. New shares may be created for the payment of capital gains distribution and occasionally rights to purchase additional stock are issued to shareholders. But there is no continuous offering of new shares, as in the case of most mutual funds. Thus, new buyers of closed-end shares ordinarily can obtain shares from only existing holders; investors who wish to dispose of shares must find a buyer. In other words, whether one is buying or selling closed-end shares, the price is determined by supply and demand—just as prices of other listed and unlisted securities.

In recent times, most of the closed-end funds have been selling at a substantial discount. The *Wall Street Journal* shows each Friday the "Net Asset Value" and the "Stock Price" for closed-end funds.

Dual-Purpose Funds

Another type of closed-end investment company is the dual-purpose fund with portfolios consisting mainly of common stock. The ownership of each fund's portfolio is divided equally into two groups of shares—half for investors who want income and half for investors who want capital gains. The funds offer a lot of leverage to each group. Owners of the "income shares" who have paid for only part of the stock receive *all* of the fund's dividends; owners of the "capital shares" who have paid for the other part

EXHIBIT 22

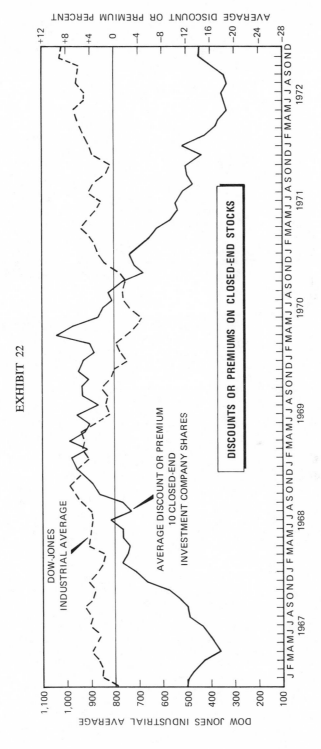

DISCOUNTS OR PREMIUMS ON CLOSED-END STOCKS

AVERAGE DISCOUNT OR PREMIUM PERCENT

DOW JONES INDUSTRIAL AVERAGE

DOW-JONES
INDUSTRIAL AVERAGE

AVERAGE DISCOUNT OR PREMIUM
10 CLOSED-END
INVESTMENT COMPANY SHARES

SOURCE: Wiesenberger Financial Services, *Investment Companies*, 1933, p. 22.

get all the capital gains. Dual-purpose funds, introduced in 1967 to the United States, have not been in operation long enough to provide a performance record that would be meaningful. However, to date, the dual-purpose funds, as a group, have not done well.[5]

Selecting an Investment Company

There are a great many investment companies to choose from when selecting one for your investment purposes. Probably the most difficult thing to do, when deciding which company is best for you, is to determine your investment philosophy and the purpose for which you are making an investment. For example, you may wish to set up a college fund for your children, a retirement fund, or just an ordinary investment with no specific purpose in mind except possibly income or maximum growth. But once you have determined your investment objective, you can substantially reduce the number of investment companies you have to evaluate. For example, you may feel that inflation is going to be the overriding economic factor in life in the future and that our currency is going to be periodically devalued. If you believe that, then you might wish to consider a company that invests primarily in gold mining shares, such as International Investors.

Once you have decided what your investment philosophy is and have narrowed the companies down to ones which appear to match your philosophy, find out as much as you can about the companies you are considering. Remember, you are buying shares that you will presumably hold for a long time. As one mutual fund broker relates:

> "I tell my customers that they may be holding these shares longer than they'll hold their husbands or wives. So I advise them to investigate the shares thoroughly, as though it's a once-in-a-lifetime proposition." [6]

Get a Prospectus

A prospectus is probably the most objective statement about the fund that you can find anywhere. Since mutual funds always offer their shares to the public, they are constantly in registration. Therefore, they must prepare a

---

[5] *See* "Another Look at the Dual-Purpose Funds," *Fortune,* April 1973, pp. 25–27; "A Warrant on a Bull Market," *Forbes,* July 1, 1974, p. 82.

[6] Springer, *The Mutual Fund Trap,* p. 169.

new prospectus every year for the examination of perspective shareholders. Typically, a prospectus tells you what the fund sales person would not dream of revealing. You will find a lot of useful information by reading and analyzing the prospectus.

The fund's prospectus will outline the investment objective of the fund, the fund's investment advisor, and background information on the fund's officers and directors. It will also tell you how to purchase your shares— how to make initial investments, how to make subsequent investments, and how the price of share is determined. It will show you how to redeem shares, what the dividend distribution policy of the fund is, and what the recent purchases and sales in the investment portfolio security have been. The prospectus will also show you the fund's current portfolio.

In addition to examining the prospectus, it also would be useful to get the most recent annual and quarterly report from the fund. This gives you a list of holdings explaining what the fund's investment philosophy is and the kinds of recent investments that have been made.

In other words, the prospectus and annual and quarterly reports provide information that you, as a prospective purchaser of an investment company's shares, should evaluate and analyze before purchasing.

Size of the Fund

Size has an important bearing on the performance of funds. Most recent studies have suggested that the best performers among the funds generally are those in what is called the middle asset category—above $10 million and below $300 million in assets. Funds in this bracket generate large enough advisory fees to attract competent portfolio managers, thus overcoming a major handicap of the smallest funds, and have sufficient funds and total assets to provide for the annual administrative accounting and management expenses.[7]

The large funds, on the other hand, suffer from their sheer size. They typically have to worry about the impact of a particular stock in their portfolio if they make a trade in that stock. Because funds are generally restricted to owning no more than 10 percent of the voting stock of any one company, a billion dollar fund could invest no more than a piddling 1/10 of 1 percent of its assets in a $10 million company. Even a big rise in the stock would not do the giant much good. Thus, the smaller funds enjoy far greater flexibility than the large ones. You may say that by not investing in any

---

[7] *Investment Trust and Funds,* American Institute for Economic Research, p. 22.

fund over, say, $300 million, you rule out some of the best performing funds in the recent past. But as one advisory service, Richardson and Roebuck, suggests, that is exactly what you should do, for the past record may no longer be meaningful. "The important truth about these giants is that at the time they enjoyed their greatest growth they were more like midgets—small aggressive funds with stock in maybe only 20 or 30 young dynamic companies." [8]

Performance

Probably the most important factor in selecting an investment company is to examine the performance records of the various funds you are considering. Performance results provide an especially valuable measure of management's ability, which in the final analysis is going to make one investment company outperform another. The past performance record of an investment company is of course no guarantee of future prospects, but it is perhaps the best available basis on which to estimate future expectations.

Perhaps the most widely used measure of performance of investment companies is determined by:

  • comparing the net asset value or market value of the fund's share at the beginning and end of the period being reviewed and ascertaining the increase or decrease; and
  • adding the amount of all dividends paid during the period.

The following example may serve to illustrate this calculation:

	Fund A	*Fund B*
Asset value at beginning of period	$15	$15
Asset value at end of period	$22	$12
Dividends paid during period	$ 3	$ 9
Increase	67%	40%

Once you have selected a measure of performance, you have to consider the "relevant" performance period. Some analysts argue that the per-

---

[8] W. A. Richardson, and M. L. Roebuck, *Choosing a Mutual Fund for Maximum Growth* (Greenwich, Conn.: Richardson & Roebuck, Inc., 1970).

formance period should be sufficiently long to include at least one and preferably several complete, cyclical movements. In addition, performance comparisons should be made among a broad cross section of funds and against a recognized measure of stock-price averages. One recent study performed by the American Institute of Economic Research evaluated what the researchers believe is a representative group of investment companies, including closed-end companies and open-end or mutual fund companies. They called these representative companies the "American average." Exhibit 23 shows the companies they included in the American

---

EXHIBIT 23

As presently constituted, the American Average includes the following companies:

Adams Express Co.	Keystone S-2 Fund
Affiliated Fund, Inc.	Lehman Corp.
American Business Shares, Inc.	Loomis-Sayles Mutual Fund, Inc.
American Express Inv. Fund	Madison Fund, Inc.
Anchor Income Fund	Mass. Investors Growth Stock
Axe-Houghton Fund A, Inc.	Massachusetts Investors Trust
Axe-Houghton Fund B, Inc.	Nation-Wide Securities Co.
Axe-Houghton Stock Fund, Inc.	National Investors Corp.
Broad Street Investing Corp.	National Securities Income Series
Bullock Fund, Limited	Niagara Share Corp.
Carriers and General Corp.	Price, T. Rowe Growth Stk. Fd.
Colonial Fund, Inc.	Putnam, Geo. Fund of Boston
Consolidated Investment Trust	Putnam Investors Fund
Dividend Shares, Inc.	Scudder, Stevens & Clark Fd., Inc.
Dominick Fund	Selected American Shares, Inc.
Eaton & Howard Balanced Fund	Sigma Investment Shares
Eaton & Howard Stock Fund	State Street Investment Corp.
Fidelity Fund, Inc.	Tri-Continental Corp.
Fundamental Investors, Inc.	United Income Fund
General American Investors Co.	United States & Foreign Securities
Investors Mutual, Inc.	Vance Sanders Common Stk. Fd.

Wellington Fund, Inc.

---

average. Figure 7-1 shows the performance of the American average compared to a widely recognized stock-price average, Moody's 125 Industrial-Stock average. The two lines parallel each other quite closely. The initial deviation shown in Figure 7-1 is partly due to the loading charge applicable to many of the open-end funds included in the study.

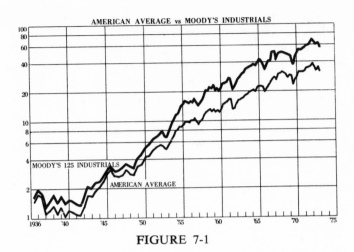

FIGURE 7-1

Figure 7-2 shows the American average compared with the results that would have been obtained from investments of similar amounts left to accumulate at various rates of interest, compounded annually.

Another significant observation of the study is that representative closed-end investment companies have provided consistently more favorable investment results than those obtained by the better open-end funds. Over a span of more than three decades, encompassing four major cyclical movements, the closed-end companies have produced more favorable results during periods of advancing stock prices as well as during periods of markedly declining stock prices.[9]

"But damn it, in the long run I will be dead," you say. What about more recent performance?

Recent Performance

Some argue that statistics covering long periods should always be supplemented by more recent performance results. The size of the fund, the management, or the investment strategy may have changed considerably over a long period, thus giving long-term statistics questionable predictive value.[10] For example, it is interesting to note the changes in the top

---

[9] American Institute for Economic Research. *Investment Trusts and Funds,* March 1974, pp. 29–37.

[10] "Some observations on the Consistency of Mutual Fund Performance," *Mutual Fund Reporter,* November 1973.

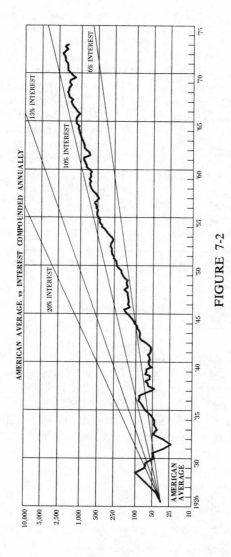

FIGURE 7-2

145

performers over the last 10 years. Exhibit 24 shows the mutual fund leaders over the 10-year period ended December 31, 1973.

EXHIBIT 24
MUTUAL FUND LEADERS FOR 10 YEARS 1964 TO 1973

	Gain *		Gain *
1. Rowe Price New		11. Ivy	147.2%
Horizons (NL)	255.7%	12. Pioneer	143.6
2. Enterprise	233.1	13. Oppenheimer	137.9
3. Security Equity	207.0	14. Johnston (NL)	135.6
4. Over-the-Counter		15. Imperial Growth	123.8
Securities	182.5	16. Investment Co. of	
5. Axe-Houghton		America	122.9
Stock	175.8	17. Financial Industrial	
6. Investors Research	168.5	Income (NL-I)	121.6
7. Istel	155.2	18. Provident Fund for	
8. Chemical	152.9	Income (I)	118.3
9. Vanderbilt	150.7	19. Harbor (I)	118.2
10. Putnam Investors	149.8	20. Putnam Growth	117.2

* With dividends added back and capital gains reinvested.
(NL) No-load.
(I)   Income fund.

SOURCE: Arthur Wiesenberger, Investment Companies, Wiesenberger Services, Inc., New York, 1974.

Exhibit 25 shows the top 10 performers in more recent periods. Note the considerable changes in companies included as the top performers. It is interesting to note that among those funds listed in Exhibit 25 the largest were International Investors (almost $150,000,000 at March 31, 1974) and Value Line Special Situations (about $64,000,000). Many portfolios of the top funds reveal a commonality in their investments in gold shares.

Sources of Information

Obviously the number of investment company possibilities requires that the prospective investor do some homework before making a choice. Fortunately, there is much information available about investment companies, and these sources should be consulted prior to any purchase. As mentioned previously, the most useful source might be the prospectus which open-end investment companies are required to furnish to potential purchasers.

EXHIBIT 25

MUTUAL FUND LEADERS

For three months ended March 31, 1975

		Gain or (Loss) *
1.	Scudder Development (NL)	57.0%
2.	Value Line Special Situation	50.5
3.	Amcap	45.0
4.	Financial Venture (NL)	44.1
5.	Sequoia (NL)	43.4
6.	Oppenheimer Time	41.3
7.	Edie Special Institutional (NL)	40.7
8.	Comstock	40.0
9.	Edie Special Growth (NL)	39.9
10.	General Securities	39.5

For year 1974

1.	International Investors	10.9%
2.	Lexington Income (I)	8.2
3.	ISI Trust	7.7
4.	Research Capital	3.8
5.	Partners	3.2
6.	Mutual Trust (NL-I)	1.6
7.	Rowe Price New Income (NL-I)	0.9
8.	American Birthright Trust	0.5
9.	ISI Income (I)	(0.7)
10.	Vance Sanders Income (I)	(1.4)

For 5¼ years ended March 31, 1975

1.	International Investors	294.7%
2.	Templeton Growth	85.3
3.	Founders Special	43.3
4.	Istel	35.5
5.	Pioneer II	35.1
6.	Investors Selective (I)	34.2
7.	Keystone B-1 (Investment Bond) (I)	32.8
8.	Colonial Income (I)	32.3
9.	Keystone B-2 (Medium Grade Bond) (I)	31.4
10.	Eaton & Howard Income (I)	30.9

* With dividends added back and capital gains reinvested.
(NL) No-load.
(I)   Income fund.

SOURCE: Arthur Wiesenberger, Investment Companies, 1975, supplement entitled Management Results to March 31, 1975, Wiesenberger Services, Inc., New York 1975.

Closed-end companies, since they are not in continual registration, provide copies of annual reports and other pertinent documents on request.

Perhaps the "bible" in the industry is Arthur Wiesenberger's book *Investment Companies,* which is published annually by Wiesenberger Financial Services. This book contains detailed information about most closed-end and open-end companies, together with much useful information about the general subject of investment companies. The annual publication is kept up-to-date by monthly and quarterly supplements. This service is authoritative and very objective.

In addition there are other sources of information that you may wish to use:

• *Forbes Magazine* publishes a mutual fund survey issued every August 15. Included in its tabulations are all publicly distributed funds with total assets of $2 million or more. The publication includes easy-to-grasp performance comparisons for specific periods of time and for up and down markets.

• *Fund Scope* is perhaps the most complete publication available to individual investors. It provides continually updated figures on fund performances, and it issues an annual guide containing the record of each major fund over the past 10 years. It is possible using the data provided in the surveys to compare funds having similar investment objective by contrasting their increases or decreases in asset values, dividends, and capital gain distributions. Since *Fund Scope* is not an advisory service, they do not recommend individual funds, and presumably are objective in presenting their facts.

• *Mutual Fund Performance Analysis* by Lipper Analytical Services, Inc. This publication provides weekly and quarterly performance figures providing a computer comparison of the relative standing of funds.

Chapter 8

REAL ESTATE

If stocks are uncertain and bonds are ravaged by inflation, the place to put your discretionary dollars may be in real estate. Here are eight reasons often advanced for investing in real estate, with some opposing arguments to consider:

	Opposing Arguments
1. Real estate is a hedge against inflation.	Inflation brings high interest rates that may make it difficult or impossible to finance development of the property.
	Inflationary increases in expenses such as taxes, interest, and maintenance may not be offset by similar increases in rent.
2. Leverage makes real estate particularly good in inflationary times. The investor gets the benefit of inflation on the total value of the real estate, while he invests only a portion of the cost, borrowing the rest.	This is great if things go well. One study has indicated that if one can pick out raw land, which will increase in value 25 percent a year, he can earn after taxes 14–28 percent a year on his investment for five years, assuming a 15 percent down payment on the purchase of the land.
	Leverage can be a disaster if things turn down. You get in the Monopoly

149

parlor-game situation of mortgaging your best properties to pay for a landing on someone else's piece of real estate. Then the next round you land on Park Place or Boardwalk, and the game is over.

3. Land is bound to increase in value, because they are not making any more. Also population is going to increase.

How about population? With the zero-population growth movement, you can't be too sure about population increases. They *are* making more land—by land fills, irrigating the desert, and building roads and airlines to previously remote areas.

It is amazing how much vacant land there is, even in the United States. Someone has computed that the world's population could be accommodated in the United States, and it would be no more crowded than West Germany is now. Even in the metropolitan areas of cities like New York, Los Angeles, Pittsburg, and San Francisco, 70 percent of the land is vacant. Get up in a high building or other place and look at any city.

4. Land which will go up the fastest in value is just one jump *out* ahead of the developers, like John Jacob Astor buying Manhattan farm land 150 years ago.

The best land may not be "out"—consider the energy crisis. Maybe it will be downtown; maybe it will be in suburbs on public transportation lines. It is hard to outguess where the customers are going to go.

5. Real estate is safer than the stock market.

This is really a matter of not being able to *tell* what is happening to the value of your real estate, as you can do with stocks by looking at the daily paper.

Real estate has a lack of liquidity which takes away a great deal of safety.

The worst situation is to own a building which is one-half rented, but 100 percent heated and mortgaged. When our firm moved one of its offices from one downtown office building to another, the former office, which occupied an entire floor, was vacant

	for three years. This meant the owner was receiving about $20,000 a year less rent, while the expenses went down very little. Taxes and mortgage interest go right on.
6. A man's property is "his castle" —isn't this what English common law taught us?	Environmental restrictions certainly prevent you from doing as you please with your property.
7. Rental property is a sure fire tax shelter for income you do not need now.	These tax advantages are always under attack. See the next chapter on Investment Partnerships.
8. A paid-up piece of rental property will support you the rest of your life.	No one can project the life and profitability of any piece of real estate very far into the future.
	The "increasing pace of change" has made it impossible to carry out the strategy 30 or 40 years ago of buying a nice brick one- or two-story building, with or without apartments, in a small city or suburban business district. This kind of property may now be bypassed in short order and become a liability.

Now that you realize that real estate is not all wine and roses, you still should consider the investment possibility.

Vacant Land

The first question is demand. Population and their demands for facilities and services are all important. With the "no growth" syndrome, however, one wonders. Environmental and energy matters do not help. A sewer moratorium in the suburbs of Washington, D.C. caused vacant land to go down in price 20–30 percent. An "open space land bank" decreed in California with no development until 1990 caused a tract earmarked for housing to decline in value 50 percent. In our home county, with slightly over 1 million people, there are at least 170 empty gas stations.

The demand factors are not all bad, however. Even if total population does not increase or increases only slightly, we know there will be a "selective" increase in the population aged 25–34. This group is scheduled to increase 35 percent in number from 1974 to 1980. These people are the home buyers, and they are going to move somewhere. With the environmental restrictions, some land will be taken out of circulation, but the land remaining should become that much more valuable.

Location

Real estate experts say there are three things to consider in buying land. These are as follows:

1. Location
2. Location
3. Location

Despite growth, inflation, and other factors, some areas of cities are selling for less than they were 50–60 years ago. Obviously these have been bypassed by the public. The economic law of supply and demand still works.

Even in urban areas, 70 percent of the people are on 1 percent of the land. This means you have to be *very* selective in your location.

What you have to do is envision a particular kind of customer, with a particular kind of project, feasible within a particular period of time.

And you have to buy wholesale, not retail. Lot purchases in a recreational subdivision may be all right for personal use, but they are not investments. You are probably paying more for selling costs than you are paying for the land.

Timing

It generally takes about five years of holding vacant land to make a profitable sale. The nature of the possible use of the property must change, due to a demand by people for facilities. The order of uses of land, from the lowest value of use to the highest, runs like this:

Farm

Recreational property

Single family residence

Industrial

Apartment house

Commercial

Vacant land does not climb in price steadily. Like moving from one rung of the ladder to the next, it climbs in spurts, as the next rung is attained.

You can help your land climb the ladder of use by some development. Most people won't pay for development to come, they have to see something happen. The sight of a bulldozer on the land helps sell lots. Even pointing to an electric pole as a source of electricity makes more customers than assuring them that the electricity is coming.

If you are subdividing residential property, remember that the old salesman said sell the sizzle and not the steak. People buy a dream, not land. If you have a creek, a beaver colony, or an old deer stand, it will romanticize the property and sell lots for you.

During your usual five-year waiting period, the value of your vacant land must at least double in order to have a satisfactory transaction. When you consider that property taxes, liability insurance, and interest on financing all total more than 10 percent a year—along with the costs of selling—any increase in value less than 100 percent will not be satisfactory.

There are some possible bright spots during this holding period. In some cases, you may be able to derive some income by growing crops or running livestock on the land while waiting. There are some tax advantages to deducting interest and taxes as ordinary deductions, and in effect offsetting them with capital gain income on the sale of the property. There are increasing problems in taking these deductions, and these are outlined in the next chapter. Also, you have to be careful not to have so many sales that you become a dealer in real estate and therefore lose your capital gain advantages.

Rental Property

Single family homes are no good for producing income. An old rule of thumb is one should rent a house for 1 percent a month of the value of the property. This is little enough today when you consider you could get 8 or 9 percent a year net on high-grade bonds and do nothing. Out of your 12 percent a year house rental, you have to pay taxes, maintenance, insurance, and maybe some utilities, to say nothing of vacancy problems.

It is hard even to get the 1 percent, particularly with high-priced homes. There is great resistance by a renter to paying $500 or $750 a month rent. Anyone with the financial capabilities of paying sums like that is probably also in an income tax bracket where it makes it more desirable to own, and deduct interest and taxes.

The bright spot of owning and renting a single family home is inflation, particularly if you have leverage. Even with a 4 percent assumed annual increase in the value of the house, it can be a satisfactory investment. There is also some tax shelter from depreciation deductions.

The headaches of this kind of investment, in addition to trying to come out financially, are the physical ones of maintenance and vacancies. One owner of this kind of property, *now* experienced, has inserted in his latest lease a provision that the tenant is responsible for repairs like the dishwasher and garbage disposal. He says there is nothing like the incentive system to stop the tenant from putting corn shuckings, artichoke leaves, and the like down the garbage disposal, resulting in a $100 plumbing bill. Do you really want the phone call claiming the hot water tank has sprung a leak, the furnace has gone off, or whatever else the problem may be?

Apartment Houses

If you get one big enough to afford a manager, maybe you can look at your investment only as a financial matter, with no concerns about the physical aspects like maintenance.

This *can* be the best kind of real estate if, again, you get a good location and a up-to-date building. The adverse side is declining income, due to vacancies or rent cutting, while expenses continue to rise. In our area, during a recession a few years ago, the rent cutting was ruthless, with competing apartment house owners nearby soliciting the tenants and offering them similar units at $20 a month less rent. What do you do then? Do you meet the cut, and thereby reduce your income, or do you let the tenant move out, and have zero income from that apartment for some time?

As with single family houses, a little inflation helps the yield. For example, a study of a 23-unit garden apartment, with a price of $420,000 and a 75 percent mortgage, showed an annual yield of 7–12 percent, depending on interest rates on the mortgage. Cranking in a little inflation, with an assumed 3 percent annual increase in rental income, partially offset by a 1.335 percent increase in operating costs, and then adding a 2.5 percent annual increase in property value, boosted the annual returns to the 10.7 to 18.2 percent range.

The annual yield is computed by using the following formula—assuming an apartment house purchase for $375,000, the purchaser paying $100,-000 cash and taking on a $275,000 mortgage, with 8½ percent interest and a 20-year term.

Gross rental income (100% occupancy)		$67,000
Less vacancy allowance (5% is generally used, but check this yourself on each project)		3,350
Net rental income		$63,650
Less—		
Taxes	$ 7,500	
Other operating expenses	17,500	
Debt service ($5,820 principal, $22,800 interest)	28,620	53,620
Cash flow		$10,030

The annual cash flow can be compared with your investment to determine the annual yield. For example, $10,030/$100,000 = 10.03 percent. Cash flow is converted into taxable income as follows:

Cash flow	$10,030
Add back principal portion of debt service payments	5,820
	$15,850
Deduct depreciation at 4% (25-year life on $300,000 building)	12,000
Taxable income	$ 3,850

Receiving $10,030 a year in cash, while paying taxes on only $3,850, demonstrates the tax sheltering capacity of depreciation. This is particularly true in a leveraged situation, such as our example, where you invest $100,000 but are taking depreciation on $300,000.

There is generally more tax shelter in the area of apartment houses than any other kind of real estate. One study has computed the average annual yield from apartment houses at 10.9 percent of equity investment. Of this total, 10.8 percent is from tax shelter, due to depreciation, debt financing, capital gains, and leverage. The ratio of building value to land value is about twice that of an office building and about three times that of a shopping center. This is important in giving you the maximum amount of your investment to depreciate. Also, you have much more favorable rules on use of accelerated depreciation methods than you do with commercial properties.

Commercial

When you get into commercial properties, the surrounding area is much more important than in any other kind of real estate. What you are looking for is an easily accessible building which serves an affluent neighborhood in a growing community. This means you look at some of the following:

- Community—Is population and employment growing or at least stable? Declines in either of these are red flags.
- Neighborhood—An affluent neighborhood will have manicured lawns, two car garages, bustling shopping centers with fairly new cars in parking areas, and perhaps high rise apartments or industrial buildings going up.

Bad features are too many vacant shops, too many homes for sale, or jalopies in shopping center parking lots.

- Immediate Surroundings—A commercial building should be in a commercial area to draw business. On the other hand, a medical building need not be since it draws from residential areas.
- Financial Standards—Occupancy should be 95 percent.

Operating expenses should be about 42 percent of gross rents, and not over 45 percent.

Debt service should be 40–50 percent of gross rents.

Combined operating expenses and debt service should not be over 90 percent of gross rents. This results in—

Cash flow being at least 10 percent of gross rents.

REITs

The initials REIT stand for Real Estate Investment Trust. REITs are like mutual funds except they own mortgages, pieces of real estate, or combinations, instead of securities. They give a small investor a chance to own a "piece" of mortgages or properties with only a single income tax. The REIT itself pays no tax if it meets strict statutory tests.

REITs have been through a shakeout since 1973, due to high interest rates, inflation, delays in construction, and other problems. They may still offer possibilities if you can pick one that will come back. One expert has suggested that some of them will yield 8 or 9 percent, with a chance of a 10 percent or greater growth in earnings per year in the next few years.

Tax Free Exchanges

One big advantage of investing in real estate, instead of securities, is the possibility of exchanging one piece of real estate for another without paying tax on any increase in value. For example, if you have a small apartment house you bought ten years ago for $100,000, and it has now depreciated to $65,000, you might exchange it for an equity in a much larger apartment building. Assume the market value of the equity you receive is $150,000. You have realized a gain of $85,000 on the exchange, but you do not have to recognize any of this gain for tax purposes. Books have been written about how to build up your net worth from $1,000 to $1,000,000 by "trading up" with real estate. A big factor is that part of your capital is not siphoned off by taxes every time you make a trade. It has been estimated that gains not recognized on these exchanges may be as much as $20 billion a year.

Home Ownership

That's right, we have not yet talked about the most prevalent type of real estate ownership, which is home ownership. Actually, 63 percent of nonfarm families own their own homes. There are certainly personal reasons for this wide home ownership, such as families desiring some roots, the pride of ownership, and the practical feature of not having to move.

In addition, the economic and tax features of home ownership are quite favorable. The tax advantages are principally the deduction of real estate taxes and interest on mortgages. Renters pay their shares of these items through their rent, but the landlord, the property owner, deducts them, not the tenant. Of course, an economic factor that has really been favorable for home ownership, as well as all other kinds of real estate, has been inflation.

This inflation, plus getting rid of some worries and costs of maintenance, has caused a great growth in condominiums. The National Association of Home Builders estimated that 15.2 percent of all housing starts in 1974 were condominiums, compared with 10.7 percent in 1973. Since 1970, housing costs have been going up twice as fast as incomes. The average new house costs over $40,000; the median family income is about $13,000, not nearly enough to make mortgage payments on that $40,000 house.

Of course, nothing is all peaches and cream. There *are* disadvantages to condominiums and certain things to watch out for. One of the principal reasons condominiums are cheaper is that a unit uses less land than a house—this means that in general you are going to be more crowded, with less privacy. Also, be concerned about the common areas, the landscaping, walks, recreational facilities, and even streets, if they are owned by the development. Normally the owners have a management association to handle these common areas. You should be sure there is such an association and that it is soundly organized. You should also be sure the projected monthly fee to the association is adequate to cover the expenses of these common areas, and that the facilities in or planned are of adequate size for the total eventual development. One major cause of problems with completion and maintenance of common areas, recreational facilities, etc. is unsold units. If you do not have the planned number of owners paying into a pool for these facilities, you are going to have real trouble getting them done and maintained. Be sure the condominium unit owners own the recreational facilities, parking facilities, etc. If these facilities are rented from the developer, it may turn out to be much more expensive. See the publications listed in Chapter 16 under Real Estate for more detailed advice about condominiums.

Cooperative apartment houses are a form of common ownership similar to condominiums. In a co-op, instead of owning your individual unit as real estate, you own stock in a corporation, which in turn owns the apartment house. The possible inflation and tax advantages are much the same as with a condominium. For some reason, co-ops are not so popular in recent years—their heyday was 40–50 years ago.

Home ownership was left to last because the personal features should be paramount, not the business and financial ones. After all, a home should be primarily for you and your family to enjoy. This can be proven from the classification system used by a large city public library, which keeps books on *buying* homes in the art department, and books on *selling* homes in the business department.

But you can't disregard the business and financial aspects. The average home is sold every five to seven years. Even if you personally don't expect to be transferred, or otherwise move out of the city, the neighborhood or your family may change, and the home become unsuitable for your use. So you want to think about what will make this house attractive to a large number of buyers. Now, let us consider location. Are you close to schools, shopping, churches, and public transportation? Are you a sufficient distance from major highways or heavy industry? The "gimmick," the "sizzle" which sold you, may sell someone else but don't count on it appealing to everyone. The "darling" one bedroom, rose-covered cottage 10 miles from public transportation and five miles from the nearest store will have a limited market when you get around to the selling stage.

Chapter 9

INVESTMENT PARTNERSHIPS

"Invest your tax money instead of sending it to the government!" "Get into a can't-miss Mexican vegetable rollover, catfish farm, or pistachio grove!" Come ons such as this are common in selling tax shelters or investment partnerships. Let's see what they're all about.

Tax Benefits Available

A tax shelter will offer some or all of the following:

- Deferral of reporting income for tax purposes:
  If the reporting of income can be deferred for 10 years, and the tax savings invested, these tax savings can be at least doubled before the time the income must be reported.
- Availability of current deductions
- Recovery of income at more favorable capital gains tax rates, or even tax-free.

If there is more than one investor in a tax shelter venture, a partnership or a Subchapter S corporation must be used so that the benefits, such as deductions and credits, will flow through to the individual investors. The partnership is the most common vehicle. Immediately one worries about the old definition of a two-man partnership as an organization where one man has experience and the other capital, and after a couple of years they change places! A limited partnership is used so that the investors will be liable only for the possibility of losing their investment.

Some tax shelters are not for anyone. First of all, the venture must be a sound business investment. Then, if there are some tax savings or deferrals available, that is frosting on the cake.

Even the good tax shelters are not for all individuals because of competition and supply and demand. Obviously, tax savings and tax deferrals are more significant to an individual in the 70 percent bracket than one in the 20 percent bracket. The result of demand from high-bracket taxpayers is to price tax shelter partnership offerings so that they are not generally considered desirable for you if your top individual tax bracket is not at least 50 percent.

Types of Investments

The simplest form of tax shelter is for you to walk into your boss's office and ask him or her for a $5,000 cut in salary for the current year. Your taxable income is reduced by $5,000, and you, therefore, save taxes at your top individual rate on $5,000. Your objective in trying to pick a tax shelter investment is to come out with a better result than you would with a salary cut. This means that you have to look at the investment and economic features of each tax shelter offered to you.

We will look in some detail at oil and real estate, two of the principal types of tax shelters. Some of the other shelters available include the following:

> Trees (citrus, almonds, pistachios, etc.)
>
> Crops
>
> Cattle
> > Feeding—Only a deferral of taxable income
> > Breeding—Deferral plus possibility of capital gains on sales of animals
>
> Chickens and eggs
>
> Catfish—This industry has grown 2,000 percent in 10 years and is now estimated at $100,000,000 a year in retail prices.
>
> Timber
>
> Movies
>
> Plays
>
> Scotch whiskey
>
> Equipment leasing

Oil

An investor in an oil drilling fund can receive more tax benefits than from any other tax shelter. About 80–90 percent of what he invests for his interest is deductible in the year of the investment as intangible drilling expenses. He may also get some investment credit against his individual tax for investments by the partnership, and some depreciation on the tangible assets of the partnership. Then, if his drilling venture is one of the fortunate ones that hits some oil and/or gas and has some income, some of this income may be tax-free because of percentage depletion. He may then be able to get some of the taxable income in the form of tax-favored capital gains.

There are at least 200–300 oil drilling funds being sold to the public. Like anything else, they vary—a subject we will discuss later.

Real Estate

We covered real estate investments in general in Chapter 8, and will now deal with the tax shelter type of real estate investment, which has obviously increased tremendously. U. S. Treasury Department figures show a change in net results of real estate partnerships over a recent six-year period, from a total $304 million profit to a total $1 billion loss. The attraction of real estate investment can readily be seen when it is considered that this kind of investment can be tax-exempt for 15–20 years and still throw off some cash return to investors.

Generally, desirable real estate investments are too large for one individual investor to handle alone. The question is, how big should the group be? The advantage of the small group, say six or eight of your business associates or friends, is that all the money invested goes into the real estate. But then the question arises as to who manages the group—who makes the decisions? A larger group, those "sold" to investors, will furnish management but then gives additional problems. For example, are you paying too much for this management? Is so much being taken out by "front end load charge" that your net investment going into real estate is reduced sharply?

Some of the common types of real estate found in tax shelter partnerships are:

Raw land
Apartment houses

Office buildings

Hotels

Shopping centers

Of these, housing real estate receives the best tax breaks. There will be more depreciation with housing for a given amount of investment because of a higher ratio of buildings to land. Also, a more accelerated rate of depreciation can be used for housing than for commercial real estate, and there is a more favorable provision as to the portion of gain on sale that may be ordinary income instead of capital gain.

Provided you meet the ever-present requirement of location, a subsidized housing project, such as an FHA 236 apartment project, can return something like 15 percent a year if the tax benefits go to a taxpayer in a 50 percent tax bracket. Like every other investment, however, there are bad points. A recent study showed a 8 percent default rate on mortgages on FHA 236 projects around the country, so not all of them are good.

Reasons for Failure of Tax Shelters

The following have been suggested as seven reasons for failure of tax shelter partnerships.

1. Excessive purchase price.

Tremendous competition for sound properties has resulted in prices so high that not only are tax advantages offset, but it is economically impossible to have a satisfactory return. For example, there have been apartment houses with debt service and other costs so high there would be a negative cash flow even if they were 100 percent occupied. One well-publicized cattle feeding program charged investors $750 each for cows that cost the promoters an average of $377. One investor in this program, after complaining to both the IRS and the SEC, settled for only a $10,500 loss rather than a larger amount the promoters insisted he pay. The promoters are now out of business.

2. High front-end load received by the promoters, resulting in too small an amount going into the actual investment.

3. Absent or poor management or failure of limited partners to contribute additional assessments.

You have to remember you are in a partnership with some strangers. Even if you are worth $40 million, the venture may go down the drain if enough of your partners cannot or do not want to put any more money in.

4. Insufficient down payment, resulting in large balloon payments which the investors cannot make.

5. Lack of experience or expertise of the promoter to select suitable properties and arrange a sound financial structure.

6. Economic factors.

One wonders about cattle feeding, for example, when a company with a name like National Alfalfa Dehydrating and Milling Co., headquartered in Kansas City, decides to go out of the cattle feeding business because it is too risky and takes a loss of $6,963,396.

Frauds

In addition to the economic and other problems for a tax shelter partnership, there are some that are just crooked. There are still "Ponzi" schemes around. Charles Ponzi was a promoter in Boston in 1920. In eight months, he induced 40,000 people to invest $15 million in a scheme to buy postage reply coupons in Spain for one cent, and redeem them in the United States for 10 cents worth of U. S. stamps. He promised at least a 50 percent profit in 45 days. The real guts of the scheme was using the investments by later investors to pay off the earlier investors with the interest. The whole scheme fell apart when an investigating newspaper discovered there had been only $1 million of these postal reply coupons issued in total during the period Ponzi was supposed to be investing $15 million.

Ever since 1920, Ponzi has been a name for a scheme where, in the pure version, the investor's money is not invested in anything or, as a variation, there is some investing of funds but new investors are still needed to fund the payoff of the old.

In a recent Ponzi scheme, a promoter publicized an idea of buying low-grade "industrial" wine in Europe and shipping it to the United States to sell to food processors. The investor would get nine-month notes with "guaranteed" returns of 30–100 percent. This scheme lasted 10 years, spreading by word of mouth by the enthusiastic early investors until it was discovered that there was no investment in wine. There were no ships, and there was nothing known as "industrial" wine.

In a more modern variation, an oil drilling fund operating under the name of Home-Stake Production Co. sold $130 million in interests in drilling funds in nine years. It may never be known how much of the investors' money actually went into drilling, but in one year only $3 million was invested out of $23 million received. Included as investors in these funds were many prominent entertainers, which is not too unlikely, but investors also included people like the chairman of the second largest bank in the United States and the former chairman of General Electric, which is unusual.

Advisory Services

One thing gives rise to another. The poor quality of many of the tax shelter "deals" and the amounts of losses has caused services that advise investors on tax shelters to spread. If you use one of these, you should be sure that their reports are not influenced by any interest of theirs.

These services have mostly looked at oil funds. One of the services, Tax Shelter Advisory Service, Narberth, Pennsylvania, looked at 200 oil funds and investigated people, expense and profit-sharing ratios, read the prospecti, checked with the Securities and Exchange Commission, and wrote to the promoters. After all this, if they were still interested, they would visit the promoters. They found, however, they ended up only being interested in visiting 10 percent. Another advisory service, ENI Corporation, 366 Madison Avenue, New York 10017 (also offices in Chicago, Los Angeles, San Francisco, and Seattle), went through many of the same procedures in looking at 180 oil funds offered to the public in 1973. They ended up recommending nine of these. Other ratings were "not recommended" and "poor."

Decreases in Tax Benefits

The Tax Reform Act of 1969 materially reduced the tax benefits of tax shelters. By imposing a maximum 50 percent tax on earned income, the 1969 Act materially reduced the incentive for "gimmicks" to reduce taxable income. At the same time, it materially increased possible taxes on capital gains and imposed a new minimum tax on tax preferences, which may provide some additional tax on tax shelter situations.

Now even further reductions of tax benefits are likely. The Treasury Department is strongly recommending an idea called "LAL" (Limitation on Artificial Accounting Losses) which would limit the deductions of tax shelter losses against other kinds of income, such as salaries, interest and dividends, or income from a business or profession. Losses would be deferred until they could be offset against gains from a particular kind of property, such as real estate, oil, gas, etc., or until the losses are actually realized by a sale or other disposition of the investment. It has been estimated that these proposals would defer deductions on 43.4 percent of the annual investment in commercial real estate construction. Again to show the preference to residential real estate, the estimate for the deferral of deductions on residential type of construction is only 6.5 percent.

Conclusion

If you think we are negative on tax shelters, we are. The odds of the average investor having a satisfactory result are not great—what with all the hurdles to surmount. The odds really logically follow the law of supply and demand. There is something about tax savings that makes an investment so attractive to individuals that they will bid up its price or buy it at a figure that makes no economic sense. There *are* good tax shelters around and economic advantage to be obtained from them, but on the average, an individual is not too likely to find one. You should look for one that seems to have a reasonable chance of either returning your investment with some profit, or giving you some income—your best chances of finding one of these may well be in the investment you make alone, or with two or three friends, rather than in the area of public offerings.

Chapter 10

PENSION AND PROFIT SHARING PLANS AND YOUR RETIREMENT

If you have read this far, you may be discouraged about building yourself a net worth by investments. Well, here's a possibility where you probably will not need to invest any money and you won't be handling the investments. Perhaps, based on your experience, that is good too!

Reasons for Popularity of Retirement Plans

About 30 million "private" (i.e., nonpublic) employees, or about one-half of the total, are covered by pension and profit-sharing plans. Of course nearly 100 percent of public employees are covered by such plans. In fact, the coverage is so good for many public employees that citizens and tax-payers worry about the plans bankrupting particular governmental bodies. These plans have about $300 billion in assets—about equally divided between the private and public plans.

Some of the reasons for the tremendous growth in numbers and coverage of pension and profit-sharing plans are:

   1. The difficulty the average citizen has in accumulating anything after taxes and living expense dollars. This is the "squirrel cage" doctrine. As an individual makes more and more money, he pays higher and higher tax rates, so he has less left. After paying higher and higher living expenses, if he does save anything, the income on his savings is taxed at higher and higher rates. A pension or profit-sharing plan operates like a semi-compulsory savings plan.

2. The need for income. People are living longer, and inflation is making it more difficult for people to have a decent income in retirement. Twenty-five years ago, insurance companies ran full page ads of a beaming couple retiring to Florida on $150 per month. After some years, they increased the desired income to $250 a month, and some years later, they seemed to give up entirely. It just wasn't feasible for many people to buy insurance policies or annuities with their own money that would give them a decent living on retirement in inflationary times.

Medicare and private health insurance plans have pretty well taken care of the catastrophic medical expense problem, the one where people used to worry about a serious illness which would cost them or their families $25,000 or $30,000 a year in medical expenses. The big worry *now* is outliving your money.

3. Labor demands. Increasingly unions are asking for fringe benefits, including pension or profit-sharing plans, instead of cash. They are savvy about tax benefits, too.

4. Competitors' plans.

5. Psychological impact of executive salaries. Even if a cash increase in salary would be better for the individual, particularly with the 50 percent maximum tax on earned income, it may sit better with stockholders and others, and not disturb pay relationships down the line, to give an executive some pension or profit-sharing plan benefits, instead.

6. Death benefits either in the form of life insurance included in the plan, or the payment to the heirs of a deceased employee of his account in the pension or profit-sharing plan.

7. Tax benefits, which are considered next.

Tax Benefits

Tax benefits of a pension or profit-sharing plan include—

1. The employer deducts contributions to the plan as business expenses, which means the government pays about half of the expense for most corporations.

2. There is no tax to the employee until he receives something on retirement, death, or other termination of employment.

3. Income accumulates tax-free on the assets of the plan. This leads to much greater compounding of benefits and is particularly important over a period of years. For example, at an 8½ percent interest rate, money will double tax-free in nine years. If an individual was receiving 8½ percent interest, and paying 50 percent of this interest out in taxes, his money would double in about 17 years. The effect of this tax-free compounding

is to build up for an employee two to three times as much capital as he would have been able to save himself from after tax dollars.

The total effect of these first three tax benefits can be seen by comparing individuals Joe and Fred, each directing $5,000 a year of current compensation to a retirement plan. Joe's employer is putting $5,000 a year in a pension or profit-sharing plan for Joe. Fred is embarked on a "do-it-yourself" effort, taking what's left after taxes from $5,000 of his current compensation and investing it. Assuming both Joe and Fred earn 8 percent annually and continue this for 25 years, the retirement funds will grow to:

Joe	$365,000
Fred	104,000

Fred could narrow the gap between his retirement fund and Joe's by setting up an IRA (Individual Retirement Account) and setting aside $1,500 a year, which would be tax deductible and earn tax-exempt income.

4. The first $5,000 of death benefits payable from the plan is exempt from income tax, even if the decedent had a vested right to the benefits at the time of his death.

5. There is no Federal estate tax on benefits from a plan paid to an heir and not to the employee's estate after death of an employee.

What Kind of Plan—Pension or Profit Sharing?

We have been talking about pension or profit-sharing plans rather interchangeably. The private plans in the country are about equally divided between the two types. What is the difference?

A pension plan is benefit-oriented. At the start of the plan, a determination is made as to what benefits will be paid on retirement of employees. Contributions to the plan are then made by the employer in amounts actuarily determined as necessary to build up the assets in the plan to an extent necessary to pay the determined benefits.

A profit-sharing plan, however, is contribution-oriented. The initial determination is a formula under which the employer will make contributions, probably as a percentage of the employer's profits. Of course, if there are no profits, there are no contributions, and the amounts of contributions vary with the amounts of profits. Therefore, each employee builds up an account in an amount which cannot be determined in advance. One thing certain is that the tax deductible contributions to the plan cannot exceed 15 percent of the salaries of the employees participating in the plan.

The best plan for you, if you have a choice, will be determined by your age and your expectations as to length of employment. If you are more than 35, a pension plan may be better, just because you have fewer years in which to accumulate your share of profit-sharing plan contributions. One study has determined that it may be possible to contribute to a pension plan 28 percent of your salary each year if you are 45 and 71 percent if you are 55. Obviously, contributions at these levels are going to build up much greater benefits than the 15 percent of salary-a-year which is the maximum under a profit-sharing plan. The pension plan also has the benefit to older employees of giving some credit to their past service. This is just not possible with the profit-sharing plan.

On the other hand, if you are under 35 or about that age, and look forward to a long period of employment, the profit-sharing plan may work out better. One additional benefit under the profit-sharing plan is that forfeitures of employees terminating their employment are allocated to the benefit of the remaining employee participants in the plan, instead of benefiting the employer's future cost—as they do with the pension plan.

Where the profit-sharing plan works right, for example with Sears Roebuck and Co., the results can be phenomenal. Many Sears employees who have retired find their dividends from their Sears stock in their profit-sharing account are greater than any salary they earned during their active service. This result has come from substantial forfeitures of terminating employees being credited to accounts of employees who stay, and from investing in Sears stock, which has done well over the years.

From the viewpoint of the employer, if you happen to be one of those, the profit-sharing plan is probably more favorable. For one thing, you have less fixed commitment to your employees to make contributions in good or bad years. Also, there may well be more incentive for the employees to do well, as the benefits are tied to some extent to productivity and profits. We have seen, for example, that cooperative plywood mills, where employees were owners of the business, had one-third higher productivity than comparable privately-owned mills. The answer seemed to be that if an employee was sitting down on the job, a fellow employee would freely offer to kick him in what he was sitting on, because he was wasting the fellow employee's money.

Can You Get in on These if You Are Self-employed?

You may have thought from this discussion that all this applies only to employees of a substantial company with a pension or profit-sharing plan. This is not the case. If you are essentially a self-employed person, you can still get the benefits of a pension or profit-sharing plan, regardless of whether you are a major stock-holder and president of a small ordinary corporation, have the same status with a professional corporation, or are legally a self-employed person as proprietor or partner.

These possibilities have arisen as a result of the growing realization that an employee has a much better status than an entrepreneur. This has resulted in all of the states passing professional corporation laws allowing doctors, dentists, lawyers, certified public accountants, and others, to incorporate. This was legally prohibited until quite recently. Legally, you are just as separate from a corporation whether you are an employee of General Motors, or whether you are John Jones, president of John Jones Corporation—the only employee and own all the stock. So if you are a corporate employee, either of a regular or a professional corporation, you can get all the benefits of a pension or a profit-sharing plan, even if you are the only employee and own all the stock.

And even if you are not an employee, but operate a business as a proprietor or a partner, or you are a self-employed professional, you can still have all the benefits of a pension or profit-sharing plan, if you are willing to cover your employees after one year of employment. The annual contribution to your plan cannot exceed 15 percent of your net income from your business or profession, or $7,500 per year, whichever is lower. This limitation was tripled by the Pension Reform Act of 1974, and has made Keogh plans an attractive method of building net worth. The following is a comparison of amounts accumulated by a 50 percent top tax bracket individual investing $7,500 a year in a Keogh plan or $3,750 a year of after-tax dollars. Either way the investment costs $3,750 of after-tax dollars, since the $7,500 contribution to the Keogh plan is deductible, resulting in a $3,750 saving in income taxes. An 8 percent return on investments is assumed.

| Years of Investment | Amount Accumulated | |
	Keogh Plan	After-tax Investments
15	$203,640	$ 75,088
20	343,214	111,667
25	548,294	156,172
30	849,624	210,318

The Keogh plan results in a reasonable number of years in 3 to 4 times the amount of net worth accumulated by after tax investments.

For about the first 12 years of the existence of self-employed retirement plans, or Keogh plans, the limitation was $2,500 per year; for the first few years, only one-half of the amount placed in the plan by the self-employed person was tax deductible. The liberation is just another indication of the growing pressure to equalize employees and entrepreneurs for tax purposes.

When Do You Want to Retire? Will You Be Able to?

Whether you have the benefits of a pension or profit-sharing plan or you don't, you need to give some thought to the timing of your retirement. Your first step in determining when you would like to retire is to think about your personal desires as to when you would like to stop working, and what you would do if you quit. One you have decided on the ideal retirement age from a personal viewpoint, you should determine whether this retirement age is feasible financially. To do this, the steps are as follows.

   1. Estimate what your expenses would be if you retired now. Then project these expenses to the year in which you plan to retire, making whatever allowance for inflation you think proper. We have provided Exhibit 26 as a worksheet on which you can accumulate your expenses, both now and when you plan to retire.

   2. Compute the amount you need to invest each year to be able to meet your retirement expenses. Your starting point is your estimated total of retirement expenses from Exhibit 26. This should be entered on line 1 of Exhibit 27.

If you wish to leave your assets to your family, you should complete Exhibit 27. On line 4, compute the amount of investments needed at retirement, assuming you get a 5 percent return. Then enter on line 5 the amount of investments you have now, and on line 6 show what these investments will grow to be in the year of planned retirement. Exhibit 28 will give you the factor by which to multiply your current investments to get the desired figure for line 6. By taking the factor opposite the number of years until your planned retirement, you can determine the proper multiplier to use. After computing your deficit in investments on line 7, determine from Exhibit 29 how much is needed to invest each year until retirement to eliminate your deficit. Exhibit 29 assumes a 6 percent return and gives you the amount necessary to invest each year to have one dollar at retirement—after you have determined the number of years remaining before retirement.

If you are not concerned with leaving assets to your family, and are

EXHIBIT 26
RETIREMENT EXPENSES WORKSHEET

	Now	On planned retirement
Food		
Housing		
Clothing		
Automobile		
Entertainment, recreation, and trips		
Books, newspapers, magazines, and records		
Medical and dental expenses		
Contributions to church and charities		
Miscellaneous		
Income tax on estimated retirement income		
Total	$	$

willing to use up principal, you can get by with a considerably smaller amount of investments. Starting with your required annual income from investments on line 3 of Exhibit 27, you can consult Exhibit 30 to determine the amount of investments needed on retirement. Exhibit 30 shows the funds necessary to invest at three different annual interest rates to produce various amounts of annual income for a period of 25 years.

No matter how you plan your retirement, you should not overlook the wonders of compound interest, which make starting early especially important. For example, one company has a retirement plan for its employees where the employees contribute $5 a week and the employer also contributes to the plan. They have computed that an employee starting this

---

EXHIBIT 27

---

1. Estimated annual expenses in retirement
   (Exhibit 26) $_____

2. Estimated annual income from Social
   Security, pensions, and annuities   _____

3. Estimated annual income needed from
   investments (line 1. minus line 2.)   _____

4. Investments needed at retirement—based
   on 5% return (line 3. multiplied by 20)   _____

5. Investments available now   _____

6. Estimated investments available at retirement
   (Exhibit 28)   _____

7. Deficit in investments (line 4. minus line 6.)   _____

8. Amount to invest each year to eliminate
   deficit in investments (Exhibit 29)   _____

---

plan at age 30 will have a pension of $741 per month at age 65. If, however, the employee does not start the plan until he is age 40, 10 years later, his pension at age 65 is reduced to $394 a month, or about cut in half. As the brochure for the plan states, "If enrollment were postponed 10 years from age 30 to age 40, the employee would keep (or spend) a few extra dollars of salary, but would sacrifice $347 a month forever."

Early Retirement for You?

Whether retirement at 50, as Bill Stoneston wants to do, at 55, or some other age, is desirable is for you to decide. From a financial viewpoint, go slow! In recent years, early retirement has become more and more usual. It has been desirable both from the viewpoint of some employees and many employers. Employers have often been interested in cost saving —the financial desirability of replacing a $25,000-a-year person with perhaps a $12,000-a-year person. Employers have encouraged retirement by offering financial incentives such as one or two years' salary, extra retirement benefits, and other bonuses. If these have not worked, they have sometimes used psychological incentives, such as undersirable work, not assigning any work, or other demeaning devices.

EXHIBIT 28

How Your Investments Will Grow
at 6%, Compounded Annually

Years	Multiplier
1	1.06
2	1.12
3	1.19
4	1.26
5	1.34
6	1.42
7	1.50
8	1.59
9	1.69
10	1.79
11	1.90
12	2.01
13	2.13
14	2.26
15	2.40
16	2.54
17	2.69
18	2.85
19	3.03
20	3.21
21	3.40
22	3.60
23	3.82
24	4.05
25	4.29
26	4.55
27	4.82
28	5.11
29	5.42
30	5.74

When you get around to looking at early retirement from a dollar and cents viewpoint, you should realize that the early retiree pays a triple penalty as follows.

1. He has a reduced pension.

2. He loses the benefit of any future increases in salary, which is generally the basis for computing pensions.

EXHIBIT 29

How Much to Invest Each Year
to Have $1 at Retirement

Years to retirement	Amount to invest
1	$1.00
2	0.49
3	0.31
4	0.23
5	0.18
6	0.14
7	0.12
8	0.10
9	0.09
10	0.08
11	0.07
12	0.06
13	0.05
14	0.05
15	0.04
16	0.04
17	0.04
18	0.03
19	0.03
20	0.03
21	0.03
22	0.02
23	0.02
24	0.02
25	0.02
26	0.02
27	0.02
28	0.01
29	0.01
30	0.01

3. He has longer to live on his pension and is therefore at the risk of inflation longer.

Take as an example the middle management executive of a large corporation who is now 55, has worked for this corporation 30 years, and has averaged $25,000 a year for the best 3 of his last 10 years, the basis

EXHIBIT 30

AMOUNT OF INVESTMENTS REQUIRED TO PRODUCE
VARIOUS AMOUNTS OF ANNUAL INCOME FOR 25 YEARS

Annual income	*Amount of investments required if invested at annual rate of*		
	5%	6%	7%
$ 8,000	$112,752	$102,267	$ 93,229
10,000	140,939	127,834	116,536
12,000	169,127	153,400	139,843
14,000	197,315	178,967	163,150
16,000	225,503	204,534	186,457
18,000	253,691	230,100	209,764
20,000	281,879	255,667	233,072
22,000	310,067	281,234	256,379
24,000	338,255	306,801	279,686
26,000	366,443	332,367	302,993
28,000	394,630	357,934	326,300
30,000	422,818	383,501	349,607

for computing his pension. If he retires today, his pension is $7,380 a year, a big comedown from $25,000. Social security will not start until he is 62, and he may have 30 years of inflation risk to live with.

If he can last another five years and retire at 60, his salary would probably rise 7 percent a year, bringing his average salary to $35,000. For purposes of computing his pension, he then will get $16,380 a year for life, or over double his pension at age 55. If he stays all the way to mandatory retirement at 65—and again assuming salary increases of 7 percent a year—he will retire at a salary of $49,000 a year and a pension of $26,560.

A person needs three financial props before he can consider retiring early. The first is social security, the second is a pension, and the third is capital. There are seven principles for persons thinking about early retirement, and these are listed below.

1. Retire only when you are finished with major financial responsibilities, such as putting children through college or paying off a mortgage.

2. Don't retire early if you do not have a vested pension—i.e., one that belongs to you—as well as substantial savings or investments.

3. Don't retire early if you haven't qualified to receive a sizable social security payment at age 62 or 65.

4. Be wary if your retirement benefits depend heavily on the stock market. These benefits can ruin a retiree in bad times.

5. Try to negotiate any extra benefits, such as cash payments.

6. Find out if your employer has ever raised the pensions of people already retired, to compensate for inflation.

7. Make sure the terms of your retirement plan will not stop you from working elsewhere if you desire.

Chapter 11

YOUR OWN BUSINESS

From time to time, each of us dreams of owning a business, professional practice, or whatever turns us on. Some actually put their dreams into reality as witnessed by the number of people we included in our profiles in Chapter 3 who have successfully started and developed a commercial organization or a professional practice. Many books, articles, and seminars have been devoted to the reasons why people want to do their own thing, the do's and dont's of starting and succeeding at your own thing, and the successes and failures of small organizations. It is not our intention to turn this chapter into a short treatise on "Up Your Own Organization," [1] for several reasons. The most important reason is that *someone* has done it before (see some basic references in Chapter 16). Our intention in this short chapter is to present some of the financial and investment aspects of your own business or practice.

Rewards and Risks

There are many factors that irresistably lure a person to start his or her own business or professional practice. Some may find that the satisfaction of *doing* instead of *proposing* or *justifying* to others in a larger organization

---

[1] For an excellent reference on small business, see *Up Your Own Organization,* by Donald M. Dible, The Entrepreneur Press, Santa Clara, Calif., 1971.

is the important motivating factor. Some are motivated by the idea of starting something from scratch and building a successful organization with the possibility of fame and fortune resulting from the process.

Others are motivated because they find some aspects of the large organization in conflict with their individual work habits, personality traits, and aspirations. They may be turned off by slow corporate communications resulting from hierarchical layers of management or by promotion and salary practices that sometimes do not reflect differences in individual efforts and results.

There are also financial factors involved in motivating one to go into his or her own business or practice. Certainly the possibility of building an equity in your own business is a strong motivation. Another financial factor to some is the possibility of developing an organization that can be passed on to interested family members who are capable of running what you started.

So much for some of the rewards. How about the risks? One of the first things that your friends will tell you when you casually remark you are going to start a business is: "You are out of your cotton-picking mind. Do you know what the failure rate is?" There is no question that there are substantial risks associated with starting your own company.

If you compare the financial results of small companies with those of large companies, you will find that a higher percentage of small companies are unprofitable. Approximately 85 percent of business failures are small companies. However, the good news is that of all companies showing a profit, the small companies show a higher return on investment than the large ones. The least profitable small companies do worse than the least profitable large companies and the most profitable small companies do better than the most profitable large companies. The point of this statistical analysis is that, in spite of the notoriously high mortality rate and well-publicized financial difficulties of small firms, the well-managed small company produces favorable financial results.

The owner-investor must be willing to take financial risks to gain financial rewards. He or she must be willing to pay a price. Let's explain. Typically the capital for the initial phases of a new company must come from you. Initial capital is difficult to obtain from banks and venture capital companies because, at the time the company is formed, you have no track record to show anybody. And even if you find some "deep money pockets" somewhere, they are likely to ask you how much *you* have put into the organization.

To provide this initial capital means that you need some liquid assets to start the business. We strongly recommend that the assets you use are not earmarked for your children's education or for some other special purpose. The risk is too great.

You should be prepared to run financially lean for several years because most new organizations are not profitable immediately. You will find that all the customers you counted on are hard to win away from competitors or that your new product just doesn't turn people on the way it does you. Thus, you will find that a lot of time and effort will go into making the business profitable. Running lean may mean that the handsome salary you enjoyed with the big corporation you just left may have to be reduced. And even if you are fortunate enough to maintain the same salary level, the salary rate per hour will be lower because you will put in many long, hard days to start and succeed at your own business.

Capital Sources and Financial Information

Anyone who has been successful in starting a new venture soon finds that keeping the venture successful usually requires additional capital and always requires financial information.

There are many public, private, and institutional *capital* sources that provide small businesses with money in exchange for equity or interest. There are various forms of debt capital available from commercial banks, commercial finance companies, credit unions, suppliers, equipment manufacturers, and others.[2] Equity capital may be obtained from small business investment companies, corporate venture capital companies, customers, employees, insurance companies, investment bankers, and others.

No matter what the source of capital, financial information will be required to enable you to:

1. Determine *how much* capital is required;
2. Show some evidence to those providing capital that—
   a. you have done some *financial analysis;*
   b. you have some idea what *return* you might be able to provide on equity capital or how you will be able to make interest and principal payments on debt capital.

In addition, good financial information is necessary to properly manage the affairs of your business. At a *minimum,* you should have a balance sheet prepared at least once a year and an income statement prepared annually and quarterly. These two financial statements prepared for a small box manufacturing company are shown in Exhibits 31 and 32.

---

[2] See Dible, Chapter 15, "Forty Money Sources."

EXHIBIT 31

MARYSVILLE PACKAGING COMPANY

BALANCE SHEET, DECEMBER 31, 1975

(in thousands of dollars)

ASSETS

Current Assets:

Cash		$ 140
Accounts receivable (net of allowance for doubtful accounts)		246
Inventories:		
Raw materials	$ 238	
Goods in process	94	
Finished goods	30	
Supplies	66	428
Prepaid taxes and insurance		18
TOTAL CURRENT ASSETS		$ 832
Fixed Assets:		
Manufacturing plant	$1,240	
Less: Accumulated depreciation	420	820
TOTAL ASSETS		$1,652

LIABILITIES AND CAPITAL

Current Liabilities:		
Notes payable	$ 128	
Accounts payable	54	
Unpaid estimated federal income taxes	10	
TOTAL CURRENT LIABILITIES		$ 192
Long Term Debt		340
Capital:		
Capital stock	$1,000	
Retained earnings	120	1,120
TOTAL LIABILITIES AND CAPITAL		$1,652

In addition to a balance sheet and income statement based on actual historic results, it is beneficial to prepare *pro forma* financial statements to represent how things *might be* during some future period. *Pro forma* financial statements are very important to providers of capital because they represent financial projections of current assumptions and information. For example, we could prepare a *Pro forma* Balance Sheet and Income

EXHIBIT 32

MARYSVILLE PACKAGING COMPANY

INCOME STATEMENT, 1975

(in thousands of dollars)

Sales		$1,457.2
Less: Sales returns and allowances	$11.2	
Sales discounts allowed	28.0	39.2
Net Sales		$1,418.0
Less: Cost of goods sold		$1,108.6
Gross profit margin		$ 309.4
Less: Sales and administrative expense		240.4
Net operating profit		$ 69.0
Less: Interest expense		40.0
Net profit before federal income tax		$ 29.0
Less: Estimated income tax		14.0
Net Profit after federal income tax		$ 15.0

Statement for the next year for Marysville Packaging with the following estimates of operations for the next years.

1. *Sales:* All on credit $1,630,000; sales returns and allowances, $14,000; sales discounts taken by customers, $30,000.

2. *Purchases of goods and services*
   a. New Assets
      Purchased for cash: manufacturing plant and equipment, $62,000 prepaid manufacturing taxes and insurance, $24,000. Purchased on accounts payable: raw materials; $154,000; supplies, $50,000.
   b. Services used to convert raw materials into goods in process, all purchased for cash: direct manufacturing labor, $304,000; indirect manufacturing labor, $112,000; social security taxes on labor, $18,800; power, heat, and light, $83,200.
   c. Sales and administrative service, purchased for cash: $468,000.

3. *Conversion of existing assets into goods in process:* Depreciation of building and equipment, $52,000; expiration of prepaid taxes and insurance, $16,000; supplies used in manufacturing, $58,000; raw materials put into process, $518,000.

4. *Transfer of goods in process into finished goods:* Total cost accumulated on goods that have been completed and transferred to finished goods inventory, $1,098,000.

5. *Cost of finished goods sold to customers:* $998,000.
6. *Financial transactions*
   a. $180,000, borrowed on notes payable to bank.
   b. Bank loans paid off, $420,000.
   c. Cash payment of $35,000 for interest on debt.
7. Cash receipts from customers on accounts receivable: $1,614,000.
8. *Cash payments of liabilities*
   a. Payment of accounts payable, $498,000.
   b. Payment of 1975 income tax, $10,000.
9. *Estimated Federal income tax on 1976 income:* $41,000, of which $18,000 is estimated to be unpaid as of December 31, 1976.
10. *Dividends declared for year and paid in cash:* $22,000.

Based on the estimates above, a *Pro forma* Balance Sheet and Income Statement can be prepared as shown in Exhibits 33 and 34.

Cash Flow

In addition to basic financial statements, it is extremely useful to prepare a cash flow analysis to determine sources and uses of cash in the coming period. The cash flow analysis is important to determining how much short-term capital may be needed or, hopefully, how much cash is generated by operations for growth, investment, or other purposes.

A "Sources and Uses of Cash" statement for Marysville Packaging Company is shown in Exhibit 35.

The cash flow analysis presents two types of information—the sources of cash and how the cash will be used. Sources of cash normally include your capital and capital from sale of stock, from sales, and from loans. Uses of cash normally include inventory, equipment purchases, payment of loans, etc. The cash flow analysis should be made for a period such as a year to determine company liquidity. A *cash budget,* month by month during the year, should also be prepared to show not only the total amount of cash needed or generated but when it is needed or generated as well. We discussed the cash budget in Chapter 5.

Don't Kid Yourself

One of the disconcerting aspects of many small businesses is the inability or unwillingness of the owner-manager to recognize "opportunity costs." One of the most important costs attributable to running your own busi-

---

EXHIBIT 33

MARYSVILLE PACKAGING COMPANY
PRO FORMA BALANCE SHEET AS OF DECEMBER 31, 1976
(in thousands of dollars)

ASSETS

Current Assets:

Cash		$ 34	
Accounts receivable		218	
Inventories			
Raw materials	$174		
Goods in process	158		
Finished goods	130	462	
Supplies		58	
TOTAL CURRENT ASSETS			$ 772
Prepaid taxes insurance			26
Fixed Assets:			
Manufacturing plant	$1,302		
Less: Accumulated depreciation	472		830
TOTAL ASSETS			$1,628

LIABILITIES AND CAPITAL

Current Liabilities:

Notes payable		$ 68	
Accounts payable		60	
Unpaid estimated federal income taxes		18	
TOTAL CURRENT LIABILITIES			$ 146
Long Term Debt			340
Capital:			
Capital stock	$1,000		
Retained earnings	142		1,142
TOTAL LIABILITIES AND CAPITAL			$1,628

ness is the *foregone* opportunity of working somewhere else or doing something else. Thus, every person running his or her own business should recognize the opportunity cost by including as one of the expenses of the business a salary cost at least equal to what could be earned elsewhere as a salaried employee.

Column 1 of Exhibit 36 shows the net profit as determined by many owner-managers in preparing an income statement. The profit of $25,000 does not include the opportunity cost of the salary he or she could earn elsewhere.

EXHIBIT 34

MARYSVILLE PACKAGING COMPANY
PRO FORMA INCOME STATEMENT FOR 1976
(in thousands of dollars)

Sales		$1,630
Less: Sales returns and allowances	$14	
Sales discounts allowed	30	44
Net sales		$1,586
Less: Cost of goods sold		998
Gross profit margin		$ 588
Less: Sales and administrative expense		468
Net operating profit		$ 120
Less: Interest expense		35
Net profit before federal income tax		$ 85
Less: Estimated federal income tax		41
Net Profit after federal income tax		$ 44

EXHIBIT 35

MARYSVILLE PACKAGING COMPANY
ESTIMATED CASH-FLOW STATEMENT 1976
(in thousands of dollars)

SOURCE OF CASH

From operations:			
Net income	$44		
Depreciation	52	$96	
Increase in taxes payable		8	
Decrease in amounts receivable		28	
Increase in accounts payable		6	$138

USES OF CASH

New plant acquired	$62	
Dividends	22	
Increase in inventory	92	
Decrease in notes payable	60	
Increase in prepaid assets	8	244
Decrease in cash		$106

Although the net operating profit of $5,000 in Column 2 of Exhibit 36 recognizes the foregone salary of the owner-manager, it still does not rec-

	EXHIBIT 36		
	EASY TIMES INC.		
	INCOME STATEMENT		
	Column 1	*Column 2*	*Column 3*
Sales/services	$100,000	$100,000	$100,000
Cost of sales/services	50,000	50,000	50,000
Gross margin	$ 50,000	$ 50,000	$ 50,000
Operating expenses:			
Owners salary	–	$ 20,000	$ 20,000
Other salaries	$ 18,000	18,000	18,000
Advertising	1,000	1,000	1,000
Depreciation	1,000	1,000	1,000
Other expenses	5,000	5,000	5,000
	$ 25,000	$ 45,000	$ 45,000
Net operating profit	$ 25,000	$ 5,000	$ 5,000
Return for owners capital			1,000
Net profit			$ 4,000

ognize another opportunity cost, namely the return on the capital the owner-manager has invested in his or her organization. For example, assume Mr. Easy has invested $20,000 of his capital to get Easy Times, Inc. started. Obviously, he has other opportunities in which to invest the $20,-000 for which he would receive some return. At the minimum risk, he could have deposited the money in a bank and received 5 or 6 percent on the savings. So the income statement should reflect "return for capital" as shown in Column 3. The profit of $4,000 in Column 3 represents a truer picture of what Mr. Easy is earning from his business.

So, don't kid yourself. Know what the financial consequences of running your own business are and recognize the return for your labor (the opportunity salary cost) and the return for your capital (the opportunity investment cost).

Getting Your Capital Out

At some point, you should consider how you can get the capital that you have invested in your business out—for retirement purposes, extended travel, whatever. Getting your capital out sometimes is not easy. In many personal services organizations—accounting, consulting, law, medical, and dental—the continuation of the organization is dependent upon the servicing of the clients. So if you are the owner of the personal services firm, your capital may be difficult to extract unless you sell the firm to someone who is attractive to your clients and who can service the clients in a manner similar to you.

Assuming you obtain a buyer, the next hurdle is to determine the value of your equity. Normally, a closely-held company does not have widely traded capital stock for which it is easy to determine the per share value. So there has to be some objective evaluation of the worth of the business that is acceptable to the buyer and the seller.

Getting your capital out of the company requires some planning on your part to insure the continuity of the business and to determine the value of your investment. One way of providing a value for the company is to register your securities or your shares and to sell them to the investing public. This provides a vehicle for trading your securities and selling them when it is legal to do so. This process requires the assistance of a CPA, attorney, and underwriter and should be discussed well in advance of the registration with each of them.

One other way of getting your money out is to merge with another organization which will provide cash for your business or will provide securities that are widely traded and salable at some point. If you have a partnership organization, you may have buy-sell provisions in your partnership agreement that enable you to sell your interest to your partner at some desirable point.

BUT WHAT IF. . .
(Hyperinflation, Recession, Devaluation. . .)

There are a growing number of people who believe that we are caught in a process called continuous inflation that has several alternative sequences of events, all of which end up in a depression of one kind or another. With such a possible scenario, some experts suggest that traditional investments, particularly those involving the stock market, are inappropriate (with the exception of gold stocks). They feel your attention should be turned elsewhere.[1] In this section, we focus on other investments which are important primarily for the preservation of capital.

The Inflationary Problem

The American Institute of Economic Research (AIER) indicates in its publication *What Would More Inflation Mean to You* that in the four decades following the worst

---

[1] *See* Harry Browne, *You Can Profit from a Monetary Crisis* (New York: Macmillan Publishing Co., Inc., 1974), Parts I and II; Donald Hoppe, *How to Invest in Gold Stocks and Avoid the Pitfalls* (New Rochelle, N.Y.: Arlington House, 1972), Part I.

years (1932–1933) of the Great Depression, Americans have seen the dollar gradually lose two-thirds of its buying power. This inflation, the thesis goes, is the process of issuing currency and checking accounts, called purchasing media, in excess of the goods and services offered in the markets. When the purchasing media in excess of those needed to represent goods offered in the markets are created and issued, demand for goods will rise. Everything will cost more than it used to.

Continued inflation has caused several consequences within the domestic economy and in the country's financial relations with other countries of the world. People have been encouraged by the "easy-money" policy to incur more and more debt for houses, cars, appliances, etc. at higher and higher prices. Businesses have embarked on new capital investment programs that may not have been profitable under stable monetary conditions. Others have speculated in real estate, commodities, and the stock market because these have been termed good "hedges" against inflation.

As a result of our policies in foreign countries, we have had extensive spending programs with the unfortunate result that other nations now hold net short-term claims more than four times the Nation's gold reserves. The international position of the dollar has weakened in recent years and some other major currencies have become stronger than the dollar. In addition, the gold standard has been abandoned, and the United States Treasury's Gold Reserves have decreased from 69.4 percent of the world's gold reserves in 1949 to 23.4 percent in 1973.[2]

Specifically, some of the obvious consequences of continued inflation to individual investors have been rather alarming, to say the least: [3]

> 1. Loss by savers and holders of life insurance of nearly $1 trillion since 1939.

---

[2] Board of Governors, Federal Reserve System, Banking and Monetary Statistics (Federal Reserve Board).

[3] AIER, *Understanding the "Money Muddle"* (American Institute for Economic Research), pp. 2–3.

2. Loss of purchasing power by—
   a. All retired and elderly persons dependent on savings, pensions, and proceeds of life insurance.
   b. Salaried individuals and others whose relatively fixed income lag behind the rise in prices.

3. Loss of investment dollars by all businesses whose depreciation and inventory charges are based on lower historical costs which are sorely inadequate for the replacement of plant, equipment, and inventory at higher prices. (Witness the recent controversy over "illusory" earnings of companies.)

4. Loss of tax dollars by millions of individuals because increasing tax rates take more of an individual's inflationary generated income.

5. Gains from speculating when financial rewards gravitate to those who use others' money (debt) and promote get rich schemes, land development and other deals to get something for nothing rather than providing any legitimate services.

There are other consequences that could be cataloged in a somewhat ponderous way, but we think the point has been made. It is now more important to evaluate the effects of continuous inflation on different types of investments and to assist you in formulating a program that takes into account the possibility of one of two future scenarios taking place: [4]

1. A recession that may well become so severe that it could become one of the nation's few major depressions.

2. More inflation to the extent that the dollar would increasingly depreciate and would lose virtually all its value in exchange for the necessities of life during the next few decades.

To an extent, we have seen both of these events occur in the last year when we have been in a period some have called "stagflation." Such a combination may again exist in the future or perhaps double-dig it inflation will reappear.

---

[4] AIER, *What Would More Inflation Mean to You?* (American Institute for Economic Research), p. 38.

There is no way to know which events will occur—if they do occur—the sequence of events that will take place, or the rapidity with which the events will take place. If you do not believe such events will occur, it is still useful to develop contingency plans—i.e., to play the "what if" game. The next few chapters aid in formulating a contingency plan. If, on the other hand, you believe that the probability of these events occurring is high, then the next section will assist you to develop the majority of your investment plan.

Chapter 12

THE ESSENTIALS

The first criteria for any investment program, in a broad sense, is to start with the essentials. These include your livelihood, your home, your savings or the reserve fund which can be used in the case of an emergency, and life insurance. To these, we will add debt because the more perilous the times, the more flexibility one should have. Large amounts of debt usually mean loss of flexibility to the debtholder.

Your Livelihood

With prospects of hyperinflation and depression, job and income security should be evaluated. Some believe you should make plans for an alternate way of employing yourself if you are dependent for your income on some large corporation. Obviously, this is impossible for everybody, but everybody can develop plans to be more self-sufficient—repair of household items or gardening are examples.

For those who have more flexibility in job choice, you should evaluate the services your organization currently provides and determine whether or not it depends on a healthy, booming economy. For example, a sales or marketing organization dealing with leisure time activities dependent on customers' discretionary dollars would be extremely vulnerable in a depression. Organizations that provide essential personal services would no doubt have the least difficulty. These organizations would include health care, public agencies such as fire and police departments, sanitation, primary and secondary education, etc.

If your present livelihood is vulnerable to a depression, try to develop alternatives that would not necessarily maintain your present standard of living, but provide at least food, clothing, and shelter.

Your House

There are several schools of thought regarding home ownership in a period of hyperinflation and depression. Some think that if you view home ownership as a form of consumption, almost like rent, there is no reason not to own a home. However, if you consider home ownership as an investment, you may be kidding yourself. The equity in your house is tied up, and you have a substantial opportunity cost in addition to the problem of liquidity in periods of monetary crisis. For example, if you have a $100,000 house and your equity is $60,000, your opportunity cost, at 10 percent money market rates, is $6,000 (before taxes, of course). Therefore some suggest sell your house, rent a home of comparable quality in an area of your choice, and invest the proceeds in an investment providing more liquidity, flexibility, and perhaps a greater hedge against hyperinflation or depression.

There are others, however, who think that home ownership provides a high degree of personal security in periods of economic peril. Houses in stable residential neighborhoods have certainly been sound investments up to the present time, the thesis goes, and would represent a highly satisfactory hedge against long-term inflation in the case of hyperinflation. In the case of depression, your home would provide some shelter and would not be a burden, particularly if there was little or no mortgage debt on the home.

We personally favor home ownership, not as an investment but as something that appeals to our personal values, that provides security in a world of constant turmoil.

In recent times many affluent families have purchased a second home for recreational purposes. Such a purpose makes a lot of sense. In some locations you can rent the facilities for at least part of the year to help defray expenses. In addition, the second home can enable you to enjoy less expensive vacations. By renting the facilities for part of the year, your second home provides a partial tax shelter. The recreational home especially can be a retreat from the maddening pace of modern urban living, a chance to get away from the "busi-ness" of the city, and a place to reflect on true values.

With the prospect of hyperinflation and depression, there is increasingly more literature regarding such a setting as a retreat from the even more menacing aspects of life that might result. Some investment advisors are recommending that some portion of an investment program be devoted to a retreat budget to provide for emergency situations—shortages of critical foods and fuels, breakdowns in essential services, or actual rioting. They suggest that the retreat be located away from large urban centers, relatively inaccessible, and in an area where any nearby residents are relatively self-sufficient.

If you are interested in such a retreat and the use of it during periods of civil disorders that may occur, you should equip your retreat accordingly. You should also equip yourself to be more or less self-sufficient in your retreat. Your retreat should be stocked with canned foods, water, and dehydrated or freeze-dried food, both of which have an eight- to ten year shelf life. Some also suggest you give thought to power sources, cooking facilities, access to natural foods, medical supplies, and alternative means of transportation if no gasoline is available.

Cash and Savings Accounts

With an uncertain future, it is important to have funds for use at any time. We all need working capital to meet current bills and day-to-day expenses. We have discussed the need to keep cash in checking and savings accounts to a minimum because of the extremely low yield in relation to the rate of inflation. In fact, you lose purchasing power if the inflation rate exceeds the interest rate each year—as has been the case in recent years.

With the possibility of hyperinflation or depression, some suggest that any amounts in excess of funds to pay current bills should be placed in currencies other than U.S. dollars and in depositories other than U.S. banks. The thesis is that even though funds in savings accounts are insured up to $40,000, if the country really gets in trouble and depositors draw out their funds, the government's insurance reserve fund would not be sufficient to protect depositors against such consequences. The strategy then is to try to determine which countries would be depression-proof or be stronger economically and then place any excess savings in such countries. Most recently, advisors have suggested placing funds in Swiss banks, primarily on the premise that the Swiss banking industry enjoys the world's best banking reputation in periods of economic crisis.

Browne in his book *You Can Profit from a Monetary Crisis* suggests the following as being some of the advantages of using a Swiss bank account: [1]

---

[1] Harry Browne, *You Can Profit From a Monetary Crisis* (New York: Macmillan Publishing Co., Inc., 1974), pp. 186–87.

1. You will have funds outside your own country where they can't be confiscated by a government using controls in attempt to repair economic damages of its own mistakes.

2. You will be dealing with a banking system that is in some respects sounder than the United States banking system. The Swiss banks usually maintain higher reserves against their deposits. And unlike U.S. banks, the withdrawal restrictions stated for each type of account are taken seriously.

3. You can keep your wealth in foreign currencies that may increase in value as the dollar declines.

4. Your privacy will be respected; even the Swiss government has no access to information about your account.

5. You can use the account to make investments anywhere in the world, whether these investments be stocks, foreign currencies, bonds, gold, silver, other metals, commodities, or whatever.

6. You can utilize the financial opinions of the bank's management in making your investments.

Opening an account in a Swiss bank is not all that difficult. Obviously, if you are in Europe or Switzerland you can open an account in person, at which time you can get answers to any questions you have. If you are not able to open an account in person, it is very easy to open one by mail. Browne includes a list of Swiss banks in his book. The American Institute of Economic Research can provide information to you regarding opening a Swiss bank account. The three largest banks in Switzerland all have offices in New York, which can help smooth out any problems that might develop in your banking transactions. These three Swiss banks are:

Union Bank of Switzerland
Bahnhofstrasse 45
8021 Zürich

Banque National Suisse
Place Fëdérale 1
3003 Bern

Swiss Bank Corporation
1, Aeschenvorstadt
Basel

Recently the yields in Swiss bank accounts have been a little lower than in the United States; for example, during the spring of 1975 the interest rates of Swiss franc savings book accounts were around 5 percent. Also, because of wide fluctuations in exchange rates, the Swiss authorities found it necessary in the fall of 1974 to introduce restrictions on international money transactions. At present, only deposits up to 50,000 Swiss francs (about $20,000 as of May 1975) are accepted by Swiss banks on an interest-bearing basis. Deposits in excess of 100,000 Swiss francs are subject to a quarterly commission, or negative interest, of 10 percent. Thus, you may have little or no profits from deposits in Swiss banks, but the chief motive would be defensive. You would be anticipating that in a severe international monetary crisis, it would be wise to have funds outside the United States in the event that restrictions are placed on the amount of money you can take out of the country or in the event the U.S. dollar becomes weaker than some foreign currencies.

Exhibit 37 provides information as of May 1975 on types of accounts one of the major Swiss banks offers. As the exhibit indicates, there are some withdrawal restrictions and withholding tax aspects. The U.S. resident who opens a Swiss bank account, or, for that matter, a bank account in any country, has to also answer a question on his or her U.S. Federal income tax return to the effect that he or she has such an account.

You may wish to get information regarding the types of accounts that these banks offer, current interest rates, withdrawal restrictions, minimum amounts required for deposit, and the like by writing directly to a Swiss bank. Names of the Swiss banks, in addition to the ones above, may be obtained from a directory of foreign banks, usually available at many banks and libraries.

Life Insurance

As was suggested in the chapter on life insurance, first analyze your needs and keep your program flexible by having a large portion of coverage in term insurance.

If you believe U.S. insurance companies will be vulnerable to possible hyperinflation and/or depression, you may wish to have some insurance policies written in Swiss francs so that the proceeds will be paid in what may be a more stable currency. There are two large Swiss life insurance companies:

Geneva Life Insurance Co.
Obstgertenstrasse 7
8035 Zürich, Switzerland

Swiss Life Insurance Co.
General Guisenquai 40
8022 Zürich, Switzerland

EXHIBIT 37

LIST OF CONDITIONS

	½–1% *Current Account*	3½% *Private Account*
Use	Substantial volume of payments for commercial and private purposes: the key to all banking services	Comparatively small cash needs and payments for private purposes, purchase and sale of securities, credit of dividends and interest from securities, standing payment orders; salary account
Maximum balance bearing interest	No limit	No limit
Withdrawals	At any time up to entire balance	Up to Fr. 10,000.—within a month, for larger amounts three months notice required
Withholding tax	30% on interest earned	30% on interest earned
Statements of account	With particulars, half-yearly, or monthly if requested	Three times per year, i.e. for periods January to April, May to August, and September to December.
Purchase of securities	At any time for entire balance	At any time for entire balance if purchase is effected through us
Additional remarks	Rate of interest and debit of a turnover commission (¹⁄₂₀ of one percent, calculated on debit entries) in compliance with local custom. Interest is paid only if the acount holder is a resident of Switzerland	Fr. 1.50 monthly fee for maintaining the account. Suitable also for crediting Social Security benefit payments. Salary accounts are available to Swiss residents only.

5% Savings Book	6% Youth Savings Book	6% Investment Book
Payments and withdrawals in cash at our counters, through the Post Office or by bank transfer. Acceptance and issue of bank cheques. No private cheque books. Books made out in holder's name or to bearer.	Payments and withdrawals in cash at our counters, through the Post Office or by bank transfer. Acceptance and issue of bank cheques. No private cheque books. Books are made out in the name of young persons under 20 years of age.	For longer-term deposits at a higher rate of interest. Payments and withdrawals in cash at our counters, through the Post Office or by bank transfer. Acceptance and issue of bank cheques. No private cheque books.
No limit	No limit	No limit
Up to Fr. 5000.—within a month without notice, for larger amounts six months' notice required (special concessions in emergency cases)	Up to Fr. 5000.—within a month without notice, for larger amounts six months' notice required (special concessions in emergency cases)	Up to Fr. 10,000.—within a year without notice, for larger amounts 6 months' notice required. For account holders aged over 60 the same withdrawal conditions are applicable as for holders of Savings Books
30% on interest earned (interest up to Fr. 50.—per year on books in holder's name exempt from withholding tax)	30% on interest earned (interest up to Fr. 50.—per year exempt from withholding tax)	30% on interest earned (interest up to Fr. 50.—per year exempt from withholding tax).
Once a year on December 31 for books in holder's name deposited with us free of charge	Once a year on December 31 for books deposited with us free of charge.	Once a year on December 31 for books deposited with us free of charge.
Entire balance may be used at any time for the purchase of Credit Suisse bonds an ! shares through our intermediary	Entire balanced may be used at any time for the purchase of Credit Suisse bonds and shares through our intermediary	Entire balance may be used at any time for the purchase of Credit Suisse bonds and shares through our intermediary
As regards security, investor's deposits in Savings Books include certain privileges under the Banking Act	As regards security, investor's deposits in Savings Books include certain privileges under the Banking Act. Tax advantages in the cantons Zurich and Geneva	

SOURCE: Credit Suisse—Swiss Credit Bank, Schweizerische, Kreditanstalt.

These companies offer basic insurance plans, and information and premium rates can be obtained by writing to these companies. When you write, it may be best to include the following information:

- Sex
- Date of birth
- Amount of coverage
- Type of plan
- Length of the plan—if it is term insurance, the number of years
- Any other information that might help the company advise you of the appropriate insurance plan [2]

Debt and Committed Expenses

One school of thought during inflationary times is that borrowing makes a lot of sense since the debt would be paid back with cheaper dollars. However, debt often results in loss of flexibility because committed expenses (interest, debt repayments) increase along with the debt.

We believe that, in the event of a monetary crisis, debts should be kept low and should be used only for housing. A rough guideline to be used is that your payments of interest and principal should not exceed 20 percent of your monthly, after-tax income.

In addition to debt, look at all present long-term financial commitments and make plans to keep committed expenses from increasing rapidly. In the recent past, we have received warning signals on the availability and costs of oil, food, metals, forest products, and other necessities.

Cars

The gasoline situation can only get worse. Protect yourself by opting for lightweight small cars that provide basic transportation. If you "need" comfort for larger trips, rent a big car for such infrequent uses.

---

[2] Browne, *You Can Profit From a Monetary Crisis,* pp. 303–304.

Housing and Heat

Focus ideas on alternative means to conserve fuel because portable fuels, heating oil, and natural gas are headed up in price and down in availability. Electrical heating appears to be on the upswing and it is also costly. So insulation, storm windows, doors, and other ways of minimizing outside air drafts are much more important today. You can rest assured that heating can only get more expensive, not cheaper, so make all these fuel savings measures today to gain maximum benefits. The longer you benefit from insulation the more your spending plan will benefit.

Obviously, another way to reduce your heating costs is to turn the heat down. It is amazing to us how many homes (and offices) are heated much more than necessary. In some homes, unused rooms are still heated as much as the rest of the house; sweaters are not worn by the inhabitants of the house, etc. As a result, a great deal of heat is wasted.

Food

Since meat prices increased a couple of years ago, families have discovered alternative sources for balanced protein. You can protect your family by enlarging your eating habit patterns to use more of the readily available and less costly foods. Also make your purchases during the time of year when prices are lowest, and store the surpluses away for the periods when costs are higher. On an esthetic note, we might all eat less to improve health, not to mention the savings in cost.

Chapter 13

THE GOLD BUGS

In recent years there has been an explosion of interest in all sorts of gold-related investments. The attraction is that gold, and to some extent silver, has historically been the only real money with universal acceptance in the world. The gold movement has been founded by those whose thesis is that there is a pending monetary crisis, which began in 1933 when the United States stopped converting its paper currency to gold upon demand (except in international payments), and left the gold standard. At the same time, it became illegal for American citizens to hold gold bullion in the U.S. and to hold gold coins and gold certificates. After the end of convertibility of paper currency into gold, the size of the money supply became progressively less dependent on U.S. gold holdings, and the government was more free to create new money. In short, the government was able to pursue inflationary policies more easily; individuals, however, found it harder to protect themselves from inflation. Inflation, the gold bugs proclaim, will eventually lead to complete economic collapse, and paper money without gold backing will become just paper.

You may argue with this thesis, but it is difficult to argue about the performance of gold-related investments in recent years. The price of gold has soared, along with the rate of inflation. In the past four years, the price of a troy ounce of gold has risen from about $36 to a high of $197.50, with the price in May 1975 being $167. In the same period, the index of gold stocks, as reported by the *Financial Times* (London), has risen 500 percent. Silver also has tripled in value over the same period.

Although there is no unanimity among the gold bugs as to the best gold-related investments, they are in agreement that such investments include silver coins and bullion, gold coins and bullion, gold mining stocks, and foreign currencies that may not be affected by runaway inflations. Furthermore, they have more gold backing than the U.S. dollar.

Silver

Many investors are turning to silver for several reasons. First, it is a precious metal and has security value in times of monetary crisis. Second, silver is in short supply. In the past 23 years, silver consumption has exceeded new production. Third, silver has been a reliable hedge against inflation. For example, during Chile's decade of inflation, the price of silver increased more than 1,500 times. When runaway inflation occurred in Germany after World War I, the price of silver increased more than 91 billion times!!

Basically, the investor has four main ways to invest in silver: shares in silver mining companies, silver futures contracts, silver bullion, and silver coins.

Shares in Silver Mining Companies

One way to invest in silver is to invest in shares of silver mining companies. Such shares would represent ownership of a part of a company in the silver industry. Many silver mining shares in the recent past have performed well, but a wide variety of factors affect the investment, including consumption of silver, silver production, management competence, efficiency of the mine, and the like.

Silver Futures Contracts

Silver futures contracts exist in order to set prices for industrial producers and users of silver for some time in the future. For example, if you are an industrial user of silver and you know that you will need 5,000 ounces of silver a year from now, you would like to know now what the silver will cost you next year. In order to establish a price today for 5,000 ounces of silver to be delivered to you one year from today, you agree to a futures contract, or you make a deal for a purchase one year away.

In order to make it easy to obtain such a futures contract, a futures market exists in which all people with such needs gather to make contracts. When you want to make a purchase there may be no one interested in taking the other side of the contract, so speculators operate in the market.

A speculator can either buy or sell, depending upon his view of the future price of silver.

Futures contracts are primarily for people who welcome extremely high-leverage, short-term situations. They are for people who are willing to spend a great deal of time studying the silver situation and staying on top of it every day.

Basically the two other ways of investing in silver are recommended by those who have analyzed the situation quite extensively.[1] For most people, the two recommended methods of investing in silver are silver bullion and silver coins.

Silver Bullion

You can purchase bars of silver bullion in any quantity. You receive whatever number of ounces is covered by the amount of money you invest. As Browne points out there are three principal ways you can buy silver bullion: (1) in the United States and store it yourself: (2) in the United States and have the seller store it for you; (3) through a Swiss bank and have the bank store it for you.

For example in the United States, the Pacific Coast Coin Exchange can buy silver for you and store it for a storage fee. If you buy through a Swiss bank, the procedure is merely to tell the bank the number of dollars you want to spend, and the bank will purchase the appropriate number of ounces at the current market prices. The bank charges a commission when you buy or sell the bullion plus a fee for storage and insurance in the bank. Also, mint sets of silver coins stamped before 1965 and bags of circulated dimes, quarters, and half dollars, as well as silver dollars, are widely traded in the United States.

The Pacific Coast Coin Exchange has made bags of silver coins available *on margin* since 1967. You can buy these silver coins in commodity units called bags. Each bag contains about 720 ounces of silver and has a face value of $1,000.

To acquire a bag of circulated silver coins from the Pacific Coast Coin Exchange, the investor puts up the difference between the $1,000 face value of the bag and the current market price as margin. On these margin accounts, generally you need invest only 35 percent of the current market price and interest (or maintenance) on the unpaid balance. The June 1974 maintenance rate was 10 percent. Storage costs run about $10 per year,

---

[1] See for example Browne, *You Can Profit from a Monetary Crisis,* particularly Chapter 26 and Persons, *How to Make Money from Inflation,* pp. 231–34.

and there is a 2 percent brokerage fee to buy the silver coins and 2 percent to sell them.

Since the price of silver bullion is the single most important influence on the price of silver coins, prices for bags of silver tend to move together with prices of silver bullion. The price of a bag of U.S. silver coins in June 1974 was approximately $3,500. To illustrate the purchase of silver coins on margin, the Pacific Coast Coin Exchange worked out the illustration in Exhibit 38 using the June 1974 market price.[2]

Some investors may prefer to make an outright purchase of the coins, take delivery, and store the coins themselves. Using the example in Exhibit 38, the total bag price for bags purchased outright would be $3,570—three bags would cost $10,710. To take delivery from coins purchased from the

---

EXHIBIT 38
SILVER COINS PURCHASE ON MARGIN

A. Total cash available for purchasing in U.S. silver coins	$10,000
B. Base price of a bag of U.S. silver coins (approximate price, June, 1974)	$ 3,500
C. Minimum initial deposit per bag (multiply line B by .35 and round *down* to the nearest dollar)	$ 1,225
D. Commission (multiply line B by .02 and round *down* to the nearest dollar)	$ 70
E. Sum of deposit and commission (add lines C & D)	$ 1,295
F. The maximum number of bags that can be secured with a PCCE Margin Account (divide line A by line E and round *down* to the nearest whole number)	7
G. Total Cash required (multiply line E by line F)	$ 9,065
H. The unpaid balance on each bag (subtract line C from line B)	$ 2,275
I. Total unpaid balance (multiply line F by line H)	$15,925
J. Current maintenance rate	10%
K. Annual service charge (multiply line F by $10)	$ 70
L. Sum of maintenance and service charges calculated on a monthly basis (multiply line I by line J; add line K and divide by 12)	$ 138.54
M. Total amount of silver bullion secured (multiply line F by 720)	5,040 oz.

---

[2] "A Summary of the Pacific Coast Coin Exchange's Current Operations," Pacific Coast Coin Exchange, Los Angeles, 1974.

Pacific Coast Coin Exchange, you may pick them up from any of 10 depositories in the U.S., Canada, and Switzerland. They may also be delivered to the airport of your choice for a minimum shipping fee depending on the distance.

Some investors prefer to hold bags of silver coins rather than silver bullion because they feel the coins will provide added protection in the event of some extreme domestic crisis. Since the coins are 90 percent silver, they might be readily acceptable. As Harry Browne was recently quoted in *Newsweek,* "When we are in the middle of the crisis, a pound of beef may be selling for $80 million—or two silver coins. The next week, the price will be $80 billion—or two silver coins."

Gold

The three principal media for gold investments are gold bullion, gold coins, and gold stocks. On January 1, 1975, with Congress' repeal of the ban on the ownership of gold bullion, Americans were able to buy gold bullion for the first time since 1933.

Gold bullion is the safest way to invest in gold because such an investment includes gold and no other variables. F Gold bullion will be as valuable as the price per troy ounce. Bullion is usually sold in bars of 400 ounces each, but you may be able to buy much smaller bars, possibly all the way down to half-ounce wafers worth about $75 or $80 at current prices. Gold bullion prices as reflected in London are published daily in the *Wall Street Journal* and in many other daily newspapers.

One plan for buying gold bullion calls for a sales charge of 6 to 8 percent above the daily closing price. Small sizes of gold are usually charged the higher percentage. Gold may be repurchased by the same brokers at the closing price less 6 or 8 percent. The spread thus could be as high as 16 percent. Included in the sales and repurchase prices are assaying and certification of value.

Gold Coins

Gold coins can be owned by U.S. citizens if the coins were minted before 1934 and if they were held for numismatic (coin collecting) purposes. However, since the U.S. Treasury has not required you to prove your numismatic intentions, pre-1934 coins are a legal way to own gold.

There are numerous coins, issued by various governments, that may be purchased. In October 1974, all gold coins were selling at a premium over the value of the gold content, a premium ranging from about 10 percent for the South African Kruger Rand to as much as 50 percent for the British sovereign. The premium is the cost of the coin above its gold content. For example, the British sovereign which has 0.23540 ounces of gold would sell for approximately $53 when the price of gold bullion is $150 per ounce and the premium is 50 percent ($150 × 0.23540 × 150 percent). All other things equal, it is best to pay as small a premium as possible.

Gold coins can be obtained from many U.S. coin dealers, such as the Pacific Coast Coin Exchange. In addition, most Swiss banks can obtain gold coins and store them for you. In the United States, gold coins may be quoted in lots. The lots for four gold coins that can be legally obtained by U.S. citizens are:

	Number of Coins Per Lot	Actual Gold Weight Per Coin (oz.)	Gold Weight Per Lot (oz.)
US Double Eagle	20	0.96746	19.3492
British Sovereign	100	0.2354	23.54
Mexican 50 Peso	20	1.20563	24.1126
Austrian 100 Corona	20	0.98016	19.6032

Gold Mining Shares

Obviously there is a limit to what can be kept in the form of coins and bullion or what some term "hard" money. The storage problem alone would prohibit a great deal of investment in such assets. In addition, some income may be important for some investors, and income in the form of dividends or interest just does not come from hard assets. Thirdly, some would like to have the possibility of appreciation rather than preservation of capital, and would prefer to have some sort of leverage factor in their investments. Gold mining shares provide an alternative to hard assets, and most recently have provided great appreciation to those who have invested in such shares.

For example, a recent issue of *Medical Economics* indicated that T. Rowe Price, an investment advisor, recommended in 1971 that certain stocks related to natural resources would be good investments. Let's see what happened in the period 7/19/71 to 5/23/74 to the gold stocks he recommended. Exhibit 39 shows what happened.

Obviously gold stocks are more speculative than gold coins and bullion, primarily because you are betting on more factors than just the price of gold. For example, gold mining companies could be affected favorably or un-

EXHIBIT 39

SELECTED .GOLD MINING STOCKS

	Buy Price 7/19/71	Recent Price 5/23/74	Percent Change
Anglo American Corp. of South Africa	8.3/8	7	— 16
Anglo American Gold Investment Co.	20.7/8	61	+192
ASA Ltd.	23.1/8	74.5/8	+223
Dome Mines Ltd.	22	51	+132
Gold Fields of South Africa Ltd.	22.3/8	50.1/4	+125
West Driefontein Gold Mining Co.	24.1/2	61.5/8	+152

favorably by labor relations, governmental policies, management, natural disasters, etc. Some suggest that these factors are more critical, or that the possibility of these factors being adverse in North America are greater, and as such recommend only South African gold stocks. For example, a recent investment bulletin by The American Institute Counselors, Inc. suggests that retention of Canadian gold mining company shares is no longer recommended. They observe that production costs are much higher in Canada than in South Africa, and that mining tax legislation pending in several Canadian provinces will, if initiated, tend to adversely affect the profitability of the Canadian gold mining industry.

Investments in the shares of selected foreign gold mining companies may provide protection against both continued depreciation of currencies (including possible future devaluations) and severe recession or depression. Nevertheless, one should not buy South African gold stocks without careful study. Perhaps the best source for such a study would be Donald J. Hoppe's *How to Invest in Gold Stocks and Avoid the Pitfalls.* In this book he gives you an historical perspective on the case for gold, and evaluates the gold stocks of North America and South Africa. He also provides some very useful chapters on the selection and management of a gold investment portfolio. As Hoppe suggests there are three basic ways to invest in South Africa's gold resources: [3]

- The mining finance house
- The mining investment trust
- The mining company itself

---

[3] Donald J. Hoppe, *How to Invest in Gold Stocks and Avoid the Pitfalls*, p. 457.

Shares in all three types of institutions are available to American investors.

1. *The Mining Finance House.* Most of the gold mining companies located in South Africa are controlled by leading finance houses, which are in turn controlled by what is perhaps the strongest group of financial interests in the world, namely Rothschilds of France and Great Britain.[4] For example in Exhibit 39, Anglo American Corp. of South Africa, Anglo American Gold Investment Co., and Gold Fields of South Africa Ltd. are mining and finance houses.

Mining finance houses came into being primarily because the enormous initial cost and substantial risk involved in bringing a large reef gold mine into production and because of the reluctance of individual private investors to commit capital to new enterprises in underdeveloped countries.

2. *The Investment Trust.* As we discussed in our chapter on mutual funds, investment trusts are companies whose principal asset is an investment position in the shares of operating companies. The investment trusts that we are now discussing concentrate their commitments on operating gold mines, and have a much higher percentage of their assets in such shares than the finance houses that we discussed above. For example, one of the major gold mining investment trusts of South Africa is American-South African Investment Co. Ltd. (ASA Ltd.), which is also shown as a recommended investment in Exhibit 39. It is traded on the New York Stock Exchange.

3. *The Gold Mining Company.* Hoppe suggests that the individual mining company has both the highest yield and, in general, the best possibility for leverage and therefore capital gain. However, he suggests these potential advantages exist because of the greater risks of investing in individual mines. As the American Institute Counselors Inc. state, investors should understand the dividend and value pattern of the hypothetical gold mine shown in Exhibit 40. Their Investment Bulletin of May 20, 1974 advises that investors considering gold stocks should understand the following:

"The operating life as portrayed is about 25 years. Dividends begin about the fifth year, increase through the 20th year, then decline until the last year when a liquidating dividend is paid on break-up value. During prime life the dividend increases at a rate approximating 6%. The share value, reflecting the present value of future dividends, increases at an increasing rate from the time of the mine's incorporation until the dividend growth pattern becomes sustainable. Thereafter the increase proceeds at a decreasing rate, the peak value tending to coincide with the end of the first third of the mine's life.

---

[4] *Gold and the Gold Mining Industry,* American Institute Counselors Inc. Investment Bulletin, Volume XLI, No. 10, May 20, 1974.

EXHIBIT 40

DIVIDEND AND VALUE OF A HYPOTHETICAL GOLD MINE

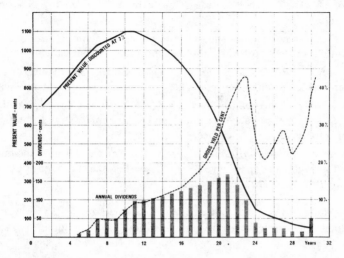

SOURCE: Reprinted from November 1970 *Mining Journal* by permission of Mining Journal, Ltd.

Discounting reduced mine life and the fruition of expected production, the share value decreases at an increasing rate during the middle and most productive third. This combined with successive absolute dividend growth causes gross yield (current dividend divided by present value) to increase at an increasing rate until the relatively coincident peak of production, earnings, and dividends is reached.

In the last third, discounted mine value and dividends both decrease at a decreasing rate, tapering off toward the final year. This causes a marked early decrease in gross yield that then tends to level off and finally to rise in anticipation of the liquidating dividend at the end of the mine's life.

The foregoing description shows that share ownership in a gold mining company resembles ownership of an annuity, the value of which ultimately becomes zero. Variants may occur such as unexpected enrichment from discovery of new gold deposits or those of other metals or losses from some physical disaster to the mine.

Whether or not a substantial further increase in the official gold "price" soon occurs, increasing industrial demand for gold augmented by that of investors can be expected to sustain a gradual upward trend of the free market "price." This should alter somewhat the yield basis of valuation, which until recently, tended to resemble a straight annuity, to one having qualities of a variable annuity. This is because heretofore improved yield expectations reflected profit growth from increasing production only whereas now and in the foreseeable future it should additionally reflect profit growth attributable to an increasing "price." The influence of this "growth aspect" tends to be accentuated the longer the life of the mine. Also, it should lengthen the life of most mines by extending their span of profitability.

The life-of-mine diagram suggests a basis for grouping the different mines according to their suitability to meet the following investment objectives:

1. *Maximum Income for 12 to 15 Years.* For the elderly and/or retired, generous income may be obtainable for either several or many years.

2. *Moderate Income for 20 to 30 Years.* For those desiring qualities of both a satisfactory rate of income and reasonably assured continuation of operations for 2 to 3 decades.

3. *Little Income but Long-term Growth.* For those whose incomes are taxed at high rates, participation in the earlier stages of growth provides an opportunity to accumulate capital.[5]

This same investment bulletin also included some 26 South African companies for purchase as well as retention, broken out into three major groups:

- High income group
- Moderate income-growth group
- Low income, long-term growth group

Their recommendations are shown in Exhibit 41. Of these 26, ASA Ltd. is available on the New York Stock Exchange; the remaining 25 South African companies recommended in Exhibit 41 are traded in the over-the-counter market in the United States.

Foreign Currencies

Some of the gold bugs, most notably Harry Browne, suggest that the most stable form of value for savings is a strong currency; in the opinion of some, there are some foreign currencies that are stronger than the U.S. dollar. Browne suggests that currencies be evaluated for long-term investment using these criteria:

1. If you believe that gold is the only real money, the first measurement must be the *gold backing* of the currency.

---

[5] *Gold and the Gold Mining Industry,* pp. 38–39.

EXHIBIT 41
RECOMMENDED GOLD MINING COMPANIES

Recommended for *Purchase* as well as *Retention*
High Income Group

Blyvooruitzicht Gold Mining Company, Limited
Free State Geduld Mines, Limited
Kinross Mines, Limited
Libanon Gold Mining Company, Limited
President Brand Gold Mining Company, Limited
West Driefontein Gold Mining Company, Limited
Western Deep Levels, Limited
Western Holdings, Limited

Moderate Income-Growth Group

Anglo American Gold Investment Company, Limited
Buffelsfontein Gold Mining Company, Limited
Doornfontein Gold Mining Company, Limited
St. Helena Gold Mines, Limited
Western Areas Gold Mining Company, Limited
Winkelhaak Mines, Limited

Low Income, Long-Term Growth Group

ASA, Limited
* Anglo American Corporation of South Africa, Limited
East Driefontein Gold Mining Company, Limited
Elsburg Gold Mining Company, Limited
* Gold Fields of South Africa, Limited
Hartebeestfontein Gold Mining Company, Limited
Kloof Gold Mining Company, Limited
President Steyn Gold Mining Company, Limited
Randfontein Est. Gold Mining Co., Ltd.
Southvaal Holdings, Limited
* Sentrust Beperk
Vaal Reefs Exploration and Mining Company, Limited
* Mining and Finance house

2. Is it *convenient* to obtain and hold the currency? Is it readily available in Swiss banks, for example?

3. Is there a *large enough market* for the currency to enable you to convert it back to dollars whenever you choose?

4. How *reliable* is the currency? Is it possible that its present gold

content is only a temporary condition? What is the government's history regarding currency manipulation and monetary freedom for its citizens? The prime consideration is the gold backing. When you find several currencies that appear to be solid in that respect, you can then choose among them to satisfy the other standards.[6]

Browne did an analysis of the gold backing for 26 major currencies, using the amount of currency in circulation and the size of the gold reserve. Exhibit 42 shows his ranking of 26 major currencies as related to gold backing. Based on his analysis, he comes out with the following recommended currencies:

1. the Swiss franc
2. the Dutch guilder
3. the Belgian franc
4. the Austrian schilling
5. the German mark
6. the Lebanese pound

If you believe that foreign currencies will provide a more stable form of savings, it is not difficult to have funds kept in foreign currencies since this can be done through Swiss banks. Previously we discussed how you can open a Swiss bank account. If you wish to have deposits in the bank account held in a foreign currency, just tell the bank which currency you wish to have your funds held in. All funds deposited in that account will be converted automatically to the currency of your choice.

Recommended Portfolio for Gold-Related Investments

Although there may be unanimity among enthusiasts for gold-related investments that such investments should constitute a bulk if not all of your portfolio, there is less agreement as to the mix of the investments within the portfolio. Exhibit 43 compares an investment portfolio of $50,000 as recommended by Browne, Hoppe, and the American Institute of Economic Research, three widely quoted sources of gold-related investment recommendations.

All three advisors suggest some U.S. currency, presumably for emer-

---

[6] Browne, *You Can Profit from a Monetary Crisis*, p. 213.

EXHIBIT 42

Gold Backing for 26 Major Currencies
(As of December 31, 1972—all amounts in millions)

Rank	Currency	Demand Deposits	Currency Outside Banks	Total Money Substitutes	Gold Reserve	Gold Backing (%)
1.	Lebanese pound	1,215	1,034	2,249	1,078.02	47.93
2.	Dutch guilder	11,890	11,410	23,300	6,681.01	28.67
3.	Swiss franc	31,500	17,930	49,430	11,879.79	24.03
4.	Portuguese escudo	85,570	36,120	121,690	27,823.05	22.86
5.	South African rand	2,170	627	2,797	533.16	19.06
6.	Austrian schilling	53,350	45,470	98,820	18,454.03	18.67
7.	Belgian franc	203,200	216,800	420,000	73,410.10	17.48
8.	German (West) mark	85,600	45,700	131,300	13,973.10	10.64
9.	French franc	174,550	84,130	258,680	19,573.14	7.57
10.	Turkish lira	9,630	16,940	26,570	1,904.04	7.17
11.	Greek drachma	25,490	50,560	76,050	3,984.09	5.24
12.	Swedish krona	6,490	14,360	20,850	1,044.43	5.01
13.	Italian lira	36,052,000	8,471,000	44,523,000	1,820,136.31	4.09
14.	Canadian dollar	16,890	4,550	21,440	830.46	3.87
15.	Mexican peso	37,900	26,880	64,780	2,350.06	3.63
16.	United States dollar	250,180	56,600	306,780	10,400.00	3.39
17.	Spanish peseta	723,800	327,800	1,051,000	34,881.06	3.32
18.	Israel pound	3,550	2,040	5,590	182.28	3.26
19.	Australian dollar	5,227	1,665	6,892	220.40	3.20
20.	English pound	9,342	4,079	13,421	307.03	2.29
21.	Yugoslavian dinar	31,400	23,400	54,800	952.02	1.73
22.	Danish krone	25,910	5,350	31,260	480.94	1.54
23.	Norwegian krone	10,500	8,750	19,250	247.21	1.28
24.	Japanese yen	26,820,000	7,706,000	34,526,000	246,714.50	0.71
25.	New Zealand dollar	956	238	1,194	0.88	0.07
26.	Irish pound	301,800	191,300	493,100	6.52	.0013

SOURCE: Reprinted with permission of Macmillan Publishing Co., Inc., from *You Can Profit from a Monetary Crisis*, by Harry Browne, pp. 216–217. Copyright © 1974 by Harry Browne.

EXHIBIT 43

GOLD RELATED INVESTMENT PROGRAM

$50,000

	Browne [1]		Hoppe [2]		American Institute for Economic Research [3]	
	%	Amount	%	Amount	%	Amount
U.S. currency	1.25	$ 625		$ x [4]	8.0	$ 4,000
Retreat budget	17.50	8,750		x [4]	—	—
Silver coins	18.75	9,375	4.0	2,000	2.0	1,000
Gold coins or bullion	12.50	6,250	16.0	8,000	10.0	5,000
Foreign currencies:						
Swiss francs (in Swiss bank)	37.50	18,750				
Dutch guilders (in Swiss bank)	12.50	6,250				
Gold stocks			80.0	40,000	50.0	25,000
Metric Accounting Unit Storage Agreement					30.0	15,000
	100.00	$50,000	100.00	$50,000	100.00	$50,000

[1] Browne, *You Can Profit from a Monetary Crisis*, p. 314.
[2] Hoppe, *How to Invest in Gold Stocks*, p. 526.
[3] AIER, *Investment Bulletin—Quarterly Review of Investment Policy*, July 15, 1974, p. 54.
[4] x = Some amount but not specified.

gencies and current bills. Both Hoppe and Browne suggest a retreat budget, but Browne is much more concerned about the need for a retreat budget. All suggest some silver and gold coins, with Browne suggesting more than 31 percent of the portfolio in such assets; Hoppe 20 percent, and AIER 12 percent. Each of them differs quite markedly in their recommendations on the major part of the portfolio. Browne suggests 50 percent should be invested in foreign currencies; Hoppe suggests 80 percent in gold stocks; AIER suggests 50 percent in gold stocks and 30 percent in the Metric Accounting Unit Storage Agreement (MAUSA), which operates like a mutual fund in precious metals and mining company stocks. The minimum investment is $10,000, which is sent to the Swiss Credit Bank in Zürich.

KEEPING YOUR PARTNER, SAM'S, "TAKE" AT THE MINIMUM

In all your attempts to accumulate some net worth, even in your attempts to distribute what you have, you have an invisible partner in the U. S. Government, sometimes known as Uncle Sam. You also may have minority partners in your state and local governments, but let's concentrate on Sam, the partner we all have.

We do not advocate trying to cheat Sam. For one thing, the percentage of alleged tax evaders who are convicted is extremely high. More important, we happen to think an individual gets enough good out of this country and its government to pay his share of running it, despite the gripes. But this doesn't mean you should pay more than your share. And your share was defined years ago by a leading Federal jurist as "what you legally owe as a result of transactions that took place, not those which might have happened."

This is where planning comes in. You have many different ways to arrange your financial affairs, and some arrangements are much better tax-wise than others.

Remember, your after-tax dollars are the only ones you can spend for that trip to the Caribbean, your new sports car, etc. And saving a tax dollar is much more important than making another dollar of taxable income. If you're in the 50 percent income tax bracket, a dollar of tax savings is just as good as two dollars of additional salary, dividends, or other taxable income. That's why dollars of tax saving are referred to as "100-cent dollars"—you have no tax to pay, and you keep 100 cents of the dollar to do with as you please.

As inflation continues, tax planning becomes more important. Even if your "real" income (in purchasing power) stays the same or even decreases, you are getting more dollars and therefore climbing higher in the progressive income for brackets. Look back at Exhibit 9 in Chapter 2 to see what inflation will do to the tax liability of the Stonestons.

So let's examine some things you might do to keep your tax liabilities at a legal minimum and try to keep the government from being your majority partner.

Chapter 14

TAX PLANNING

Basic Objective

The big problem in individual income taxes is the progressive nature of the rate structure. For example, a married man with $44,000 of taxable income in one year will pay 50 percent income tax on any additional income, while the same man with only $12,000 taxable income in a year will pay 25 percent tax on his next few thousand dollars of additional income. This was dramatically brought out in the case of Xavier Hollander, well-publicized author of *The Happy Hooker*. The Internal Revenue Service is claiming that Ms. Hollander owes about $70,000 additional 1970 income tax on about $90,000 of unrecorded income. Ms. Hollander, in her petition to the Tax Court, says in effect that "no way could I have made more than $120,000, which I reported, from practicing prostitution in New York for nine months in 1970."

The basic objective, then, is to avoid having large amount of ordinary income taxed to one individual in one year.

Methods of Meeting the Basic Objective

1. *Tax-Free Income.* Interest on municipal bonds, social security benefits, and the other relatively few types of tax-free income are obviously more attractive because of their tax exemption.

2. *Tax Favored Income.* Capital gains, only one-half of which are

subject to tax, or income from oil or gas wells or other natural resources, a portion of which may be tax-free because of percentage depletion, are more attractive than fully-taxed income.

3. *Spreading Income Among More Entities.* This will get you into methods of dividing income among members of the family by gifts, etc., perhaps dividing income between an individual and his corporation, and the possible use of trusts to create more entities and therefore more taxpayers.

Joe Lund, one of our Chapter 3 profiles, is a good candidate for saving some income taxes by spreading some investment income around to members of his family. Joe is paying a top income tax rate of 42 percent, while his grown children don't get higher than the 25 percent bracket. Thus, every $1,000 of investment income transferred to the children by giving them some stocks or bonds would save the family as a whole $170. Joe and Peggy are at a point where they can consider permanent gifts, rather than the kind of "Indian giving" where the assets come back, as we are going to suggest shortly for the Stonestons and Jack Martin. By making permanent gifts, Joe can realize some estate tax savings, as we will see in the next chapter.

A big non-tax reason for Joe making these gifts to his children is getting some extra income in their hands when they can really use it. The two married children have young families who are going to require greater amounts. A thousand dollars a year extra income now will mean a lot more to them than having it 15 or 20 years in the future when Joe and Peggy are gone, and their own incomes are probably up substantially.

4. *Spreading Income Among More Years.* The more evenly an individual can receive his total income for a period of years, the less tax he is going to pay. It is often desirable, therefore, to defer income or accelerate it, as the case may be, in order to get an even flow of income by years.

It may be particularly desirable to accelerate income into the current year if you are eligible for income averaging. Your test is whether your income for the current year will be more than 20 percent over the average taxable income of the four previous years. If you meet this test, you can spread the excess over the current year and the four previous years, which has the effect of having the excess income taxed over five years instead of one, and therefore in much lower tax brackets.

In most instances, with only modest fluctuations in income, it is desirable to consider deferring tax for a year, merely because of the use of money concept. This means that it is generally desirable to defer income and accelerate deductions near the end of the year. To determine whether this is a good idea or not in your individual situation, however, you really need to sit down about November 1 and fill out Exhibit 44. This form gives you a place to list your actual income and deductions for the first 10 months of the year, and your estimates of these items for November and December.

EXHIBIT 44

	January through October (Actual)	November and December (Estimate)	Total
Income:			
Salary	$_____	$_____	$_____
Interest	_____	_____	_____
Dividends			
Net earnings from business or profession	_____	_____	_____
Capital gains (only one-half of long-term)	_____	_____	_____
Other	_____	_____	_____
Total income			$_____
Deductions and Exemptions:			
Standard deduction (16% of total income, maximum $2,600)			$_____
OR			
Itemized deductions___			
Taxes (state and local income, real estate, sales and other)	_____	_____	_____
Interest paid	_____	_____	_____
Contributions			
Medical and dental expenses	_____	_____	_____
Casualty losses	_____	_____	_____
Other	_____	_____	_____
Total itemized deductions			$_____
Larger of standard or itemized deductions			$_____
Total deductions and exemptions			$_____
TAXABLE INCOME			$_____

Totaled, the form gives you the estimated total income and deductions for the year.

After you have arrived at an estimated taxable income figure for the year, compare this with your actual taxable income for the four previous years (to see if income averaging might be in the picture) and with your expectations of taxable income for the future. Let's assume your estimated taxable income is about the same as it will be next year, so that you will be in the same top tax bracket. It may then well be worthwhile to consider using your tax money for a year longer by deferring some of your taxable income to next year. Here are some of the factors you might consider.

If you are self-employed in a business or profession, you should consider deferring sending out bills or collecting items of income for the balance of the year. Of course, you should not carry this to the extreme of creating some uncollectible accounts, but at least put some income over into January.

On the other side of the books, it would be desirable to pay up any business and professional expenses before the end of the year rather than carrying them over to next year. If there are any business or professional assets you have been considering acquiring, you would do well to make the purchase before the end of the year. This makes you eligible for both special first-year depreciation of 20 percent of the cost of the assets and the investment tax credit of 7 to 10 percent of the cost of the assets, which is a dollar for dollar deduction on your tax bill.

If you have had some capital gain and loss transactions during the year, or have some potential gains or losses you might take, you should fill out Exhibits 45 and 46. Remember that losses are deductible against gains, and that a net loss of $1,000 a year is deductible against other income. Only one-half of a long-term loss is deductible against other income. If you have a substantial potential loss, it might be well to take the loss, so you can start using it up at the rate of $1,000 a year. You can carry forward the loss indefinitely.

Exhibit 44 shows you how to compare your probable standard deduction with your possible itemized deductions. If your itemized deductions are going to be close to the amount of the standard deduction, you might consider bunching some deductions, which would ordinarily be paid next year, at the end of the current year, as is discussed later on in this chapter under the profile of Pete Jones.

Finally, you might take a look at your personal exemptions status, and see if there are any exemptions which are doubtful. You may not be furnishing more than half of the support of the individual. Maybe a few dollars additional contributed before the end of the year will give you an added $750 exemption. A special problem here is the newly married son or daughter, whom you have been supporting all year. If the young couple

EXHIBIT 45

CAPITAL GAINS AND LOSSES TO DATE FOR YEAR 19___

Amount or Number of Shares	Stock, bond, etc.	Bought Date	Price	Sold Date	Price	Short Term Gain	Loss	Long Term Gain	Loss
			$		$	$	$	$	$
Capital loss carry-overs from five prior years									
Capital gain dividends (long term)								——	——
TOTALS								===	===

EXHIBIT 46

YEAR-END TAX STRATEGY FOR CAPITAL GAINS AND LOSSES

List your possible capital gains and losses here. Consider these together with your totals of realized transactions from Exhibit 45 to determine your year-end strategy for improving your tax situation by offsetting gains already realized this year and making the best use of capital losses.

Amount or Number of Shares	Stock, Bond, etc. That Can Be Sold for Tax Advantage	Bought Date Price	Current Price Unit Total	Possible Short Term Gain Loss	Possible Long Term Gain Loss
		$	$ $	$ $	$ $

1. Total possible gains and losses
2. Total realized gains and losses from Exhibit 42
3. Expected year-end totals (line 1. plus line 2.)

files a joint return, you will not be able to claim an exemption for your son or daughter, nor will your son's or daughter's father in-law.

The answer here is to make sure the young couple files separate returns. Then, if you furnish more than half the support of your own child, you can claim the exemption. Finally, you can create some additional entities for whom you can claim personal exemptions by December 31. If you are going to acquire some new children, it is certainly better to acquire them in December rather than in January. This is a little late in the year to do any planning for natural births, but you might be considering adopting a child. Maybe you can speed up the paper work and get that done in December instead of January.

Tax Planning for the Stonestons

As a sample of tax planning, consider the Stonestons, whose financial situation was explored in Chapters 1 and 2. In Exhibit 5 of Chapter 2, there is included under Committed Expenditures about $7,000 to $10,000 a year for social security and income taxes. This indicates a top income tax bracket of 36–42 percent.

The first question is whether it would be desirable for Bill Stoneston to incorporate his management consulting practice. The tax advantage would be using the 22 percent corporate tax rate for the first $25,000 of corporate income. Bill might draw enough salary from his corporation to leave $10,000 a year net income in the corporation to be taxed. If this $10,000 was taxed at the corporate rate of 22 percent, instead of Bill's top rate of 36–42 percent, there would be an apparent tax saving of $1,400 to $2,000 per year.

But there are drawbacks! After the corporation pays its tax, it will have $7,800 a year of corporate earnings locked up in the corporate treasury. Bill and his family can't use this money for any personal purposes without a second tax. If Bill were to get this $7,800 out someday as a capital gain—perhaps by liquidating the corporation—Bill would probably pay at least 25 percent tax or, $1,950. So the $1,400 to $2,000 a year tax saving has disappeared. However, the $1,950 "second tax" could be postponed for some years, and there is some value of use of money to consider. There could also be some tax-free fringe benefits to Bill, as a corporate employee, such as group insurance and reimbursement of medical expense, but there is expense and responsibility connected with a corporation, such as keeping books, filing tax returns, being sure the corporate income is at the right level, etc. There is also additional payroll tax expense now that Bill is an employee instead of an entrepreneur.

So, incorporating may not be a very good idea. If Bill had more income, so he was in the 50 or 60 percent top tax bracket, and could afford to "lock up" some income not needed for living expenses for some years, it might be worthwhile.

Bill's income is too level over the years to receive much benefit from deferring income or using income averaging. Can *anything* be suggested to the Stonestons?

The best bet for increasing the after-tax income of the family would be to use the children as taxable entities—use up their personal exemptions and low-tax brackets each year. If Bill and Sally were to transfer to their children some income from stocks or other investments, they could save all of the income tax on this investment income. For example, if each of the three children received $750 a year income, they would pay no tax, and $2,250 a year would be removed from the parents' top bracket. At a 36–42 percent top tax bracket, this means a tax saving of $810 to $945 per year.

The investment income could be transferred to the children in one of two ways. The securities could be transferred to the children outright, perhaps in the name of an adult relative as custodian. This probably would not be desirable since Bill and Sally are probably not ready to part with any assets permanently.

A better solution might be the use of short-term trusts. The securities could be transferred to three trusts, one for each child, with instructions to the trustee to transfer the income each year to the child and, after a period of years, to return the securities to Bill and Sally. The trust must last more than 10 years, so Bill and Sally will have to part with the securities for that period. They will have to weigh that and the temporary decrease in their discretionary income against the fact that the family will be accumulating nearly $1,000 a year in tax savings to use for educating the children or other worthwhile purposes.

Tax Planning for Linda Hanson

Linda Hanson, one of our Chapter 3 profiles, could certainly profit from a division of her business income between a corporation and her individual tax return. She is expecting to increase her present $25,000 annual income from her shop to $40,000–45,000 a year, consisting of a $35,000 "salary" and $5,000–10,000 a year net earnings after salary.

Let's assume she has taxable income of $45,000 a year. The comparison of her annual income taxes as an individual proprietor and as sole owner of a corporation would be as follows.

	Proprietorship	Corporation
Individual income tax		
On $45,000	$17,190	
On $25,000 salary		$ 7,190
Corporate income tax		
On $20,000 at 22%		4,400
Total annual income tax	$17,190	$11,590

Linda could clearly save $5,600 a year ($17,190 − $11,590) by incorporating. This is well worth doing!

There are two reasons a corporation fits Linda's situation much better than Bill Stoneston's. First, she reaches the 60 percent tax bracket at $44,000 individual taxable income because of being single. We are assuming that she will draw a $25,000 annual salary from her corporation and leave the remaining $20,000 of annual profits to be taxed to the corporation. Her corporation will pay a 22 percent tax on this $20,000, compared to an average 50 percent Linda would pay individually if the $20,000 were piled on top of her $25,000 salary. The savings would be 28 percent (50 − 22 percent) of $20,000, or $5,600 a year.

Second, Linda isn't too troubled about the "second tax" on getting the money out of the corporation. She is probably going to be increasing the sales volume of her business, meaning she is going to require more and more capital for inventory, accounts receivable, store fixtures, etc. So she probably isn't going to be able to take out all of her business income and spend it anyway. She is much better off having 78¢ of each dollar of the top part of her income accumulated in her corporation than to have 50¢ of each dollar individually.

With a prospective saving of $5,600 a year, Linda can afford to get into the problems and expenses of corporate books, tax returns, higher payroll taxes, etc. *And* she may pick up some tax-free fringe benefits as a corporate employee which are not available to her as an individual proprietor.

Tax Features of Employment

There are tax-free items available to employees, such as group insurance, reimbursement of medical expenses, free medical examinations, and possibly use of clubs. All of these are fringe benefits which are more attractive to an employee from the tax viewpoint than additional cash compensation.

John Herman, another Chapter 3 profile, is paying out $3,800 a year of his committed expenses, from after-tax dollars, on items his employer might reimburse him for on a tax-free basis. The items are:

Insurance premiums on $50,000 life insurance	$1,000
Medical and dental expenses	800
Entertainment (including club dues)	2,000
	$3,800

John's employer could give him a group insurance policy and pay the premiums, with no taxable income to John, as long as the policy is not over $50,000 face value.

The freight forwarding company could also adopt a plan of reimbursing employees for medical expenses for themselves and their families. Again the reimbursement would not be taxable income to John. This tax-free reimbursement is particularly useful because John, like other individuals, gets no tax deduction for medical expenses except amounts more than 3 percent of his income annually. At $800 medical expenses a year, John is just under 3 percent of his $30,000 salary and always just a little short of getting any tax deduction.

This is the usual result when a family has only routine office calls, shots, dental expenses, and uninsured portions of larger items. With the spread of medical insurance plans, fewer individuals are able to take deductions for medical expenses because they can only consider the costs not reimbursed by medical insurance. So John should be resourceful, shift with the times, and get his employer to adopt a plan to reimburse at least key employees for their medical expenses, including any medical insurance premiums paid by the employee. Note that the freight forwarding company *can* limit this medical expense reimbursement plan to key employees, to any group they select. Thus, the company can avoid the expense of paying these expenses for all employees.

To the extent John's club dues and other entertainment expenses are connected with business entertainment, his employer could reimburse him for these expenses without creating any income to John. This question of whether entertainment is business or personal is difficult to decide. There are thousands or millions of individual factual patterns, so you don't have general rules to go by. Ever since the IRS adopted new rules on this subject in 1962, T&E (travel and entertainment) has been one of the more hotly contested issues between taxpayers and the IRS.

One thing you can be sure of—John's employer has a much better chance of supporting a T&E deduction on its corporate return for John's entertainment expense than John would have on his individual return. There is some presumption that the employer would not pay for the expenses unless they were business expenses.

There is another presumption working in the same direction. If John claims deductions on his individual tax return for part or all of these entertainment expenses, the obvious question from the IRS is, "If these are such good business expenses, why didn't your employer reimburse you for them?

The great thing about all three of these items from the company's viewpoint is that they are all deductible as business expenses on the corporate tax return. The different types of compensation can be ranked as follows in order of tax desirability.

Tax Effect to Employee	*Tax Effect to Employer*
1. Never taxable	Immediately deductible
2. Tax deferred and may be reduced when payable	Immediately deductible
3. Immediately taxed	Immediately deductible
4. Tax deferred	Deferred deduction
5. Tax immediately or later	Never deductible

These reimbursements of fringe benefits are the number 1 item, and the best you can get from the tax viewpoints of both the employee and employer.

To help your thinking about the less desirable (tax-wise) forms of compensation, some other examples are:

2. *Qualified retirement plans.* The employer gets a deduction as money is put in the plan, and the employee's tax is deferred until he receives something on retirement, death, etc. Even then his income may be taxed on a more favorable basis, as we have seen in Chapter 12.

3. *Cash salary.* The employer deducts it when paid; the employee has immediate taxable income.

4. *Deferred compensation.* The employer gets a deduction only when this is paid some years in the future, the employee has taxable income at the same time, when he receives it.

5. *Qualified stock options.* The big problem here is that the employer usually does get a tax deduction, which about doubles the net cost to the average corporation. An offset may be that the employer compensates employees without paying out any cash.

The important thing for John to keep in mind is geting all the benefits from #1 that he can. The way to do this is to get his employer to reimburse all possible expenses.

There are also possibilities of spreading an employee's income over the years through the use of deferred compensation, as an alternative to current compensation.

In recent years the tax law has tended to favor currently earned income with such rewards as the maximum 50 percent on earned income, and such penalties on "gimmicks" as the minimum tax on capital gains. These considerations, together with the greater value of the use of money because of high interest rates, tend to favor an individual getting what he can, paying his tax, and investing what is left.

The choice of how to receive additional compensation still boils down to an individual matter. For example, one individual may be in his late fifties, married late, and is now struggling to send several children through college at the same time. He needs all the money he can get. This individual will no doubt vote for current cash compensation. On the other hand, there may be a young individual who has substantial outside income and would like a deferred compensation plan. The best approach is a "cafeteria" system under which individuals have some freedom of choice as to what form in which to take additional compensation.

Tax Planning for Jack Martin

Jack Martin, one of the people presented in our profiles in Chapter 3, has done a great job of tax planning in the areas of fringe benefits, spreading income among years, and getting some tax-favored income.

In the area of fringe benefits, Jack has a pension plan, the maximum tax-free amount of group insurance, and a healthy expense account to take care of some business entertainment, club dues, etc. He has also made some intelligent choices at the compensation "cafeteria" which, fortunately for Jack, his employer provided. Any additional current salary would be taxed to Jack at 50–60 percent. Instead, Jack chose $150,000 of deferred compensation, payable after his retirement when he would be in a much lower tax bracket, and stock options which give him the opportunity to get some capital gains. These will be taxed at only one-half the tax rate applicable to ordinary salary income.

One step Jack should take immediately is to put some of his securities in a short-term trust for his mother, Thelma. At present, Jack takes $7,500 of his investment income, pays 60 percent income tax or $4,500, and gives the remaining $3,000 after taxes to his mother for her support. As an alternative, Jack can put enough securities in a trust to produce $3,000 annually in income and provide in the trust instrument that the income will be paid to his mother during her lifetime. On her death, the trust will terminate, and the securities will be returned to Jack. Ordinarily a short-term trust must be set up for at least a 10-year life. However, this requirement is met if the trust lasts for the lifetime of the beneficiary, regardless of life expectancy or how long the beneficiary actually lives.

The result of this short-term trust will be to support Jack's mother with $3,000 before tax dollars, instead of $7,500 before tax dollars. Hence, Jack has $4,500 more of investment income for his own use and is helping his mother as much as before.

Getting the Best Tax Results from Family Status

A joint return of husband and wife is nearly always the best answer for a married couple. This follows because the tax on a joint return is computed as if each spouse had exactly one-half of the taxable income. This means, for example, that if a man had $40,000 of taxable income and his wife none, he would pay $12,140 tax on a separate return, while on a joint return of husband and wife, the couple would pay $8,760—a saving of $3,380. There are rare instances where separate returns may be better for instance where both spouses have income, where there are medical expense deductions or other problems—but these are a small fraction of 1 percent.

There are other forms of special status which may save money. An unmarried individual who qualifies as head-of-a-household, for example, will pay $9,480 tax on taxable income of $32,000, while, as a so-called single individual, he would pay $10,290 or $810 more on the same amount. To qualify as head-of-a-household, the unmarried individual must be maintaining a household that is the principal residence of some dependent relative.

Another favored tax category is that of "surviving spouse," defined as a widow or widower maintaining a household in which a dependent child or stepchild lives. A surviving spouse may use joint return tax rates for two years after the year of death of the husband or wife, if the individual remains unmarried. In situations where you are close to the head-of-household or surviving-spouse status, a little effort to be sure you furnish the necessary support for the dependent is well worthwhile.

An individual taxpayer receives a $750 exemption for each dependent he supports. This exemption must be totally claimed by one individual and cannot be divided. Ordinarily, this means that the individual claiming the exemption for a dependent must furnish the dependent's chief support—

i.e., more than one-half. There are situations, as when three brothers equally support their mother, where no individual will furnish more than one-half of the mother's support. Therefore, under the general rule, none of the three will be entitled to the $750 dependency exemption. However, there is provision for a multiple support agreement, where two of the three brothers can sign, indicating they will not claim their mother as an exemption. Obviously, this should be worked out so the brother in the highest tax bracket claims the exemption and does whatever is proper to "make whole" his two brothers.

When you get into divorces, dissolutions, legal separations, fragmentations, or whatever they call them now, there are a number of tax questions involved, such as—

- Who gets the dependency exemptions for the children?
- Should the husband pay alimony or child support?

The difference here is that alimony is taxable to a wife and deductible by the husband, while child support has no such tax effect. Who, if anyone, is going to get any child care deduction? All of these divorce-related tax questions should be obviously worked out with the individual tax brackets of all parties concerned.

The Itemized or Standard Deduction Election

When the standard deduction was introduced thirty years ago, about 85 percent of individual taxpayers used the standard deduction instead of itemizing their actual deductions. Because of inflation, substantial increases in interest payments, state and local tax payments, etc., this percentage has been dropping for many years and recently was under 50 percent.

The standard deduction has been increased from a maximum of $1,000 to a maximum of $2,600 in fairly recent years, and all indications are the Treasury Department is going to continuously seek legislation to make the standard deduction relatively more attractive, particularly in order to simplify the administration of the individual tax.

This means that more and more individuals will ordinarily be somewhat on the border line between claiming the standard deduction and itemizing each year.

There are considerable possibilities for bunching itemized deductions in some years and eliminating them from others in order to maximize the itemized deductions in the years that itemization is elected. For example, contributions can be steered into a certain year and, to some extent, interest, medical expenses, and perhaps other deductions can also be arranged. The ideal situation would be to itemize every other year and get the maximum actual deductions paid, for example, in the even years and minimize actual deductions in the odd years.

Look at Pete Jones, one of the profiles in Chapter 3, as an example. Since Pete has an income of about $45,000, his allowable standard deduction is not 15 percent of income, but the maximum of $2,000 per year. His itemized deductions might normally be as follows:

Real estate taxes on home	$1,000
Sales tax	500
State gasoline tax	50
Contributions	1,000
Medical expenses—Generally zero, as he is not likely to have more than $1,350 of expenses not reimbursed by medical insurance. The $1,350 is 3 percent of his income, and he has to get over this "floor" before he can deduct anything.	

So Pete might normally run about $2,550 in itemized deductions or $50 too small to do him any good, and he would take the $2,600 standard deduction every year.

What itemized deductions can he move from year to year? Probably not the sales tax or gasoline tax, to any significant extent, but certainly he can move contributions and perhaps real estate taxes. Assume Pete changes his itemized deduction pattern as follows:

	Even Years	Odd Years
Real estate tax	$2,000	None
Sales tax	500	500
Gasoline tax	50	50
Contributions	1,800	200
Total itemized deductions	$4,350	$750

He will then obviously itemize in the even years and take the $2,600 standard deduction in the odd years. His total deductions every two years will now be $6,950 instead of $5,200. With a top tax bracket of 45 percent, he will be saving about $800 in income taxes every two years. Even if he has to pay some interest for delaying payment of one year's real estate taxes, it will be well worthwhile. Particularly when, if he pays the interest in the even years with two years' real estate taxes, the interest will be deductible and the government will, in effect, be paying 45 percent of the interest for him!

Tax Features of Investments

As shown in the analysis of investments, there are some tax-free forms of investment income, such as interest on municipal bonds, the first $100 of dividend income, and tax-free cash flow from real estate investments, sheltered by depreciation and the like.

Pete Jones, the subject of one of our profiles, is a natural to invest in municipal bonds. He has $100,000 of stocks and corporate bonds, from which he is receiving $5,000 a year of taxable dividend and interest income. After paying income tax at his top rate of 50 percent on this income, he has $2,500 left. His alternative would be to sell the stocks and corporate bonds and invest the $100,000 proceeds in AA or AAA rated municipal bonds yielding 6 percent. These are available in recent years. With no tax to pay, Pete would have increased his income after taxes from $2,500 a year to $6,000, or by 140 percent. Another way to look at a municipal bond investment is that for a 50 percent top bracket taxpayer, like Pete, a 6 percent tax-free yield is the equivalent of a 12 percent taxable yield. And where can you get 12 percent with any safety?

The taxable yields, required at various top tax brackets, to equal a 6 percent tax-free yield, are as follows.

Top Tax Bracket (Percent)	Taxable Yield Required (Percent)
25	8.00
36	9.38
42	10.34
50	12.00
60	15.00
70	20.00

One objection often made about municipal bonds (or any kind of investment tied to the dollar) is that you will be "killed by inflation." In any event, Pete should consider some municipal bonds because even $100,000 worth would be only 20 percent of his total assets, and most of the remaining 80 percent should have some inflation hedge. This would include his contracting corporation, rental real estate, and his home.

If you are in a substantial tax bracket, the tax-free nature of some other kinds of income can make a big difference in your investment decisions. For example, the interest element of installment payments of life insurance proceeds is normally subject to tax. With insurance companies crediting interest at about 4½ percent, this is not very attractive as a taxable investment. However, a surviving spouse of an insured can exclude this interest from taxable income up to $1,000 a year. If you are a widow in the 50 percent tax bracket, this is as good as a taxable investment returning 9 percent and not a bad deal.

There are also tax-favored, long-term capital gains, which are only one-half included in taxable income. One caution in this regard is not to let tax planning run away with investment decisions. There is certainly a right time to sell securities. The old saying is that "a short-term gain is much better than a long-term loss."

Finally, investment partnerships, which have been discussed in some detail, offer considerable possibilities of tax saving by reducing losses which may be offset against other income. A warning in this regard is to be sure the claimed tax losses are not permanent economic losses. As one of our associates says, "Anyone can save taxes by throwing their money away."

Chapter 15

ESTATE PLANNING

You have followed the advice in the previous chapters so that you have accumulated some net worth and made some good investments. Now what are you going to do with this accumulation so that it profits you and/or your family?

Estate planning is the utilization part of our definition of personal financial planning in Chapter 1. Estate planning then becomes "the utilization of financial resources to obtain the maximum utility for the individual and the family during the lifetime of the planner and the effective distribution of resources after death."

The need for estate planning has become even more acute, primarily because of inflation, which has lead to higher income taxes, lower purchasing power for you and your family, highly fluctuating interest rates on money invested, and greater economic needs of your dependents.

Personal Desires

What do you want to do with your assets—this is more important than taxes or other considerations. After reading this far in this book, you may find it hard to believe that there *are* things more important than dollars. But it is true.

For example, if you have a net worth of millions, a desired action from a dollars and cents viewpoint would be to give Joe, your 18-year-old son, $1,000,000. You would save estate taxes, income taxes, and all sorts of good things. But what happens to Joe's incentives to complete his education, start a career, etc.? With $60,000–80,000 a year income, to say nothing of $1,000,000 in capital, who needs work?

The same thing is true in a less dramatic way of other money-saving ideas. One of the better methods of conserving family capital is by the use of "generation skipping" trusts. This is done by leaving your assets in a trust with only the income to go to your son during his lifetime and the remainder, or principal, to go to his children, or anyone you designate on his death. The result is that you "skip" your son's generation as to payment of death taxes. He doesn't own anything which survives his death, so there is nothing to levy death taxes on. Your grandchildren receive a lot more capital then if their inheritance were reduced by taxes on their father's death.

The value of generation skipping was highlighted in the vice-presidential confirmation hearings of Nelson Rockefeller. As he pointed out the details of the family fortune and its progress from his grandfather to his father to himself and his brothers. It was clear the *real* capital was accumulated by maintaining the same assets in trusts for 60 or 70 years.

In fact, this is *so* good from a tax saving viewpoint that it is top priority on the list of Treasury Department legislative objectives.

But there *are* nonfinancial disadvantages. Have you ever heard of a trust baby? That's a middle-aged trust beneficiary who has never matured because he has an assured income and neither worries about losing capital nor opportunities to increase it. Every trust officer has "war stories" about beneficiaries like Pete, the 50-year-old beneficiary who had two important dates each month—the first, when he got his check, and the fifteenth, when he would have drunk it up and have to start scrounging.

The main point is that there are no prescribed "right" or "wrong" objectives. You have to decide, based on your situation and family, what is best for you to do. But it *is* important for you to *have* objectives—don't float aimlessly through life like a boat without a rudder.

Liquidity

One of the first things to consider as to how your family would get along in the event of your death is "will my widow (or other heir) have enough ready cash to pay for the costs of dying?" These costs of dying come due rapidly. Federal estate and state inheritance taxes ordinarily must be paid within nine months after death, and governmental bodies want money, not pieces of buildings, stock in the family corporation, or other security. Also, money is needed for attorneys and other expenses of administering the estate, and for living expenses of the family during at least a readjustment period.

As a rule of thumb, you can figure that administration expenses will run about 5–7 percent of the estate. Federal estate tax is computed on the "taxable estate," which is after deduction of debts, administration expenses, charitable and marital deductions, and an exemption of $60,000. The estate tax is graduated, somewhat like the income tax, but you can figure 20–30 percent of the taxable estate on amounts of $50,000 to $300,000.

Let's consider Hank Brown who dies with a total estate of $300,000, of which he leaves $100,000 to his wife and the balance to his children, but with the income to his wife during her lifetime. Hank's taxable estate might be computed as follows.

Gross estate		$300,000
Less:		
Debts	$ 20,000	
Administration and funeral expenses	18,000	
Marital deduction for property		
left to wife	100,000	
Specific exemption	60,000	198,000
Taxable estate		$102,000

The Federal estate tax would be a little more than $20,000. The state inheritance tax would vary, depending upon the state. It could be more than Federal tax because of lower exemptions and no marital deduction. In the authors' home state, for example, the state inheritance tax would be about $15,000, for total taxes of $35,000. Then the administration and funeral expenses of $18,000 must be met and the debts paid off. This means a total of $73,000.

The problem then is can $73,000 be raised within nine months or so without sacrificing any assets? The $73,000 need not be cash in the bank, of course, but at least it should be in a form which can shortly be turned into cash in the bank without any sacrifices.

Here is where life insurance can be very useful. All that is required to receive the insurance proceeds is proper proof of death. Ordinarily a check can be secured in at most a few weeks. Many individuals with very substantial net worth find it desirable to carry insurance and give their estates this liquidity, since their net worth is largely tied up in business interests, real estate, and other assets might not be desirable to be liquidated in the event of their death. If the insurance policy was owned by the deceased person, then the proceeds are an asset of his estate and will produce a requirement for some estate and inheritance taxes. One way around this is to have the insurance policy owned by the wife, or someone else in the family, or by a trust. Any of this "outside ownership" will give the desired liquidity to the family as a whole, without producing more tax requirements.

An interesting way of providing some of this liquidity is to use what has come to be known as "flower bonds." These are U.S. Treasury bonds which can be used at par to pay Federal estate taxes, even though their market value may be considerably less than par. There are only 11 issues of Treasury bonds that qualify for this treatment, and no new ones are being added. As a result, availability of these will gradually diminish. Some of them do not mature, however, until the last years of this century, so they will be around to some extent for quite awhile. These bonds are listed in Exhibit 47. If Hank Brown, for example, had owned $20,000 of U.S. Treasury 3's of 1995, he could have purchased those recently at about 78, which would have given him a cost of $15,600 for the par value of $20,000. On Hank's death, his executor could have turned in these bonds in payment of $20,000 of Federal estate tax making a clear gain of $4,400. This gain would not be subject to any income tax, and a 30 percent gain over purchase price obviously has its attractions. Interestingly, the savings are even greater for smaller taxable estates than for large ones. This is true because the bonds must be included in the taxable estate at their par value, so that

---

EXHIBIT 47

U.S. TREASURY BONDS WHICH MAY
BE USED AT PAR TO PAY FEDERAL
ESTATE TAXES *

Series	Due
4's 1980	Feb. 15, 1980
2¾'s 1975–80	Apr. 1, 1980
3½'s 1980	Nov. 15, 1980
3¼'s 1978–83	June 15, 1983
3¼'s 1985	May 15, 1985
4¼'s 1975–85	May 15, 1985
3½'s 1990	Feb. 15, 1990
4¼'s 1987–92	Aug. 15, 1992
4's 1988–93	Feb. 15, 1993
4⅛'s 1989–94	May 15, 1994
3's 1995	Feb. 15, 1995
3½'s 1998	Nov. 15, 1998

---

* These bonds are quoted in each issue of the *Wall Street Journal*. The two issues maturing in 1980 are currently quoted at about 15 percent less than par. The nine issues maturing in the years 1983 to 1998 are quoted at about 21—23 percent less than par.

the increase in value *does* become subject to Federal estate tax. In Hank's estate, the additional value of the bonds would be taxed at a Federal estate tax of 22 percent, so there would be additional estate tax of $968. If Hank had left about a $2 million estate, which would have had a top estate tax bracket of about 50 percent, the additional $4,400 value of the bonds would have produced additional Federal estate tax of $2,200.

These flower bonds are attractive enough so that about one quarter of the total Federal estate taxes are being paid by using these bonds. Because of the special value of these bonds for paying taxes, they sell at somewhat of a premium over other U. S. Treasury bonds, so that they yield 1 or 2 percent less a year than comparable Treasury bonds. So if Hank were to live 10 years after purchasing these bonds, the advantage in paying estate taxes might be more than offset by the reduced investment income. The best solution is to purchase the bonds shortly before you die, although this is difficult to predict! There have been instances of death bed purchases of these bonds in substantial amounts, however. One purchase in the millions of dollars came 20 minutes before the actual time of death.

When you think of liquidity, go beyond providing for cash needs in the event of your death, and think about what kind of income will be available for your widow or other heirs. Is this enough to meet their reasonable family needs? When Hank Brown died, he left a widow, Betty, 43 years of age, with two children, 12 and 10. She figured she needed $20,000 a year to maintain the family in the way Hank would have liked for at least 10 years until the youngest child was ready for college. Here's how her available income from Hank's estate might look, using one of the insurance worksheets from the Appendix.

Gross estate	$300,000
Less non-income producing assets (house, cars, etc.)	100,000
Available assets to invest	$200,000
Less death expenses	73,000
Net available assets to invest	$127,000
Income	
At 5% on $127,000	$ 6,350
Social security benefits	6,690
Total	$13,040

This is considerably short of the $20,000 a year Betty figures she needs—in fact, $6,960 a year ($20,000 — $13,040) short, or $580 per month. Continuing the use of the insurance worksheet, it would take $46,400 of insurance proceeds to produce $580 a month in additional income for the eight years until Betty's youngest child is 18. Even if you assume Betty is going to invest the $127,000 that is available "aggressively," and earn 8 percent, or $10,160 a year, she still comes short of her income goal.

Income at 8% on $127,000	$10,160
Social security benefits	6,690
Total	$16,850

On this basis, Betty would be short $3,150 a year, or $262 a month, and it would take $25,200 of insurance proceeds to create this additional income for 8 years.

Betty should also look at her longer range income picture. Her social security benefits will be suspended when her youngest child reaches 18, so that her income would be down to $6,350 a year or $10,160 a year, depending on the rate of earnings on the assets Hank left. We say Betty's social security benefits are "suspended" because she can start drawing benefits again at age 62 as a widow. But since she will be 51 when her youngest reaches 18, that will leave her 11 years to worry about.

A big reason for Betty's problems with adequate income is the high proportion of non-income producing assets. These are only one-third of the gross estate, but they become more than 44 percent of the remaining assets after payment of death expenses. This usually happens, because the expenses come out of liquid assets which would produce income, not out of the home, furniture, cars, vacation home, etc. Betty should either convert some of these non-income producing assets into something that will add to her income, or think of going to work, or both.

Flexibility

We have seen the necessity for flexibility in considering investments. With changes in economics, interest rates, etc., you do not want to be rigid about your investment thinking.

In addition to the investment question, you should remain flexible as to provisions for your family. Think of changes in each individual in the family in relation to what they need due to inflation, taxes, etc. Above all, do not be carried away with tax saving ideas to the point where you end up with a rigid estate plan that does not fit your circumstances.

Wills

When individuals like Abraham Lincoln and a Chief Justice of the U.S. Supreme Court die without wills, it is obviously hard to motivate people to make them.

Some common reasons advanced for not having a will, and the contrary arguments, are as follows:

Reason	Contra
Estate too small	This estate *really* can't stand any unnecessary shrinkage from taxes, etc. Also, it is still important the assets go where the individual wishes. You may inherit or be given property later, so that your estate isn't that small.
Estate is simple and will all go to my wife	In many states this may not be true, as children, for example, may have a statutory right to a substantial part of the estate if no will is left.
	One-quarter of the widows are under 45 years of age and have minor children to raise. In some states, if there is no will these children may get up to two-thirds of the estate, and there are then problems of guardianship, reporting to courts, etc.
Everything is in joint tenancy	This one is tricky. There are 50 different jurisdictions in the United States, and there may be 50 different rules as to joint tenancy. When it was introduced in the State of Washington in fairly recent years, being billed as a means of saving attorney fees, the more enlightened attorneys felt it would probably *increase* their total practice, in straightening out all the messes that resulted.
	This may be good in small estates, which consist only of an equity in a house, an automobile, and the bank account. Once you get into joint tenancy, you are trapped, and you have no flexibility.

It may be *particularly* important for a single person to have a will. At least with a married person, the legal heirs may be reasonably logical persons. But with a single person, anything can happen as to who is the legal heir and whether the decendent really wanted to leave anything to that individual.

The principal reasons *for* having the will are first, to be sure your property goes where you want it; second, simplicity; and third, to avoid costs such as bonds, other administration, and possibly larger legal fees to straighten out the distribution of the estate.

One thing that should be realized is that there is more and more property of individuals passing "outside" of their will. Examples are proceeds of life insurance policies, property in inter vivos or living trusts, bank accounts in the names of two individuals with a joint and survivorship provison, retirement plan benefits, and others. These types of assets have beneficiary designations which determine who will receive the asset, but one thing to remember is that they are still subject to estate and inheritance taxes.

Some specific things *not* to do with your will, are as follows:

1. "I give to my dancing instructor" all of my "personal property," and leave the residue of my estate to my three children. There is an argument currently going on between the dancing instructor and the children of the elderly well-to-do lady who wrote this will as to what personal property means. Does this include everything except real estate, which means it includes all securities, bank accounts, etc., or does this only refer to such items as personal effects, including clothing, jewelry, and the like? Be specific—say what you mean.

2. "I leave to my three children, share and share alike, the residue of my estate." What if one of the children dies before you do? Do you want her or his share to go to her or his heirs, or go to your other children? Look ahead—consider the possibilities and provide for them.

3. "I leave to Mary, my sister, my home." What if you sell the home you were living in at the time you wrote the will, and buy a farm of 100 acres with a home on it? What if you have two homes at the time of your death? Again, be specific and keep your will up-to-date with the changes in your life.

4. "I leave $10,000 to the First Presbyterian Church, $25,000 to the Boy Scouts, and $15,000 to the YMCA." These may turn out to take a much larger percentage of your estate then you assumed at the time you wrote the will. You are much better off to leave percentages of your estate, with maximum amounts which you do not want to exceed.

Once you have a will, do not put it in a desk drawer and forget it. The late Senator Kerr of Oklahoma died with a 23-year-old will that made no use of the marital deduction, which was introduced nine years after the will was written. The use of this one technique would have saved his estate $13 to $19 million in estate taxes.

You may not be able to save millions, but make sure to review your will every two or three years. Think about not only savings, but the fact that your family situation changes. Children grow up, get married, accumulate assets of their own, or inherit some from grandparents. Be sure you *still* want your property to go as your will directs.

Some Basic Estate Plans

Let's look at three basic plans Hank Brown might have used, in leaving his property to his wife and children. Remember Hank Brown had a gross estate of $300,000, and his will provided that $100,000 of assets would go to his widow and the balance to his children, with income to his widow during her lifetime.

1. *Everything to wife outright.*
The marital deduction would be increased because it would go up to one-half of Hank's estate. This would reduce the Federal estate taxes from the $20,000 we estimated above to probably something like $10,000. However, if Betty keeps the estate at the same level, the entire amount will be taxable in her estate on her death, and this would mean a Federal estate tax bill of about $50,000.

2. *Income from the estate to my wife, Betty, during her life, with the property going on her death to our children.*
This means the entire estate is taxable in Hank's estate, as there is no marital deduction. Hank's Federal estate tax will be at about the $50,000 level. However, there would be no estate and inheritance taxes on Betty's death unless she accumulated property in the balance of her life. This results because she has no interest in Hank's property which passes to her children as a result of her death. What they are receiving has already been determined under their father's will.
One personal family drawback to this plan is that, financially, the best thing that can happen for Hank's and Betty's children is for Betty to die immediately. That way, they get their hands on their property now, instead of waiting perhaps 20 or 30 years for Betty to die. Also, there is no financial inducement for Betty's children to treat her well, as they are going to get whatever they get on her death regardless of how she may feel about it. You might think a few times before putting your widow in this situation in order to perhaps save taxes.

3. *One-half of the property in a trust as in No. 2, and the other one-half of the property in a "marital deduction trust," which Betty can draw principal from if she wishes.*

Tax result in Hank's estate is the same as in No. 1, since the maximum marital deduction is available, and the Federal estate tax will be about $10,000. The tax on Betty's death, however, will be reduced substantially under No. 3, since only one-half of the property will be taxable in her estate. This means that her Federal estate tax will also be about $10,000, assuming no change in the amount of the estate.

From a personal viewpoint, this at least gives Betty control over one-half of the property, as she can designate in her will who will get the principal of the marital deduction trust on her death, or she can use it up during her lifetime if she wishes. This gives her children some financial incentive to treat her well so they can get the share of the marital deduction trust they may feel entitled to.

Trusts

Trusts arose in the times of the Crusades. Before the knight left merrie old England, perhaps for several years, to go battle the infidels, he wanted to know what would happen to his castle and the lands in case he didn't make it back. The practice developed of the knight leaving title to his property in the name of one of his less adventurous neighbors, but "in trust" for the knight's wife or children, etc. If the knight didn't come back, the trustee was supposed to see that the property was used for the benefit of the family.

We might look at three specific kinds of trusts which are in common use.

Revocable Living Trust

In this kind of trust, you turn some assets over to a trustee, normally a bank, with instructions to pay the income to you and what to do about the principal in the event of your death. You can get the property back at any time during your lifetime by canceling or revoking the trust—hence its name.

The advantages of this kind of trust are avoiding probate on death, thus saving administration expenses and publicity which often comes with probate. For example, you can provide that no property is to go to one child, or leave him less than his share, without a lot of possible publicity. Also, you can "test out" the trustee and see what you think of the performance. If you like it, you can add more property to the trust or make it irrevocable. Finally, you can avoid the bother of handling your assets yourself. You can delegate to the trustee such matters as record-keeping, receiving dividends and interest, and investment decisions. You can go as far in this direction as you wish.

The disadvantages of this kind of trust are that there are no tax savings, either in the form of income taxes or estate taxes. For tax purposes, the property is treated the same as if you still owned it individually. Another disadvantage is that you lose the flexibility you have with outright ownership of the property. In the event of your death, it is going to be distributed as the trust instrument provides, even if you may have had second thoughts after drawing up the trust instrument.

Ten-year Trust

In a ten-year trust, also referred to as a short-term trust, you transfer assets to a trustee with instructions to either distribute the income to another person, known as a beneficiary, or to accumulate the income for the benefit of that beneficiary. You then provide that on the expiration of the trust, which must be more then ten years away, the property will be returned to you. You cannot have the income of the trust used to support your child or the income will be taxed to you. What items constitute support is uncertain, varying from state to state, with complications such as majority at age 18.

The ten-year trust can be particularly useful if you are supporting someone for a limited number of years, or if you want to accumulate income for a child, such as for a college education. A perfect example would be Jack Martin, as we saw in profile No. 12, in chapter 14.

Another example is John, a man in his thirties with a five-year-old daughter, Mary. He now has taxable income of $25,000, putting him in the 36 percent tax bracket on the top part of his income. John expects the family income to increase so that in the 1980's his marginal tax bracket will be 50 percent or more. John has $30,000 of investments. He does not need the investment income to meet living expenses, but wants to build up a college education fund for his daughter.

John puts securities with a market value of $16,000 in a trust for Mary, providing that the income of the trust will be distributed each year for 12 years to a custodian for Mary. At the end of 12 years, the trust terminates and the securities are returned to John. What is the result? Assuming a 7 percent annual return from the securities and 5 percent interest on a savings account, in which the custodian puts the annual income, a fund of $17,600 will be available for Mary at age 17. Of this total, nearly $8,000 is contributed by Uncle Sam in the form of savings of taxes John would have paid on the income. The remaining $9,600 is the after-tax income John is giving up during the 12-year period.

"Sprinkling" Trust

The "sprinkling" trust gets its name from the fact that the trustee is given authority to vary distribution of income and, perhaps, principal among a group of beneficiaries, in accordance with the best judgment of the trustee.

For example, assume Jack Martin, profile No. 12, was killed in an automobile accident and left an estate of the $545,000, previously detailed, plus $200,000 in insurance proceeds, or a total of $745,000. One-half of this estate he left to his wife, Elaine. Assume further that Pete, one of Jack's three children, is a young heart surgeon who is looking forward shortly to an income of $100,000 a year; a second child, Mary, is married to a young minister and their income is $8,000 a year; while a third child, Bill, is getting his doctorate in English poetry and expects to pursue an academic life. If Jack left one-half of his estate in a sprinkling trust, giving the trustee the authority to determine distributions of income, it would certainly make sense all around to distribute income to Mary and Bill, but not to Pete or to their Mother, Elaine.

Sprinkling trusts may be created either during your lifetime or by your will. Ones created by your will are testamentary trusts.

Marital Deduction

We have been talking about the marital deduction without really defining it. A marital deduction is a deduction for Federal estate tax purposes, in computing the taxable estate, of the value of property left to one's spouse, with a maximum deduction of one-half of the estate. Transfers to qualify for the marital deduction must either be outright, or must be in the form of a particular kind of trust. The principal of the trust must be subject to a power of appointment by the spouse—i.e., a designation by the spouse of who will succeed to the property on the death of the spouse.

Like any transfer of either income or estate from one taxpayer to another, the greatest benefit results from taking property off the top of one spouse's taxable estate and putting it on the bottom of the other's. Therefore, the more the marital deduction is used, the smaller the tax saving on successive increments. Also, savings are smaller if the surviving spouse has property of his or her own, so that the property transferred by the marital deduction will be added onto a considerable base.

However, in thinking about possible use of the marital deduction, the value of the use of money must always be considered. The tax on the second estate may be deferred for many years, and therefore a substantial saving may be available—even if the estate of the second spouse ends up paying as much tax on the marital deduction property as if it had been taxed in the estate of the first spouse to die. In considering the benefits of the marital deduction, relative ages and life expectancies of the two spouses therefore enter in.

Lifetime Gifts

Some advantages of lifetime gifts are the following:

1. Gift tax rates are about 75 percent of estate tax rates.

2. Gift taxes start at the bottom of the progressive rate structure, while the property is removed from the top of the estate tax rate schedule.

3. Any gift taxes paid reduce the taxable estate.

4. Substantial gifts may be made without paying any Federal gift taxes, as each individual has a $30,000 lifetime exemption and also a $3,000 annual exclusion for each person to whom gifts are made.

5. Any income from the property given will be taxed to the donee, generally at lower income tax rates.

6. Gifts may be a protection against the possibility of losing the value of the marital deduction benefits due to one's spouse dying first.

7. Probate and estate administration expenses are eliminated on gift property.

8. The donee gets some experience in handling property before inheriting any. Maybe when he does inherit, he won't be like the man who inherited $100,000 of a blue chip stock which split 3 for 1 shortly afterward. Seeing the market price was down substantially in the newspaper (naturally enough when he really owned three times as many shares), he sold it all before it went down any further. Following a cocktail party recommendation, he put the $100,000 in a speculative stock which a year later had a total market value of $25,000.

Gifts which are held to be "in contemplation of death" are added back to the taxable estate of a decedent. There is a presumption that gifts made within three years of death were made in contemplation of death, although this presumption may be rebutted. However, gifts may be advantageous from a tax viewpoint even if they *are* held to be in contemplation of death, since the estate at least saves the estate taxes on the gift taxes paid or due, in accordance with advantage No. 3 above.

The disadvantages of lifetime gifts may be summarized as:

1. Loss of control of the property. The donor can't get it back if he needs it for financial or other reasons.

2. Possible bad results to donees, in the form of removing incentives to work, encouraging them to dissipate funds, etc.

3. About the only possible financial disadvantage is that you pay the gift taxes now, and therefore lose the use of the money, while you might not pay the greater estate taxes for many years. Obviously your life expectancy is important here.

Assuming some lifetime gifts seems desirable, what kind of property should you give? First of all, it is generally desirable to give something with market value about equal to your cost. If you give property which has appreciated substantially in value, you lose the opportunity to have your heirs get a new stepped-up tax basis, equal to fair market value, on your death without paying any income tax for this basis. Then, if you give property which has depreciated in value from your cost, you are losing the tax value of the loss inherent in the property.

Another thing to consider is whether you should or should not give income-producing property. Is it desirable from an income tax viewpoint to shift the taxation of the income? And, from a financial viewpoint, can the donor afford to part with the income, and is it desirable for the donee to have it? One very good kind of property to consider giving is life insurance policies. These are not income-producing, and ordinarily not property you expect to dispose of during your lifetime anyway. A consideration is how the premiums will be paid in the future.

Joe Lund, our Chapter 3 profile, is an excellent possibility for lifetime gifts. The top part of his estate will be in about the 34% bracket for death taxes, so about one-third of any gifts will be saved to the family. Joe and Peggy can give each of their three children up to $6,000 a year without even filing gift tax returns. In addition, they have a lifetime exemption of $60,000 to use up if they go over their $6,000 per child per year. So they could give their children up to $78,000 in any year without paying Federal gift taxes. State gift taxes, if any, would be modest.

One thing Joe and Peggy have to consider is whether they can afford to part with the assets given away. This may be particularly a problem if Joe dies and his $24,000 pension disappears with him, leaving Peggy with probably about $18,000 a year income. This may be inadequate, con-

sidering their life style. If this is their big worry, gifts of non-income producing property, such as the special situation securities and unimproved
real estate, would make sense.

Getting these assets out of the Lund's estates would reduce the cash
needs at death by about one-third of the value, giving the survivor that
much more to invest. On the other hand, there will be no income tax savings, as there would be from the gift of liquid securities discussed in
Chapter 14. So as usual in these situations, Joe and Peggy will have to
decide what is most important to them.

Business Interests

Interests in closely-held businesses, whether they be proprietorships, partnerships, or small corporations, present some of the most difficult situations
in estate planning. First, if you have such an interest, sit down and make
some individual decisions, such as:

1. Do you want to pass on your business interest after your death,
as opposed to having it sold? Do you want the business liquidated, etc.?

2. If you do want to pass it on, to whom?

3. What benefits do you want your heirs to receive from this business
interest?

In both 2 and 3, you must distinguish between active heirs and inactive
heirs. You must make clear decisions in this area. If your son is going
to run the business, he has to be able to run it—like the captain of a
ship. He should not be like the son trying to run his late father's contracting business, who had to give up when his younger brother, who
owned a substantial percentage of the stock, refused to sign a bond that
was essential to future contracts.

4. Do you want to give away any of your business interests during
your lifetime?

If you decide you do not want to pass on your business interests, you
certainly should consider a buy-sell agreement to be effective on your death.
The value of a sole proprietorship may disappear within days after your
death, if you have made no plans for preservation. This is important for an
interest in a partnership, which legally will end on the death of a partner.
It may also be very significant for stock of a small corporation. If you
die, your salary is going to cease. Your heirs may want dividends to get
some return on your investment and be unable to get them, as it is not in
the interests of the other stockholders to pay out dividends. The great ad-

vantage of buy-sell agreements is certainty, and the fact that your heirs are able to plan their affairs knowing what they will have. Life insurance is an important tool in funding these agreements because it makes money available on the death of a business interest owner to pay for his interest. The life insurance should be owned by the prospective purchaser of your business interest. This may be a key employee, your partner, the partnership, or the corporation in which you own stock.

In the case of a professional person who is not a part of a sizable organization, a buy-sell agreement may not be very reasonable. His professional practice may not transfer very well to anyone else. While he is alive, his most valuable asset is the earning power of his professional skill and knowledge. This is his working capital, his best earning asset, and his security for the future. If·all of this is going to disappear on his death, it certainly points out a situation where life insurance may be badly needed.

One of the best methods of selling a business interest is to have stock in a corporation redeemed by the corporation on the death of the shareholder. Any time you take money out of a corporation, you have a tax worry that it is going to be taxed as a dividend. There is a statutory method of avoiding this worry in the case of stock redemptions if the estate qualifies. For this it must have more than 35 percent of its value in the stock of one corporation. This may be a very useful way of providing funds to the estate in the event of the death of a stockholder, and of course the agreement for redemption of a stock may be funded by the corporation owning an insurance policy on the life of a shareholder.

If you control a corporation, it may be very desirable to recapitalize it in order to do a better job for your family. For example, preferred stock can be used to "freeze" the value of your estate by giving you a more or less fixed value asset, while the common stock may go to your relatives, employees, etc. As a result, any future increases in value of the corporation will go to other individuals. Preferred stock can also be used to give some income to members of the family in lower tax brackets, and after your death it may be desirable to have preferred stock in the hands of your inactive heirs, and common stock in the hands of your active heirs. Such a recapitalization could have prevented the problem of the brother refusing to sign the bond, mentioned earlier.

If an interest in a business is a substantial part of your estate (the same 35 percent test as referred to above under stock redemptions), you can arrange to pay the estate tax on this business interest over a period of 10 years.

State Death Taxes

These may be estate taxes which, like the Federal estate tax, are a tax on the privilege of transferring property. In the majority of states, death taxes may be an inheritance tax which is levied on a person who receives an inheritance. In the case of inheritance taxes, the relationship of the heir to the decedent is very significant. In one state, for example, an inheritance of a certain amount is subjected to 4 percent tax if the heir is a spouse or a child. On the other hand, it is subjected to a 25 percent tax if the heir is an unrelated individual. This has even given rise to adoptions of individuals 55 years old by wealthy persons wishing to leave them property and wanting to reduce the state inheritance tax.

Many state estate tax or inheritance tax laws provide limited exemptions for proceeds of life insurance, so this may be a favored type of asset.

After-death Planning

Estate planning for an individual does not end when the individual dies. There are important decisions to be made during the period of administering the estate, which may have an important impact on the net amount finally going to the heirs. Some examples are:

1. Valuation of assets in the estate. Since the new income tax basis for the asset is the amount at which it is valued for Federal estate tax purposes, it is well to consider where one wants to value an asset, when there is some possible range of values. An election is available to value the assets of the estate at either date of death or six months after death. The lowest valuation for estate tax purposes may not always be the best answer. The income tax savings from a higher value may be much greater than the additional estate tax that results.

2. Deduction of administration expenses. Most of these may be deducted either on the Federal estate tax return or on the income tax return of the estate, which it files during its period of administration. The only way to decide this is to project the expected top estate and income tax rates to see which will result in a greater saving.

3. What fiscal year should the estate adopt for Federal income tax purposes? An estate is a new taxpayer and, as such, can file an income tax return for any year it wishes. The calendar year ending December 31 is often adopted, but it is probably not the right answer in more than one-twelfth of the cases. Some projections of expected income during

the period of administration, and the effect on the heirs, should be considered before setting the end of the year.

4. If trusts are provided for in the will, it may be desirable to set them up and distribute some of the income to these trusts so it will be taxable to the trusts rather than the estate. Remember we said under tax planning that one of the basic methods of saving taxes is to divide up total income among as many entities as possible.

You should think about these types of problems in deciding whom you wish to name as your executor and any advisors you may select to help your family.

INVESTMENT INFORMATION AND ADVICE

One of the messages hopefully conveyed throughout this book is that the best investment decisions are made after enough information has been obtained to ask critical questions and to critically evaluate the advice of others. This book has attempted to discuss most investment opportunities and areas of financial planning in sufficient detail to give you some basic knowledge. However, you may desire to investigate more extensively certain areas.

The following chapter has been included to assist you in obtaining additional material. The chapter corresponds with the chapter headings in Sections II, III, and IV. Many of the references we have included can be found in large metropolitan public libraries.

In Chapter 17, we discuss investment advisors—types, services, fees, selection criteria, effective use. In Chapter 18, we return to the profiles introduced in Chapter 3 and discuss specific recommendations for each of them.

Chapter 16

IF IT'S INFORMATION YOU WANT

If anything we all suffer from information overload or data poisoning in the area of finance. Thousands of books have been written on the stock market, investment management, real estate, and so forth. Daily newspapers, weekly financial newsletters, monthly magazines, and annual reports and services spew out digested and sometimes undigested, if not undigestable, statistical data and opinions.

The purpose of this chapter is to identify selected, useful information sources on the topics covered in this book.

General Financial Information

There are several daily and weekly sources of general financial information and analyses of specific interest. Some of the better periodicals include:

The Financial Times
Bracken House, Cannon St.
London EC4P, 4BY

(Good for daily coverage of gold mining stocks, in addition to international financial information from a British viewpoint.)

The Wall Street Journal
30 Broad St.
New York, N.Y. 10004

Barron's (weekly)
30 Broad St.
New York, N.Y. 10004

Business Week (weekly)
McGraw-Hill Inc.
New York, N.Y. 10020

(Has a "personal business" column, in addition to articles covering many economic areas.)

Changing Times (monthly)
The Kiplinger Washington Editors Inc.
Editors Park, Maryland

(Articles of consumer interest.)

Fortune (14 times a year)
541 N. Fairbanks Ct.
Chicago, Ill. 60611

(Has a "personal investing" column, in addition to comprehensive and broad business articles.)

Medical Economics (26 times a year)
Oradell, N.J. 07649

(Although oriented toward physicians, this publication contains many articles on tax planning, estate planning, and investment opportunities relevant to other affluent professional people.)

Money (monthly)
Time, Inc.
541 North Fairbanks Ct.
Chicago, Ill. 60611

(Includes articles on many personal financial matters with a how-to-do it approach; includes a regular article on "one family's finances" which discuss specific financial recommendations.)

The Morgan Guaranty Survey (monthly *and* free)
Morgan Guaranty Trust Company
23 Wall St.
New York, N.Y. 10004

Business in Brief (bi-monthly *and* free)
The Chase Manhattan Bank, N.A.
1 Chase Manhattan Plaza
New York, N.Y. 10015

In addition to the above periodicals, there are several basic books and booklets on economics and personal finance that are useful:

The American Institute for Economic Research, Great Barrington, Mass. 01230. This organization has many *low cost* publications that are extremely valuable to those who wish to gain first-hand knowledge about economics and money matters. A partial list of their more general economic publications follow:

> *How to Avoid Financial Tangles, Section A: Elementary Property Problems and Important Financial Relationships,* by Kenneth C. Masteller

> *How to Invest Wisely,* by C. Russell Doane

> *Economic Tides and Trends, Their Effects on Your Lifetime Plans,* by Editorial Staff

> *Useful Economics,* by E.C. Harwood

> *Research Reports,* presenting weekly analyses of economic developments, emphasizing their probable effects on future conditions.

Flation, Not Inflation of Jobs, by Abba P. Lerner.
Paperback, Penguin Books Inc.
7110 Embassador Rd.
Baltimore, Md. 21207.

Money (second and expanded edition), by Lawrence Ritter and William Silber.

(A book on economics for people who can't stand economics. It exposes the effect of monetary policy on the stock market and other key questions.)

The Money Tree, by Catherine C. De Camp.
Paperback, The New American Library Inc.
1501 Ave. of the Americas
New York, N.Y. 10019

(A comprehensive guide to management of every-day personal finance problems; a particularly useful introduction to basic personal financial matters.)

University of Economics: Elements of Inquiry, by Armen A. Alchian and William R. Allen
Wadsworth Publishing Co. Inc.
Belmont, Calif. 94002

(A very readable college economics textbook.)

Money Book, by Sylvia Porter
Doubleday & Co.
245 Park Avenue
New York, N.Y. 10019

(The most comprehensive basic book on personal and family finance. Covers everyday matters as well as consumer rights.)

Life Insurance

Best's Insurance Reports—Life/Health, published annually by A.M. Best Company.

(A hefty volume that contains a report on each life insurance company in the United States as well as many in Canada; provides detailed financial information and includes Best's own interpretation of various aspects of the life insurance companies evaluated.)

Life and Health Insurance Handbook, 3rd edition, edited by Davis W. Gregg and Vane B. Lucas; Richard D. Irwin, Homewood Ill. 60430.

(More of a volume for professionals in insurance and estate planning; comprehensive reference source on all major phases of life and health insurance.)

Life Insurance from the Buyer's Point of View, American Institute for Economic Research.

(Covers types of life insurance policies, life insurance settlement options, how to choose the best companies, and many suggestions for the insurance buyer, including how to determine the net cost of insurance policies and how to deal with the insurance agent.)

Social Security Information. Your local social security administration has many pamphlets regarding social security benefits, which you may wish to obtain in order to find out first-hand what your benefits are.

Investment Management

How to Invest Wisely, by C. Russell Doane; American Institute for Economic Research.

(Short, concise publication of the AIER discusses principal types of investments, how to develop an individual program, and some of the characteristics to look for in making investments in each of the phases of one's life.)

Investment Management, 4th edition, by Harry Sauvain; Prentice-Hall Inc., Englewood Cliffs, N.J.

(Deals primarily with questions of investment policy as opposed to the more technical subject of security analysis; excellent chapters on the analysis of investment requirements.)

The Intelligent Investor, by Benjamin Graham, published by Harper & Row.

(One of the classics; a very readable book; excellent on review of portfolio planning.)

The Money Game, by Adam Smith, paperback, published by Random House, 201 East 50th St., New York, N.Y. 10022.

(One of the delightful books to read about the stock market; reads like a novel and provides great insight into why so many things go wrong in the stock market.)

Supermoney, by Adam Smith, paperback, published by Random House, 201 East 50th St., New York, N.Y. 10022.

(Especially valuable for its evaluation and explanation of the stock market and banking crisis of 1971.)

Best Books on the Stock Market, by Sheldon Zerden, published by R. R. Bowker Company (1972).

(An analytical bibliography; the only such guide to investment literature; covers books on investment methods, the history of the markets, the psychology of investment, mutual funds, and several other fields.)

Investment Companies

Investment Companies; Mutual Funds and Other Types, by Arthur Wiesenberger; published annually by Wiesenberger Financial Services Inc., 1 New York Plaza, New York, N.Y. 10004.

(The "Bible" in the industry; contains detailed information about most closed-end and open-end companies, together with much useful information about the general subject of investment companies; kept up-to-date by monthly and quarterly supplements; authoritative and very objective.)

Investment Trusts and Funds From the Investor's Point of View, C. Russell Doane and Charles W. Hurll, Jr.; American Institute for Economic Research.

(A very concise and objective publication which discusses types of investment companies and the performance results of a representative number of closed-end and open-end investment trusts.)

Forbes Magazine publishes an annual mutual fund survey in its August 15 issue.

(Includes all publicly distributed funds with total assets of $2 million or more; includes easy-to-grasp performance comparisons for specific periods of time and for up and down markets.)

Fund Scope is perhaps the most complete publication available to individual investors.

(Provides continually updated figures on fund performances, and it issues an annual guide containing the record of each major fund over the past 10 years.)

Real Estate

Real Estate Investment Strategy, by Maury Seldin and Richard Sevesnik; published by Wiley-Interscience.

(A very comprehensive book covering the major aspects involved in developing a real estate investment strategy—selecting the type of real estate, financing the real estate investment, and selecting the form of investment group; contains a very extensive bibliography covering investment analysis and taxation, real estate finance, real estate appraisal, housing market analysis, non-residential markets, patterns of urban development, real estate law, and land-use control.)

Real Estate Investment Analysis, by James R. Cooper, published by D.C. Heath, Lexington, Mass. (1974).

(Detailed analyses of various types of real estate investments, with desired ratios of income, expense, cash flow, etc.)

Questions About Condominiums, published by the Department of Housing and Urban Development (HUD); write Publications Division, HUD, Washington, D.C. 20410.

(A free booklet containing detailed and honest advice for the condominium buyer.)

Condominiums and Cooperatives, by David Clurman, an assistant New York attorney general who keeps a stern eye on condominiums, published by Wiley-Interscience, New York, $15.95.

(A meaty volume, published in 1970 but still valid.)

What You Should Know About Condominiums, by Henry H. Rothenberg, published by Chilton Book Co., paperback, $2.95.

(A straightforward, chatty book full of specific advice.)

Your Own Business

Up Your Own Organization!, by Donald M. Dible; published by the Entrepreneur Press, Mission Station, 2759 Quay, Santa Clara, Calif. 95051.

(The most complete how-to-do it book for the employed, the unemployed, and the self-employed on how to start and finance a new business; contains a wealth of information including a personal resources checklist, and the sources of information available to the small businessman on how to develop a business plan, money sources and business start-up checklists; also provides a very extensive bibliography of business and financial periodicals available to the small businessman and the information available from the Small Business Administration.)

Tax Guide for Buying and Selling a Business, by Stanley Hagendorf, published by Prentice Hall, Inc., Englewood Cliffs, New Jersey.

(The purchase or sale of a business falls into certain fixed tax patterns which are explained in detail. If these patterns are understood, the purchaser or seller can plan the transaction to obtain the most favorable tax consequences, and not fall into unexpected tax problems or hidden tax traps.)

Gold and Gold Related Investments

How to Invest in Gold Stocks and Avoid the Pitfalls, by Donald Hoppe, published by Arlington House, New Rochelle, N.Y.

(Very helpful if you wish to select your own gold stocks; contains detailed background information on the gold stocks of North America and South Africa; contains section on portfolio selection and management.)

Why Gold, by The American Institute for Economic Research.

(Covers the role of gold in the evolution of commercial banking, the benefits of the gold standard, the origin of the present inflationary situation, and the relationships between inflating prices, devaluation, and gold production.)

You Can Profit From a Monetary Crisis, by Harry Browne, Macmillan Publishing Co., 866 Third Ave., New York, N.Y. 10022.

(An excellent book on why gold and gold-related investments make sense and how to set up a recommended investment program; contains good bibliography and information sources on Swiss banks, silver and gold coins, silver bullion, gold stocks, and retreats.)

Kaffir Chart Service, published by Indicator Chart Services, Palisades Park, N.J. 07650.

(A weekly service which lists the daily prices of all important South African gold stocks along with information on prices for the last six months, recent years' highs and lows, and earnings and dividend information.)

Currencies

Pick's Currency Yearbook, by Franz Pick, Pick Publishing Corp., 21 West St., New York, N.Y. 10006.

(Lists information for each currency in the world; published annually.)

International Currency Review, 11 Regency Place, London SP1P, 2EA.

(A bi-monthly journal which includes a currency review of all major currencies in the world in addition to articles on economic, monetary, and currency affairs.)

Tax and Estate Planning

A Complete Estate Planning Guide, Robert Brosterman, The Mentor Executive Library, 1301 Ave. of the Americas, New York, N.Y. 10019.

(An excellent book for the general reader that explains the main aspects of estate planning, including tax saving opportunities, fringe benefits, the pros and cons of avoiding probate; also includes an estate planning checklist.)

Estate Planning For Wives—A Family's Financial Guide, by Merle E. Dowd, published by Henry Regnery Company, 114 West Illinois St., Chicago, Ill. 60610.

(Provides an easy to read straightforward discussion of handling wills, property ownership, inheritance taxes, trusts, etc.; also deals with the need to educate the wife in financial matters.)

Prentice-Hall Federal Tax Course, published by Prentice- Hall, Inc., Englewood cliffs, N.J. 07632.

(An annual publication which provides up-to-date information for filing your annual tax returns, and a comprehensive tax return checklist; includes easy-to-read sections on all the important tax regulations.)

The April Game, by Diogenes; paperback published by Playboy Press, 747 Third Ave., New York, N.Y. 10017.

(Written in sprightly style, this book deals with the administration of the income tax regulations; author, who hides his identity with a pseudonym, is alleged to be a revenue agent of the IRS; contains some solid down-to-earth advice on being inventive in the preparation of tax returns and how to behave during an IRS audit.)

Dow Jones-Irwin Guide to Tax Planning, by Ray Sommerfeld, published by Dow Jones-Irwin, Homewood, Ill. (1974).

(Explains the general ways in which major tax savings are achieved so the reader can first, review his own situation and discover what might be done to realize greater tax savings in the future; second, assess the quality of the tax advice he has been receiving, and third, alert him to the tax traps into which the uninformed and overeager may fall.)

Widow, by Lynn Caine, published by William Morrow & Co., Inc. (1974)

(Recommends each husband and wife having each year a Contingency Day, an annual review of the financial state of the family, at which they could discuss steps to be taken if either should die in the next twelve months.)

U.S. Master Tax Guide, Commerce Clearing House, Inc., 420 Lexington Ave., New York, N.Y. 10017.

(Published annually, this contains a number of useful checklists, and an explanation of most provisions of the Internal Revenue Code. It is well-indexed and a good starting point for tax information.)

Investment Newsletters

There are many investment newsletters available. Many brokerage houses provide letters to their clients, as do investment counseling firms. Some specialize in certain kinds of investments. Many of these newsletters are advertised in general financial media such as the *Wall Street Journal* and *Barron's.* If you are interested in one that seems to fit your investment objectives, we suggest you write and ask for a sample copy. One of the best newsletters providing a continuing presentation and explanation of economic issues and information is:

Investment Bulletin
American Institute Counselors
Great Barrington, Mass. 01230

Chapter 17

INVESTMENT ADVICE AND
INVESTMENT *ADVICE*

A primary objective in writing this book has been to equip you with knowledge of how to develop your own personal financial plan and to analyze the various investment opportunities available in obtaining your financial plan. Our stress has been more on a how-to-do-it kind of involvement on your part—how to pursue each investment alternative in such a way that you become knowledgeable about the opportunities and pitfalls involved.

Most of us, however, no matter how much knowledge we have about financial opportunities, seek additional knowledge from time to time from various professionals operating in the investment advisory field. This chapter examines the services offered by various investment advisors and the role advisors play in personal financial planning. Professionals who have some role in the personal financial planning process are discussed, including the life insurance agent, the security broker, the CPA, the attorney, the bank trust department, and the independent investment counselor.

The Life Insurance Agent

The primary tool used by a life insurance agent in financial planning is a capital needs analysis as discussed in Chapter 4. The primary objective of this analysis is to insure that after the insured dies and the expenses of selling the estate are paid, the remaining estate assets will be sufficient to allow the family to maintain the.present or desired standard of living.

Often, the insurance advisor regards himself as a catalyst in the financial planning process. He is in a position to contact clients, observe problem areas, offer suggestions, and initiate appropriate action in the financial planning field. Attorneys and CPAs operate under a code of ethics that prohibits their soliciting business, and therefore they are not in an aggressive position to contact clients (or are unwilling to do so). Most people (except you, of course) will not do any serious estate planning until someone can make an appointment with them and impress upon the individual the importance of such planning. The insurance agent is one of the professional advisors who can ethically take such action.

Hopefully, a good insurance advisor will review the client's financial affairs and will call in other financial advisors when appropriate. If the client's business transactions are beyond the complexity that the insurance agent feels comfortable dealing with, he hopefully will consult with CPAs regarding possible tax advantages, with a trust department or an attorney when a client's will has to be changed or when a trust has to be set up.

The role of the life insurance agent as a financial advisor is a difficult one because of an obvious conflict of interest. The insurance agent is expected to make an objective analysis of the client's need and to recommend the appropriate insurance coverage. However, the agent is compensated strictly on a commission basis; the more insurance he sells, the greater his income. In our opinion, it would be the exceptional insurance agent who is able to give truly objective advice to an individual client.

Many insurance agents would counter this view with the idea that regardless of the pressure to sell insurance for the premium commission, the agent will not do so because it is not in his enlightened long-run self interest. In other words, the agent will only recommend insurance based upon the client's actual need. Any other approach, the insurance agent will argue, will create a dissatisfied client, a poor reputation, and a loss of business in the long run. However, how does the average individual, ignorant of the intricacies of life insurance, ever realize he has too much insurance, and thus become dissatisfied. He may be forced to rely on the good judgment and advice of the life insurance agent, unless he does his own independent analysis, as we suggested in Chapter 4.

The insurance agent may be motivated not only to recommend insurance where the need does not exist, but may be motivated to recommend the wrong type of life insurance. In Chapter 4 it was mentioned that the most popular type of insurance was straight life insurance, because it supposedly provided both protection and a savings feature. We suggested, however, that the benefits from such a policy may be more illusory than real, and that term insurance provides not only the lowest cost insurance, but the most flexibility to the insured.

In light of such arguments against holding a straight life insurance and in favor of term plus a savings account and other investments, why is whole life the most common type of life insurance? One factor is undoubtedly the relative commission the insurance agent receives. The agent will earn approximately three to five times more commission by selling whole life than by recommending term insurance. The effect of such motivation obviously makes it difficult for the insurance agent to make an objective analysis of an individual's insurance need.

The Stockbroker

The stockbroker appears to be another individual to whom many turn for investment advice. In recent years, however, there have been fewer stockbrokers around. A good stockbroker should first perform an analysis of your investment needs, starting with your present assets and then becoming familiar with your investment objectives. The stockbroker should know whether you wish to emphasize capital gains or income, short-term or long-term investments, safety or speculation, etc. Such objectives are usually very subjective and not easily qualified. They often depend not only on your financial situation but also on your personality and investment philosophy. In essence, the broker attempts to find out what types of investments you would feel comfortable with. After reviewing your personal data, present financial situation, and investment objectives, the stockbroker should develop an appropriate investment plan based on your thoughts on a desirable and acceptable rate of return and risk.

The broker is prepared to offer a variety of investments, including stocks, corporate or tax-free government bonds, puts and calls, commodities, and tax shelters. The broker is also prepared to offer basic tax advice; however, if the situation is sufficiently complex, he should suggest that you consult a competent tax advisor.

The primary difficulty with relying on the stockbroker as an investment advisor is that he, like the insurance agent, has a definite conflict of interest. He is paid on a commission basis that has led, in some cases, to the practice of "churning" the accounts of customers where the broker has discretionary power to buy and sell securities.

The security salesman, even if he can overcome this inherent motivation to create unnecessary trading, must rely on his firm's research analysts for advice. The quality of research and advice provided by security analysts at brokerage firms is, however, questionable. One observer indicates that "In 1963, after studying the practice of Wall Street's security analysts, the SEC concluded that Wall Street research, far from being a guide to investing, was merely a selling tool." [1]

Even if the research analyst was competent and wanted to do a proper job, he also faces a conflict of interest. Many brokerage houses have a direct financial interest in the performance of certain securities and thus are concerned with an analyst's recommendations regarding these securities. An individual, dependent on his stockbroker for advice, who is in turn dependent on his firm's research analyst for recommendations, may very well fail to receive competent, impartial investment advice.

The CPA

The CPA usually becomes involved in personal financial planning because of his knowledge of taxes. Almost any financial decision an individual makes has tax consequences. Thus, tax planning must be an integral part of all financial planning. Much of the advice the CPA gives is in the form of analyzing the tax effects of various alternatives. However, the CPA should attempt to get the client to take a long-run view and make tax and financial planning a continuous activity. Thus, the CPA is in an advantageous position to initiate comprehensive financial planning for the person. Also in connection with assisting the client in the preparation of his or her tax return, the CPA is able to keep informed of the person's changing financial needs. The CPA is thus in a position to not only initiate financial planning but also to play a lead role in helping an individual with financial planning.

However, the CPA also has certain limitations as a personal financial advisor. First of all, he must operate under the constraints imposed by a code of ethics. He is prohibited from obtaining clients through solicitation or advertising. Also a CPA is not permitted to operate in a manner that indicates specialization. Thus, even if the individual recognizes the need for professional advice, he faces the uncertainty of choosing a CPA with expertise in his or her area of concern. The CPA must also refrain from any activity that might impair his independence and objectivity in rendering professional services.

Although such constraints may limit the scope of the CPA's role, these constraints do not have to restrict the CPA from taking the initiative in

---

[1] Christopher Elias, *Fleecing the Lambs* (New York: Fawcett World).

recommending financial planning for existing clients. The CPA's independence, objectivity, and knowledge about financial and tax matters put him or her in a position to provide advice on the tax consequences and economic substance of proposed investments, in addition to advice on income and estate tax matters.

The Attorney

Many individuals first become acquainted with a lawyer not to ask his advice on financial planning but to obtain assistance on a legal problem. For instance, an individual may be filing for divorce, have had an auto accident and be filing a claim, or may be a defendant in a liability suit. It is in connection with solving these other problems that the lawyer may become acquainted with an individual's overall financial situation, recognize areas where problems exist, and suggest appropriate action. Of course, some individuals' first contact with the attorney may be in connection with their personal financial planning; often, they want to prepare a will and need legal assistance to do so.

The attorney's approach in financial planning should be first to determine the individual's objectives. The lawyer must know what property is to go to which beneficiary, if the individual wants professional management of his estate after death, and what guidelines the person has for the disposition of the estate assets. Of course, the attorney will offer advice and counsel to the individual in attempting to determine what action will be in the client's best interest.

The lawyer will usually ask for a complete listing of the client's assets and liabilities. He will review the person's insurance holdings in view of the liquidity needs of the estate at death. Also, possibilities for minimizing estate taxes will be discussed with the client. The attorney at this point may call in a CPA who is more familiar with the details of tax matters. If necessary, other advisors will be consulted. Finally, the attorney will draft the necessary legal documents to achieve the client's objectives.

The lawyer is able to act as a "catalyst" in the financial planning process. His knowledge of the client's affairs, combined with his legal training and experience, make him uniquely qualified to recognize problem areas. He can then discuss these areas with the client, offer suggested solutions, and guide the client to other professional advisors as necessary.

The attorney must also operate under the constraints imposed by a code of ethics. He is prohibited from soliciting business and thus is not able to take the initiative that is often necessary to get an individual to do any financial planning. He is also prohibited from "holding himself out" as a specialist. It is thus difficult for an individual to choose an attorney who is competent in estate planning or in the area of concern to the individual. Of course, most attorneys are able to prepare the legal documents such as a will or trust that the individual may require. However, in our opinion, very few lawyers are really qualified to perform creative, comprehensive estate and personal financial planning. Indeed the education and orientation of many lawyers seems to result in a desire to only "practice law" and thus play a passive role in personal financial planning.

The Bank Trust Department

A bank trust department is able to perform several fiduciary duties; it can act as executor, guardian, or trustee for an estate. Everyone with a will must name an executor whose duty it is to marshall the assets of the estate, pay any debts and estate administration expenses, and make the appropriate distribution of the assets. The bank trust department can perform this service. If a court is controlling the distribution of the estate, the bank may be named by court order as guardian and perform the above duties.

The area in which the bank performs most of its services is trusteeship. When the bank is named as a trustee, it manages the property placed in trust and makes distribution of property and any investment income from the property in accordance with the specific written instructions contained in the trust. The bank trust department has specialists in real estate, investments, and taxation to assist the trust administrator in best managing and investing the property placed in trust. The bank also has attorneys available to assist the client's counsel in drawing up the legal documents.

The bank is always on the alert for customers who might be able to use the services of the trust department. The bank will then contact these people either personally or through brochures to explain the trust services they are equipped to perform and the potential benefits to the person. The bank has no legal or ethical restriction on soliciting business to act as a trustee.

Investment Counselors

By now you are probably saying "OK, OK—the insurance agent and the stock broker may not be exactly objective in their advice; the CPA and attorney may be somewhat specialized in their approach to my financial planning needs; so who the hell do I turn to?"

Unfortunately it is difficult to find someone who can provide comprehensive financial planning in an independent, objective fashion. More often than not, it is a combination of several professionals, working in an independent but coordinated manner to provide the kind of assistance you need. One type of firm that may provide a good part of what you may be looking for is the investment counseling firm.

Investment counseling firms provide a range of services. Many provide only investment management of a portfolio of securities. Others provide much more comprehensive financial planning, covering net worth planning, insurance analysis, investment management, and tax-sheltered investment advice. Many investment counseling firms also have a minimum size portfolio. As a rule it is not economical to pay a fee for investment counseling if the total value of the assets to be managed is under $50,000. Some firms will not accept a portfolio less than $100,000. Some have a $250,000 or higher minimum. However, there are some investment advisory services for portfolios as low as $10,000; these are usually provided by investment management departments of large banks.

Good financial advice does not come cheap. If an investment counseling firm is handling just security portfolio management, they will charge some percentage of the value of the portfolios. This percentage may run from a minimum of 1–2 percent of the minimum amount retained, $50,000 for example to ½ percent for larger portfolios. Investment counseling firms that provide more comprehensive investment counseling may charge an initial fee for an analysis of your situation, a fee which may run between $3,000–5,000, with a minimum fee each year for continuing supervision. Many investment counseling firms are not interested in a one-shot analysis, but wish to have a continuing, long-term relationship with their clients. For such a fee remember, however, that you should be getting plenty of attention. The firm should offer a full spectrum of financial services, including analyzing all your current assets, as well as tax and estate planning. All this takes several specialists, not just one man, and therefore substantial fees are justified.

Normally, in using an investment counseling firm, it makes sense to give the professional manager the power to buy and sell investments without your consent. Remember the professional counseling firm is being paid for its judgment. If you do not want the firm to exercise its judgment, you should probably not pay for investment management. However, you certainly should review the performance of the investment counseling firm periodically and either retain or dismiss the firm based on its *performance*.

Since there are so many investment counseling firms available, one of the biggest problems is the selection of a firm that makes sense for you. One approach is to check the banks in your area to see if they provide an investment counseling service. Often they do. If they don't, they might be able to give you a list of investment advisors who may help you. In addition, your CPA and attorney should have knowledge of investment counseling firms, which they can recommend to you. Sometimes stock brokerage firms have knowledge of investment firms, since investment counseling firms have to work through a stock broker in order to buy and sell securities for the client. In fact, some brokerage houses have done analyses of many investment counseling firms and may be able to provide you some information about the performance of investment counseling firms in your area.

No matter what your source of information and no matter how many names of firms you obtain, go about the selection of an investment counseling firm the same way you would with any trusted personal advisor. Here are some questions you should raise in discussing an advisory relationship with any individual or firm:

1. How does the firm determine a plan to meet your own particular needs? A firm should be willing to analyze all your current assets, stocks, bonds, real estate, insurance, etc., and find out what your personal goals and objectives are. It should insist on seeing all your documents, including your income tax returns and your will.

2. Is the firm totally objective? As we suggested before, be aware that its income depends partly on selling you something—sometimes a pretty difficult thing to find out. Many counselors are asset sales organizations pretending to be financial planners to increase their sales. Their financial counseling plans are but a ruse to sell life insurance, cattle feeding programs, and land schemes. Have them give you an organization chart or better still an annual report, to see how objective they really are.

3. Will the investment counseling firm refer you to other clients? Make sure you get a list that includes independent references—CPAs, lawyers, banks—and not just hand-picked happy customers—with whom you can go and discuss the investment counseling firm to find out something about their past performance.

4. How will the counselor measure the performance of the management of your investments? Measuring the performance of the management of your account is a matter that should be carefully explored with your investment counselor before you give him the right to assume responsibility for your account. Find out the exact formula he will use in performance measurement, and whether it will properly relate the portfolio structure to your investment objectives. For instance, if you want a portfolio of long-term growth stocks, the investment advisor should be evaluated upon his ability to meet that objective, and to build your portfolio out of such long-term growth stocks. The short-term market fluctuations will not be an appropriate criteria. Ascertain that the same performance measurement formula will be consistently applied in all the reports to you.

5. How frequently and in what form will the reporting of the per-

formance of your portfolio be given? Investment advisors should keep you informed of activities in your account. A schedule of regular meetings should be established and should be supplemented by informal contacts with you as required. The advisor should also be accessible to you so that your questions can be answered as they arise.

You should also know what written reports and accountings you will receive periodically. You should certainly receive, each quarter, a list of currently held assets, showing the original cost of each holding, the income from dividends and interest, and the current market value. The report should also show the performance measurement formula that was discussed with you at the time your account was opened.

6. What research capability does the investment counseling firm have, or have access to? Generally, you can expect an investment advisor's decisions to be no better than his or her research. Feel free, therefore, to ask about research capabilities. What sources of information does he use, such as direct company contact, industry analyses, investment banking firms, brokerage houses, or whatever? You should be interested in knowing how much original research the advisor's staff conducts. What direct contact do they make with decision makers in the companies they are studying, to evaluate the companies' management? What experience does the analyst or the counselor have in the industry in which he or she specializes?

Obviously, the alternative to original research is second-hand research, in which reports and evaluations made by others are collected and digested by the counselor. If second-hand research is used, find out what are the primary sources of the research. Check out these sources with people who should know something about investment research, such as banks, CPAs, attorneys, brokerage houses, etc.

7. How much competence does the investment counselor have in making economic forecasts? How much does the counselor use economic forecasts? The use of forecasts to make investment decisions is a very important matter, since specific investment decisions cannot be made without an overview of what the entire economy is expected to do and what various industries are doing. Good investment counselors must be able to anticipate what the stock market will do, rather than just reacting to it. Typically, such anticipation of market moves and changes is done after a sound analysis and forecast of what the economy will do. Economic forecasts also provide a means of comparing different investment opportunities. In some economic conditions, certain kinds of investment, such as securities investments, may not be most favorable; whereas other kinds of investments, such as the bond market or the money markets may provide more favorable investment alternatives. The investment counselor should have information to make an informed choice between competing investment options at various points of the economic cycle.

Chapter 18

RECOMMENDATIONS TO OUR "CLIENTS"

In Chapter 3 we introduced 14 financial profiles of people ranging in age from 25 to 68 and in different occupations and stages of life. In our discussion of specific investment opportunities and tax and estate planning, specific recommendations are discussed for several of the profile situations or "clients." In this chapter, we want to take a more detailed look at each client and present some specific recommendations for each. Hopefully, you can identify with some of our clients and benefit from the recommendations we provide.

For each client we have provided a summary of information presented in Chapter 3. You may wish, however, to reread that part of Chapter 3 related to the client profiles. Note that for each client situation we have followed the basic approach presented in this book:

- Determine present net worth
- Analyze income and expenses and segregate committed expenses from discretionary expenses
- Evaluate the four firsts—annual income potential, housing, savings account or reserve fund, and life insurance
- Evaluate investment and tax planning opportunities in light of individual objectives, needs, and constraints

Linda Hanson, Entrepreneur

As you may recall, 25-year-old Linda Hanson owns and manages a growing fashion-conscious apparel shop for women. Her present net worth includes:

Savings account in a commercial bank	$ 1,500
Marketable securities	$ 1,000
Furnishings in her apartment	$20,000
Equity in her business	$20,000
	$42,500

Her annual income from the shop is $25,000. With prospects of increasing volume, she believes she can increase her income to $35,000, and also the equity in her business. Her committed expenses are running about $23,000.

As to the four firsts, Linda's income potential is good, and she obviously enjoys her livelihood. (If she puts in "90 hour" weeks she better enjoy what she is doing.) As to housing, she might evaluate the possibility of buying a condominium or cooperative apartment for two basic reasons:

1. To build equity in something she is living in.
2. To shelter from taxes some of her expenditures for housing.

She is paying $350 per month for her apartment, or $4,200 a year. Using a capitalization rate of 8, she probably could afford a $30–35,000 condominium. Most of her $350 (now a mortgage payment rather than a rental payment) would be interest in the initial years and would therefore be tax deductible, which is not the case at present. Most, if not all, of her rental payment of $350 is not tax deductible unless she claims and proves that some of her apartment is used for business purposes.

The only obstacle in purchasing a condominium apartment might be the amount of down payment required. At present, she only has $2,500 of liquid assets available, and that amount may not be sufficient to provide the required down payment. If it is not, our recommendation would be to build up her liquid assets to the amount required.

She might think of building up her savings account for emergency purposes to about $5,000 (20 percent of income), but maintaining a substantial portion in a financial institution paying interest rates higher than those paid by a commercial bank. She might also evaluate short-term money market investments, including the cash management funds discussed in Chapter 5.

However, most of these investment media require a minimum of $5,000.

As to insurance, she apparently has no financial responsibility for anyone but herself at present; presumably all she might need insurance for would be death expenses. She has no estate tax requirement since her estate does not come up to the minimum of $60,000. Thus, her insurance requirements are minimal at present.

Linda's situation is one characteristic of many owner-entrepreneurs. All or most all of her resources are and *should be* committed to making her business successful. Her greatest investment opportunity is herself and her shop. Her hard work and skills should pay off through increasing success of the business and increasing equity in her business.

Somewhere along the line, Linda has to think about what she's going to do with her business in order to get her equity out, but at age 25 she has some years to decide. If her business is successful, obviously her income will also continue to increase. In the meantime, she should continue to work hard and enjoy her life.

The Hustling Harts

Bob and Joanna Hart, 26 and 25, are a hard-working, success-seeking, ambitious college-educated couple. Influenced by the zero-population movement, they have agreed to wait to have children for a few years. It is interesting to note the changing values that have occurred in our society over the past few years; for example contrast the Harts' values regarding women working and children to the values of the "fifties" when everybody wanted a split-level home, a ranch wagon, and four tow-heads. A woman's "place" was in the home.

The Harts' net worth is approximately $27,000 and includes:

Savings account in a commercial bank	$1,500
Marketable securities	$5,000
Cash value on Bob Hart's life insurance policy	$ 800
Equity in the house	$8,000
Furnishings for the house	$8,700
Automobiles	$3,000

Their annual combined incomes are $31,500, of which $17,000 is Joanna's earnings as a system-analyst programmer in a computer center in a major metropolitan bank. The Harts' committed expenses are $18,400.

Their insurance program includes a $25,000 whole life policy on Bob Hart; Joanna is covered by a group policy at the bank, and the amount of her coverage equals the amount of her salary. The prospects for increased income for the Harts are good. Both are interested in getting additional education to enhance their careers. They do not plan to have children for another five years and, thus, have the possibility of increasing their net worth.

As to the four "firsts," the changes we recommend would be in their savings account and insurance program. Their $1,500 savings is probably too modest. They might want to increase their savings to approximately $10,000, if not higher, and put most of it into short-term money market investments where the rate of return is much greater than in a commercial bank.

As to insurance, there is no need for further coverage. In fact you might question whether the Harts need what they currently have, primarily because both of them are capable of earning enough to support themselves as individuals. Based on the insurance analysis approach discussed in Chapter 4, it appears that the Harts need only about $22,000 of insurance. Certainly term insurance is a better buy for the Harts than whole life. Considering inflation, many investments probably would be a better inflation hedge than straight life insurance, so the Harts should take the savings from buying term and invest it in more inflation-hedging kinds of investments than straight life insurance.

As to additional investments, we suggest the Harts evaluate investment trusts. A total of $5,000 in marketable securities is not sufficient to have adequate diversification, and even if the Harts have a considerable amount of money to invest beyond the $5,000, the question is whether they really have the time (with both of them working) to properly manage any investment program. At this point the size of their portfolio is not sufficient to have an investment counselor, so investment trusts might be useful for diversification and investment management purposes.

One of the keys to the financial future of Bob and Joanna Hart is the excess of revenue over committed expenses that they currently enjoy. Currently they have some $13,000 of excess that can be used for discretionary purposes. Obviously, some of it is earmarked for education, furnishings, and vacation trips. However, if the Harts can use some of that exceess for investment purposes during the next five years when they are both still working, they could be well on their way to developing a substantial net worth.

One of the important criteria of some investments for the Harts has to be liquidity, given Joanna's interest in obtaining her MBA. She should evaluate the possibilities of obtaining the MBA full-time or part-time. If it is full-time, obviously some savings would have to be used for educational purposes. If she can go to an MBA program part-time, then perhaps the education could be financed out of current income. She should also explore some of the financing arrangements that might be possible from her employer if she wishes to go on a full-time basis. More and more firms now are providing educational leaves of absence from the job and are even interested in arranging financing for people who might have a long-range future with the organization. It appears that Joanna is a very good employee, with skills that are needed by the bank, and it is possible that favorable financing could be arranged with the bank for her education.

The Packing Professor

Ken and Carole Cast have a one and a half year-old-son and a family lifestyle that tends to keep committed expenses fairly low. Ken is an assistant professor in a major business school on the west coast. Ken's income from the university is about $16,000, and in addition, he earns about $10,000 from a variety of consulting assignments and executive development programs.

The Casts' net worth is approximately $47,000, which consists of:

Savings account in a savings and loan association	$10,000
Marketable securities	$10,000
Equity in the house	$ 9,000
Furnishings for the house	$ 7,000
Automobiles	$ 5,000
Death benefits in the university's retirement program	$ 6,000

For the present, the Cast's income prospects are tied somewhat to the university, and the expectations are that any salary increases will be related to cost-of-living adjustments. Ken is currently writing a book with one of his colleagues, and perhaps the book will generate some additional income. Carole is a college graduate and worked previously as a teacher in a nursery school. She hopes, when her children are past the early child-raising years, that she can return to a teaching career.

Because Ken and Carole's lifestyle includes a lot of outdoor activities that do not demand a lot of monetary expenditures, they have been able to keep their committed expenses at about $18,000; thus they have an excess of income over committed expenses of about $8,000.

The Casts' insurance program includes a $10,000 whole life policy on Ken and a $50,000 group term policy available through the university's insurance program.

Our first observation is that the Casts have a pretty good net worth already. We recommend that they do an evaluation of their insurance. It appears as though the insurance coverage might be a little bit low. Our analysis, using the approach discussed in Chapter 4, suggests that the Casts may require about $70,000 of insurance, and their current insurance is $60,000. If they get additional insurance, we suggest that it be term insurance. Perhaps they have the possibility of increasing the term coverage through their group policy at the university. Normally group insurance has a much lower rate than the rate available in an individual program from an insurance company.

If Ken actually publishes the book he is working on and generates some royalties, he might consider setting up a "Keogh" program, which would provide some tax shelter on self-employment income. For example, he is currently generating about $10,000 of self-employment income, and therefore he could contribute $1,500 of that to a "Keogh" program with the $1,500 contribution deductible on his tax return. Another possibility would be to set up a living trust with the trust asset being the royalty contract. The income from the book royalties would be paid to the trust's beneficiary, who would be the Casts' son. The Casts' son might have to pay some taxes on such income, but the tax rate would be much lower than the tax rate on income earned by the Casts.

The Casts have a pretty good investment program started. The $10,000 in the savings and loan association appears to be a reasonable amount, given the Casts' income level. They might look into the possibility of putting that $10,000 into short-term investment opportunities that pay more than the savings and loan association. They also may wish to think in terms of further diversification of their investments, and put additional income into income-producing real estate. They have the potential of using approximately $8,000 of income, in excess of committed expenses, for investment. Real estate would be a pretty good inflation hedge, and as Ken's income—particularly from outside sources—increases, it may make sense to have some tax shelter investment such as real estate. Depending upon Ken's handyman's skills and interest in such activities, the Casts might look at the possibilities of investing in single family dwellings, in an established area of the city in which they live. They would be able to keep their eye on the property and maintain such dwellings rather easily, given the flexibility that Ken has in his university teaching position.

The Young Executive

John Herman is a 32-year-old marketing executive with a freight forwarding company. John's economic undergraduate degree, coupled with an MBA, has enabled him to rise rapidly in his organization. John and Jane Herman have two children—a girl aged 10, and a boy aged 8.

John's current salary is $30,000, and he expects it will increase to $45,000 in current dollars by the time he reaches 45. He also expects annual raises approximately equal to increases in the cost of living. The Hermans' basic committed expenses are about $26,000; in addition, the Hermans regularly take a winter ski vacation costing approximately $2,000, and are purchasing a summer home with monthly payments—including taxes and insurance—of $300 per month, or $3,600 a year. Furnishings for both homes require about $3,000 each per year as well.

The Hermans' net worth is approximately $60,000 as follows:

Savings account in a commercial bank	$ 2,000
Equity in a $60,000 home	$20,000
Equity in a $40,000 beach home	$ 6,000
Furnishings for both homes	$20,000
Company sponsored stock program	$10,500
Cash value in life insurance	$ 1,500

John has a $50,000 whole life insurance policy on his life. The Hermans have thought rather extensively about their goals, which include the following:

- Put both the children through four years of college.

- Retire at age 55 with a desired annual income of $21,000 (in current dollars).

- Sell their personal residence after retirement and move to their beach property.

Our first observation is that the Hermans had done quite well in dealing with the two of the four firsts—annual income potential and housing. But possibly because they have done so "well," they are not really that well off. Their savings program is quite low, given their propensity to consume and payments on the beach property. Our initial recommendation would be to increase their savings to at least $10,000.

Our next recommendation would be to analyze their insurance program.

Using the approach discussed in Chapter 4, we find their current insurance program of $50,000 to be very inadequate. Our analysis suggests insurance coverage of approximately $350,000. Again, we would recommend the purchase of term insurance for whatever additional coverage they decide upon.

Our third recommendation would be to determine if John has any retirement program in his company and, if so, what the benefits would be both upon early retirement and upon retirement at age 65.

Our fourth recommendation would be to analyze their spending patterns, and see if they can hold to their present level of committed expenses and possibly even reduce the amount in order to increase their savings, to increase insurance coverage, and to generate sufficient funds for education of their two children. At present, their spending patterns exceed income by approximately $3,000. Entertainment and a winter ski vacation require about $4,500, and perhaps these two expenditures are candidates for reduction in the near future.

John Herman has indicated a desire to retire at age 55 with an annual income of $21,000. Assuming the company has some retirement program, the Hermans must determine what amount must be accumulated to provide the annual income of $21,000. Let's assume that John's retirement payment at early retirement will be $10,000 a year. At that age, he will not be eligible for social security, and so the additional $11,000 desired will have to come from return on income-producing assets. Let's further assume that he sells the personal residence, which in 23 more years will have increased in value from $60,000 to $119,850 (assuming an increase of 3 percent in real terms rather than inflationary terms). Assuming a return of 5 percent on the proceeds from the then fully-paid house, the Hermans would have an additional $6,000.

The remaining $5,000 of income would require assets of approximately $100,000 earning, a return of 5 percent at the time of John's retirement. (Remember, in this illustration, we have kept all amounts in current dollars.) It would take an investment of approximately $3,000 a year for the next 23 years earning an interest rate of 3 percent to accumulate to $100,000; at 5 percent, approximately $2,400. If the Hermans wait until the youngest child is 22 (14 years from now) before starting to accumulate the retirement fund, they will have to invest approximately $9,800 a year or nine years at 3 percent to accumulate $100,000 by age 55; approximately $9,000 a year at 5 percent interest.

So John Herman's goal of retirement at age 55 with $21,000 appears feasible, if they are able to generate income in excess of committed expense sufficient to accumulate the net worth required at age 55.

The Sailing Surgeon

Bart Boney, orthopedic surgeon, 36, is an avid sailor and skier. His wife, 35, is the mother of four active children—two daughters 10 and 7, and two sons 5 and 1. Dr. Boney is one of four orthopedic surgeons in an incorporated professional practice and currently derives a salary of $40,000 from the practice.

The Boneys' net worth is approximately $57,200. The major asset is a home with a market value of approximately $90,000, of which $26,000 represents the Boney's equity. In addition, they have $12,000 in furnishings and $900 equity in automobiles. The remainder of the net worth is represented by $10,000 in a regular savings account in a commercial bank; $2,300 equity in some raw land which Dr. Boney purchased years ago; $800 cash value of life insurance; and $1,400 in silver coins. Dr. Boney also has a $3,800 interest in the profit-sharing and retirement program of his surgical practice.

Dr. Boney's income prospects are rather good, since orthopedic surgeons are in great demand in his part of the country. The Boneys' basic committed expenses are approximately $29,500. However, when the Boneys purchased their home just recently, they financed the purchase price and the remodeling expenditures with a $40,000 long-term mortgage and a five-year note for $24,000. The annual payment on the note is $5,800.

Dr. Boney has $140,000 of life insurance on his life, of which only $10,000 is whole life.

In discussing financial goals with the Boneys, we were able to determine that they would like to:

- Make additional improvements on their home—landscaping, a new dock, additional furnishings. They estimate such expenditures to require about $10,000 for next three years.
- Provide four years of college education for each of their four children.
- Have $20,000 annual income for Mrs. Boney if Dr. Boney were to die.

Our first recommendation is to construct a yearly cash flow for the next five years to reflect the financial consequences of the Boneys' objectives for home improvements. Exhibit 48 is a cash flow analysis using the income and basic committed expenses. This analysis suggests that the Boneys require $15,600 over the next three years in order to meet committed expenses and to make the desired additional home improvements. Our recommendation would be that the Boneys reduce their planned home improvement expenditures to approximately $5,000 during the next five years until the five year note is completely liquidated.

			Year		
EXHIBIT 48					
	1	*2*	*3*	*4*	*5*
Salary (in current dollars)	40,000	40,000	40,000	40,000	40,000
Basic committed expenses (in current dollars)	29,500	29,500	29,500	29,500	29,500
Excess	10,500	10,500	10,500	10,500	10,500
Repayment on short-term note	5,800	5,800	5,800	5,800	5,800
Planned expenditures (remodeling, landscaping, and furnishings)	10,000	10,000	10,000		
Total other expenditures	15,800	15,800	15,800	5,800	5,800
Excess (deficiency)	(5,300)	(5,300)	(5,300)	4,700	4,700

Our second recommendation is to obtain more insurance to provide $20,000 of annual income to Mrs. Boney if Dr. Boney dies. Our insurance analysis indicates that approximately $330,000 of insurance coverage is required to provide such an income. The current coverage of $140,000 is significantly below the estimated amount required.

There are several factors favoring the Boneys' financial fortunes. First, the Boneys income is significantly in excess of basic committed expenses. At present, they have committed most of the excess to an investment of joy to the family, an investment which should retain its value over the years, and an investment which provides a tax shelter to boot. In addition, Dr. Boney has a retirement program started which, if continued at $5–6,000 a year for the next 25 years, will accumulate to over $200,000.

After the Boneys have completed the home improvements, they might consider short-term living trusts to provide for the education of the four children. Obviously, they must have some assets to put into the trust in order to have sufficient trust income for educational purposes. Because of their home improvement plans, they may not have any significant funds remaining to put into such trusts for at least five years. Let's assume that the excess of income over committed expense continues to approximate $10,000 five years from now and that eight years from now their oldest child begins college. Exhibit 49 shows a possible educational trust program

EXHIBIT 49

CHILDRENS' TRUST PROGRAM—DR. AND MRS. BONEY

	Year 6	Year 7	Year 8	Year 9	Year 10	Year 11	Year 12	Year 13	Year 14
Annual amounts available five years from now (at end of each year)	$10,000	$10,000	$10,000	$10,000	$10,000	$10,000	$10,000		
Amount accumulated at end of each year at 5%	10,000	10,500 10,000	11,025 10,500 10,000						
	10,000	20,500	31,525 $31,525						
Amount invested in a ten year trust						$31,525	$10,000		
Funds available for childrens' education (trust earns 5%)									
—Oldest child									
Age	15	16	17	18	19	20	21	22	
					Starts college				
Amount—from 1st trust				$1,575	$1,575	$1,575	$1,575		
—from 2nd trust						$1,575	$1,575	$1,575	
—Second oldest child									
Age	12	13	14	15	16	17	18	19	20
								Starts college	
Amount—from 1st trust								$1,575	$1,575
—from 2nd trust									$1,575
—Third oldest child									
Age	10	11	12	13	14	15	16	17	18
Amount—from 1st trust									
—from 2nd trust									
—Youngest child									
Age	6	7	8	9	10	11	12	13	14
Amount—from 2nd trust								$500	$500
—from 3rd trust									

EXHIBIT 49—Continued

CHILDRENS' TRUST PROGRAM—DR. AND MRS. BONEY

	Year 15	Year 16	Year 17	Year 18	Year 19	Year 20	Year 21	Year 22
Annual amounts available five years from now (at end of each year)								
Amount accumulated at end of each year at 5%								
Amount invested in a ten year trust								
Funds available for childrens' education (trust earns 5%)								
—Oldest child								
Age	21	22						
Amount—from 1st trust	$1,575	$1,575						
—from 2nd trust	$1,575	$1,575						
Starts college	Starts college							
—Second oldest child								
Age	19	20	21	22	23			
Amount—from 1st trust		$1,575	$1,575	$1,575				
—from 2nd trust	$1,575	$1,575	$1,575	$1,575	$1,575			
Starts college	Starts college							
—Third oldest child								
Age			17	18	19	20	21	22
Amount—from 1st trust					$1,575	$1,575	$1,575	
—from 2nd trust			$1,575	$1,575	$1,575			
Starts college					Starts college			
—Youngest child								
Age	15	16	17	18	19	20	21	22
Amount—from 2nd trust	$500	$500	$500	$500	$500	$500	$500	$500
—from 3rd trust						$1,575	$1,575	$500

which will cover a substantial portion of the educational expenses of the four children. Three trusts would be set up under the program, with income from the trusts going to each of the children as shown on the exhibit. The last trust of $10,000 to be used for the youngest child's education would be set up before the youngest child begins college, and therefore the income would accumulate to $3,500 at the time the youngest starts college. Thus, the amount available to the youngest would be almost the same amount available to each of the three older children ($8,650 compared to $9,450).

The Anxious Aerospace Engineer

Dick Peterson, a 37-year-old aerospace engineer, is married with three children, ages 16, 11, and 8. One of Dick's concerns is that he does not believe that his income prospects are very great in the aerospace industry. He is also worried about job security. However, because of his love for the lifestyle that he can enjoy in his part of the country, he is not interested in seeking employment outside the region.

The Petersons' net worth is $40,700, of which $28,700 is represented by $18,000 equity in the house, $7,400 equity in furniture and personal property, and $3,300 in the market value of two automobiles. In addition, the Petersons have $6,900 equity in some land in the nearby mountains; $4,700 in a regular savings account; and 100 shares in a speculative over-the-counter security with a current market value of $400.

Dick is currently earning $20,000, and his wife, who works part-time, earns $5,000. In his present employment there are little prospects for significant raises in income other than raises to keep up with the cost of living.

The Petersons have been able to keep their committed expenses, including income and social security taxes at about $15,000. Their life insurance consists of $35,000 in a group insurance policy with Dick's employer and $10,000 whole life insurance. Dick is not interested in acquiring any more insurance.

The Petersons' financial goals are not too specific except that Dick is interested in finding employment that is a little more stable and perhaps combines his interest in the outdoors with his engineering skills. The Petersons are interested in educating their children, but believe that the children can help defray most of their educational costs by working and saving before and during college.

Dick and Ellen Peterson are a couple facing a situation that many people face. There are little prospects for significant raises in income that more than offset the cost of living. Also the Petersons, like many people, are interested in staying in the particular location in which they live, primarily because of the roots that they have established and because of the life-style that they enjoy. Dick's lack of interest in moving, his lack of interest in his current job, probably contributes even more to his job insecurity, since Dick probably does not exhibit enthusiasm to his present employer. For example, he may not be willing to spend long hours in his job that typically upward mobile engineers are willing to do, primarily because Dick has some outside interests that he would rather pursue. Dick is probably not a candidate to start and develop his own business because he does not seem to be interested in putting in the long hours required— hours that would take him away from the outside pursuits.

One positive factor in the Petersons' situation is that their committed expenses are rather low, approximately $15,000. Thus, in the present situation, they are generating some $10,000 in excess of their committed expenses to use for some purpose. Perhaps one thing that the Petersons should do, given their concern with job security, is to increase their short-term investments to at least $10,000 before thinking of any other investment possibilities. Certainly the Petersons should stay clear of any front load mutual fund investments, speculative real estate, or any investments where there is a substantial risk involved. By building up their liquid investments, the Petersons will have some security knowing they can cover at least one year's committed expenses if anything happens to Dick's job situation. In the meantime Dick should evaluate possibilities that take advantage of his engineering skills and his interest in the outdoors. Given the level of the Petersons' committed expenses, Dick really could take a job that combines his interests at a substantial reduction from his current salary. For example, assuming that Ellen continues to work, the Petersons would still cover basic committed expenses on a $10,000 salary for Dick.

Given the fact that they think their children can defray most of their educational costs, the Petersons really are not in bad shape. They have a modest net worth. They have an enjoyable lifestyle, and with any luck at all, Dick will find a job that interests him more and that will allow him to have a substantial amount of time available for outdoor interests. As the children grow older and leave home, Dick's wife probably can turn to full-time work versus part-time. Given their propensity to keep their committed expenses low, their combined incomes probably will continue to exceed committed expenses, and over a 15- or 20-year-period (after the children are grown), their net worth could grow substantially. It could develop assets for retirement purposes and allow them to take more advantage of the outdoors as they grow older.

Conspicuous Consumption

Remember Dr. Gorden Piet, 42, who has splurged so much that most of his monthly income is needed to pay loans. He is making good income, approximately $48,000 before income taxes, but he has accumulated a staggering amount of commitments which drain away $3,750 per month, leaving only about $250 for living expenses for a family of five—his wife and 3 children, ages 11, 8, and 6.

Let us again review this somewhat sorry situation. To begin with, Dr. Piet purchased a $82,000 residence near his country club—the mortgage payments and related insurance and property tax expenditures amount to $750 per month or $9,000 per year. He pays for income tax payments due, home furnishings, expensive vacations and country club living by taking out loans. He currently has several loans amounting to $35,000 and is supposed to be paying them off at a rate of $1,100 a month. Actually he is paying only the interest on some loans. His insurance program is mostly expensive insurance, for which he pays a monthly premium of $250 or $3,000 per year for $150,000 worth of coverage. In addition he is making payments of $400 per month on installment loans on medical equipment and lease payments on late model large automobiles. Income tax payments of $1,200 per month and church contributions of $50 per month bring the total to a staggering amount of $3,750 or $45,000 per year.

All this lavish spending has not created any substantial net worth other than related to personal assets. He currently has $20,000 equity in the house and $30,000 worth of furnishings. The only other assets the Piets have is $8,000 over-the-counter "promising" securities and $10,000 cash value of life insurance. Fortunately, Dr. Piet is in good health, and his income prospects still are bright.

To begin with, we recommend that someone analyze Dr. Piet's medical practice to find out if he could generate more income. This could be done by analyzing his office expenses to see whether they are within the normal range for his type of practice, and whether his collection process is such to make sure that he is generating a good cash flow and not developing delinquent accounts receivable.

The next step would be to take each one of his expenses and see whether any adjustments could be made. Some expenses are somewhat fixed, and no adjustments can be made; for example, income taxes of $1,200 cannot be reduced except by reducing income. His home mortgage payments and related insurance and property tax expenditures amount to $750 per month, or $9,000 per year. These do not have any room for reduction either because of the nature of the commitments—assuming, of course, he wishes to maintain his current residence. It is also difficult to reduce the $400 per month of installment loans on medical equipment and lease payments on the late model automobiles. So it is very difficult to reduce approximately $2,350 of the $3750 monthly expenditures. (This example shows you that committed expenses are sometimes very difficult to adjust in the short run.)

The only real possibility for reduction is to analyze the several loans outstanding and see if they can be consolidated, and to examine his insurance program to see whether any reductions can be made in the monthly premiums.

First, the loans. If it is possible to get Dr. Piet's friendly banker to consolidate the various loans and extend the time involved in repayment, it would be possible to reduce the amount of the monthly payments. This might mean a reduction of 25–30 percent of the monthly payment, but obviously it would extend the time of payment. But a reduction of, say, 25 percent might mean an increase of $275–300 to add to the meager amount of $250 per month the Piets currently have for living expenses.

Next, the insurance. Since most of the insurance the Piets have is expensive permanent insurance, some cash surrender value has built up— approximately $10,000. He could borrow against his cash value and use the amount to pay future premiums. Almost all whole life policies can be turned into what is called a minimum deposit plan.[1] Such a process would reduce his monthly premiums on insurance substantially and thus free some more money for living expenses.

What the Piets need most of all is control over their living expenses. Perhaps by virtue of the above adjustments they could increase the amount available for living expenses to $650 a month. But the important point is to live within that amount. As we suggested in Chapter 5, which discussed cash flow, it is important to control the amount of total living expenses. We are not in favor of having a detailed budget, in fact most doctors we know probably would rebel against such a suggestion. However, we would suggest that the Piets budget an amount for living expenses each month, and then keep within that budgeted amount. This might mean that the Piets would have to give up some unessential kinds of expenditures, such as country club membership, charge accounts, outside cleaning help, etc. But the Piets are in financial trouble, and there has to be some discipline and control built into their financial lifestyle to get out of the trouble they are in. By reducing their committed expenses, they have a reasonable prospect of having income in excess of committed expenses in the near future. Until they get their committed expenses reduced and under control, there is no need to discuss investment opportunities for the Piets.

---

[1] "Life Insurance That Lends You the Premiums," *Money*, October 1974.

Dreams of Your Own Business

When we left 42-year-old Robin Enderson, married with two boys ages 17 and 16, he was contemplating starting his own business and leaving his position as an administrator in a state agency in which he has spent some 18 years. His current income is approximately $26,000 and his wife, Ann, earns approximately $7,000 from her job in a local bank. Last spring Robin decided he would like to chuck his career as an administrator and start his own business. He thought he had reached the top of his career ladder and no longer found his job a challenge. He has done considerable thinking about his financial situation, and he does not think that his income will increase substantially in the next few years because he is at top of the salary level for his position.

The Endersons' committed expenses are approximately $22,700, so their combined income of $33,000 is significantly above committed expenses. Robin does not think that their committed expenses will increase significantly; however, his two sons are about to start college, so there will be some educational expense involved soon.

The Endersons' net worth includes $50,000 equity in their home, which has a market value of $70,000; a piece of raw land worth approximately $25,000; and $1,000 worth of savings. Mrs. Enderson expects a share in an inheritance of $50,000 of property from her parents, but she feels the inheritance may be a long way off since her parents are still in good health. When Robin Enderson reaches 50, he will be entitled to a pension of approximately $10,000 a year for the rest of his life. However, if he leaves before age 50, his benefits will be very little. Mr. Enderson has a $10,000 whole life insurance policy on his life.

Our first recommendation to Robin Enderson is to "hang in there, baby." In another seven years, he will receive the pension of $8,000 a year for the rest of his life. This would give him a lot of financial flexibility, and seven years is really not much longer to wait. Most of us reach a point where we do not, for a variety of reasons, find our current job challenging. In some cases, it makes sense to leave a job and find one that is more stimulating. However, in Robin's case, we do not believe it would be a good decision to forego the pension of $8,000 a year to embark on a business in which he may have financial trouble for a few years. If he did have trouble it would come right during the period when the Endersons' committed expenses might increase, given the educational requirements of two boys.

Our recommendation would be that if he really is interested in consulting, then use the next seven years before retirement to do a detailed analysis of consulting opportunities and perform appropriate start-up activities.

At age 50, he could then start such a business with the security of his pension, his wife's income, and the knowledge that he has accumulated. In addition, seven years from now, the sons will have finished college, and the Endersons' committed expenses might be substantially less.

The Endersons might also do an insurance analysis. It appears that their total insurance needs are approximately $88,000; their coverage of $10,000 is substantially lower.

Divorce—Financial Opportunities and Problems

Paige Wynn is an energetic financially astute divorcee with three children, two girls 18 and 15, and a son 8. Paige, 48, was recently divorced and received a substantial settlement from her successful lawyer husband. In the divorce settlement she received a large beautifully landscaped residence with a fair market value of $96,000. In addition, she has $35,000 in savings accounts in savings and loan associations; $80,000 of marketable securities, currently yielding about 2 percent; a late model station wagon worth about $5,000; and household furnishings worth about $45,000. Paige receives $600 per month ($200 per child) for the children's support which will continue until age 19 for each child. In addition, she receives $1,500 a month in alimony which will continue until her death or until she remarries.

She also receives $400 a month as a trustee for a living trust which her father, a successful businessman, created. Her father also pays her premiums on $100,000 life insurance policy on her life. Educational trust funds have also been set up by her former husband, and these funds are to be used for college financing. The income from investments, alimony, child support, and trustee duties is approximately $33,000; her committed expenses are running about $28,000, of which $7,000 is related to expenses in maintaining the beautiful residence (taxes, gardening, insurance, housekeeper). The childcare support of $200 per child per month of course will go down as the children reach age 19. The first child reaches that age in another year, and in 11 years the $600 per month of child support will completely disappear.

Because of the somewhat fixed nature of her income, Paige is concerned about rising expenses and the eventual loss of childcare payments. As a result she is interested in what she could do differently. The first thing that she might think about is to reduce her committed expenses by moving into a more modest home. She has an equity of $96,000 in the house and presumably, if she moved into something more modest, she could take some portion of that equity and invest it in income-producing assets. For example, even if she were to move into a fairly substantial home worth let's say $50,000, that would free up $46,000 of equity which, if invested at 6 percent, would generate $2,700 of income. In addition, a more modest home would also result in a significant decrease in the amount of committed expenses related to housing, such as property taxes, part-time housekeeper, gardener, utilities, fuel, and insurance, which are running very high at this point—approximately $650 a month.

Our second recommendation would be to try to get a higher yield for the assets that she currently has invested. She certainly can find marketable securities yielding more than 2 percent. She should possibly seek the counsel of either her father or an investment counselor to manage the amount that she has available. With investment assets of $115,000, she has a portfolio of sufficient size to both afford and to profitably use the services of an investment counselor.

The Utilizers

Our last five clients are somewhat in a different class. These are people in their fifties and sixties. They have generally been working hard for 30–40 years to accumulate capital. Our next five clients are not so interested in building up net worth. They want to get to the utilization of financial resources included in our definition of personal financial planning in the opening pages of this book. None of them have any real responsibility to help children financially, and they are now interested in doing the best they can with what they have for themselves and their families, considering the approaching possibilities of retirement or death.

The All-American Businessman

Pete Jones is a fairly typical, successful, not-so-small businessman who has spent the last 30 years building up a construction corporation which he now controls. At the age of 55, Pete and his wife, Mary, look around and ask what they are going to do with what they have accumulated. Pete's son and son-in-law are both key members of the construction business.

Pete's net worth is now $500,000, comprised of the following:

Controlling 51% interest in construction corporation	$225,000
Cash	25,000
Listed stocks and bonds	100,000
Rental real estate	50,000
Life insurance (face value)	50,000
Home and furnishings	50,000
	$500,000

Pete's income is about $45,000 a year, including his $35,000 salary from the construction business and $10,000 from investments. His committed expenses are about $35,000, so he has about $10,000 of discretionary expenditures.

Pete and Mary seem to have no problems from the viewpoint of income. If necessary, Pete's salary from the construction corporation could no doubt be increased. Even if Pete should die, Mary would have something like $400,000 in assets available after paying death taxes and estate expenses, and she should be able to derive sufficient income from those assets.

Pete and Mary have no housing problem—their home is quite modest for their financial circumstances, but it suits them. They also have very adequate savings.

Pete's life insurance is modest in comparison with the size of his estate, but he really has no need for additional insurance. His death taxes would be a maximum of about $100,000 if he leaves nothing to his wife, and about $50,000 if he leaves at least half of his assets to his wife, thereby using a full marital deduction. In addition, there might be $25,000 of administration expenses, so there would be a need for $75,000 to $125,000 of liquid assets. With cash, listed stocks and bonds, and life insurance totaling $175,000, there seem to be no liquidity problems.

In addition, Pete's $225,000 of construction corporation stock qualifies for both installment payments of the Federal estate tax attributable to this stock, and for a tax-free redemption by the corporation from Pete's estate. The $225,000 stock interest now qualifies because it is 50 percent of Pete's gross estate of $450,000. (Life insurance proceeds of $50,000 are not included because policies are not owned by Pete.)

Pete's *real* decision is whether he is really interested in transferring more of his construction business to his children. He says he is, but then goes on to indicate his primary concern is to retain control of the business. Since he only has a 51 percent interest, he cannot give away any of his common stock without losing control to a group consisting of his children and his business associate who owns 35 percent of the stock.

One solution would be to recapitalize the corporation with voting preferred stock, and give Pete this voting preferred for his common stock, so that he would retain voting control of the corporation. The value of his interest, however, would be "frozen," since increases in the value of the corporation would go to the common stock, and not to this preferred. One difficulty with this plan, in Pete's case, is that a majority of the value increase would go to an "outsider"—that is one outside of Pete's family— namely, his business associate. Pete would have to decide whether or not this would be desirable.

If Pete is not willing to go for this preferred stock recapitalization, he will have to face the issue of whether to give up control, or whether to hang on until he dies. The latter may make things difficult for his children and business associate trying to operate the corporation.

Pete and his wife, Mary, might well consider annual gifts of listed stocks or bonds or cash to their children. At least they could make gifts up to $12,000 a year and be within their annual gift tax exclusions. To the extent these exclusions are not used each year, they are really wasted. Gifts of these amounts would about offset the annual increase in Pete's estate due to the excess of income over expenditures.

On the subject of investments, Pete might take a look at municipal bonds. His top income tax bracket is close to 50%, which means that a municipal bond paying 6 percent interest is as good a net of taxes for him as a taxable investment yielding 12 percent. Certainly some of his $25,000 in cash might be placed in these bonds, and he could give consideration to whether it is desirable to change any of his listed stocks and bonds into municipals.

The Old Time Baby Doctor

Doctor Frank Richards is a 59-year-old obstetrician who has unfortunately suffered two heart attacks and is unable to obtain additional insurance. He has two married children, and fortunately one of them is a son trained in obstetrics, just completing his tour of duty in the armed services.

Frank and his wife, Sue, have a net worth of $250,000, consisting of $20,000 accounts receivable from his practice, $8,000 in cash, $30,000 in marketable securities, $130,000 in rental real estate, life insurance with a face value of $30,000, and a home and personal effects totaling $32,000.

Frank and Sue have a current income of $29,000 a year, and their committed expenses just about equal their income. This situation presents their major financial problem, since nearly three-fourths of their income will disappear if Frank can no longer carry on his practice—either because of incapacity or death. They figure that in the event of Frank's death, Sue could get along with about $12,000 a year, but she would actually have available $8,000 or less.

Fortunately, Frank's son is in a position to step in and take over the practice. The best method of arranging this seems to be a partnership of father and son, with provisions for the son in effect paying his father for the practice. If Frank were insurable, partnership insurance providing funds to pay for his interest in the event of death would be desirable.

Since Frank is not insurable, the partnership agreement should provide for retirement type payments in the event of his retirement, or to his wife in the event of Frank's death. These payments might be at the rate of $12,-000 a year. The payments could be for the life of Frank, with 10 years of certain payments in the event of a premature death. Frank has not increased his fees to keep up with inflation. His son could probably collect better fees, and increase the net income to $40,000 a year. From this, the son could pay his father or mother $12,000 a year and still have more income from the practice than Frank is now receiving.

Frank and Sue have no housing problems. Their savings situation is satisfactory, and there is no use thinking about life insurance since he can't get any.

Frank and Sue should think of reinvesting the $30,000 they now have in marketable securities in income type securities yielding about 8 percent. This would increase their income from these securities from the current $1,000 to $2,400 a year. On retirement they will have available to invest the $20,000 now tied up in accounts receivable of the practice. If they invest these funds in income securities yielding 8 percent, this will give them another $1,600 a year of investment income. With this total of $4,000 a year, $12,000 of retirement payments and $7,000 rental income, Frank and Sue will have income of about $23,000 a year. This is a few thousand dollars less than their committed expenses, but they could live from capital for a few years, if necessary, or borrow on the rental real estate which is free and clear. In the event of Frank's death, Sue would be in good shape from an income viewpoint, with something over $20,000 of income, much greater than the $12,000 she feels she will need if she is alone.

Executive Suite

Jack Martin is a rather typical big company executive, who is never going to have the top job, but certainly have a substantial position with a very large company. At age 52, his children are all self-supporting. His only financial responsibility, other than his wife, Elaine, is his mother, Thelma, to the extent of $3,000 a year to meet her expenses.

Jack and Elaine have a net worth of $615,000, as follows:

Checking account	$ 3,000
Savings accounts	40,000
Listed securities	100,000
Unimproved investment real estate	25,000
Permanent life insurance	50,000
Employer's stock (net of bank loan)	100,000
Stock option	12,000
Pension plan	60,000
Present value deferred compensation	105,000
Equity in $175,000 home	115,000
Automobiles, etc.	5,000
	$615,000

Jack's income is $102,000 a year, and his committed expenses run about $80,000 a year, so he has $22,000 of discretionary expenditures.

On the four firsts, Jack and Elaine have little problem. Their income is certainly adequate. Housing is taken care of, although Elaine might want to dispose of the big house in the event of Jack's death, or the two of them might want to dispose of it 10 or 15 years from now. Savings are in good shape, and life insurance is quite adequate. Jack has $150,000 of group life insurance through his company and $50,000 of his own permanent insurance.

Jack does not seem to have any liquidity problems. His taxable estate would be something like this:

Net worth shown above	$615,000
Group life insurance	150,000
	$765,000
Less administration expenses	35,000
Taxable estate	$730,000

Jack's will leaves his wife one-half of his assets, so he qualifies for the maximum marital deduction. The cash needs of his estate might be estimated as follows:

Bank loan	$100,000
Household bills and funeral expenses	5,000
Federal estate taxes	78,000
State inheritance taxes	14,000
Administration expenses	35,000
Total cash needs	$232,000

To meet these needs, Jack's estate would have available the following:

Savings accounts	$ 40,000
Listed securities	100,000
Employer's stocks	100,000
Life insurance	200,000
Total cash available	$540,000

If Jack lives to retirement, he and Elaine should have little in the way of financial problems. Their annual income might look something like this:

Social security benefits	$ 5,000
Deferred compensation	15,000
Pension benefits	25,000
Dividends and interest	12,000
Total estimated income	$57,000

The first thing Jack should do is put some of his securities in a short-term trust, with the income to go to his mother, Thelma, as we discussed in Chapter 15 on estate planning.

Jack could also give some thought to some tax-sheltered investments, since his top income tax bracket is close to 60 percent. His unimproved real estate is of this type, but he could also consider putting at least part of his $40,000 in savings accounts into municipal bonds or an interest in an investment partnership, if he thinks he can find a good one.

At the time of retirement if Jack feels the need for additional income, he might convert his employer's stock into a security producing a higher rate of income. In the event of his death, Elaine might also want to make this kind of conversion.

The Well-off Widow

Ivy Smith is a 60-year-old widow with three married children and no financial responsibility to anyone other than herself.

Ivy has a net worth of $210,000, made up of $65,000 in savings accounts, $45,000 in listed securities, $65,000 in rental real estate, and $35,000 combined in home, personal effects, and a small life insurance policy. Her current income is about $23,000, and her committed expenses are $16,000 a year, so she has about $7,000 a year of discretionary expenditures.

Ivy also has little trouble with the four firsts. Her income is very adequate; her housing is satisfactory. As long as she is physically able to live alone and maintain the house, her savings are also more than adequate. She seems to have no real need for any more life insurance. One thing she certainly should have is some major medical insurance to bridge the gap in years until she will be eligible for Medicare. She will never get any social security benefits, as she and her husband were never employed, and they lived on inherited wealth.

Ivy certainly should be doing better with the $65,000 she has in savings accounts. If she were to invest perhaps $60,000 of this in some combination of the money market investments discussed in Chapter 5, she could no doubt get a 6 percent return. This would give her something like $1,000 more income than she is now receiving on the savings accounts, and she could keep about $625 a year of this added interest after paying the additional income taxes which would result.

Her return on her listed securities is only 3⅓ percent but perhaps she should hang on to these as an inflation hedge. At her age, she has the possibility of living 20 years or more, so inflation may be a serious problem. Hopefully, her rental real estate will be helpful, but it might still be well for her to keep the listed securities which would give her some balance to the money market investments suggested to replace most of her savings accounts.

Added income would make Ivy capable of being better able to make gifts for her children and grandchildren. She should consider giving away at least her excess income over expenditures each year so she is not adding to her estate and therefore her cost of dying.

The Retired Executive

Joe Lund is a retired executive aged 65, living principally on a $24,000 a year pension. He has a wife, Peggy, 64, and three grown children, with no responsibility for any of them.

Joe and Peggy have a net worth of $500,000, made up as follows:

Checking account	$ 5,000
Savings accounts	40,000
Listed securities	245,000
Special situation securities	45,000
Unimproved investment real estate	50,000
Self-employed retirement plan	25,000
Equity in $85,000 home	60,000
Summer home	30,000
	$500,000

Joe and Peggy have social security benefits of about $4,000 a year, and dividends and interest of $15,000 a year to add to Joe's pension, making total income of $43,000 a year. Their committed expenses are about $35,000 a year.

Joe and Peggy have no income problems as long as Joe lives, but his $24,000 a year pension dies with him. Peggy's income might then be something like $18,000 a year, made up of $2,000 social security benefits, $14,000 dividend and interest income from investments, and $2,000 a year withdrawal from her self-employed retirement plan. Her needs are probably going to be something like $20,000 a year so she is going to be a little short. She should go through the following three step analysis suggested for retirees.

1. Determine income "guaranteed" for life, such as social security benefits and pensions.

2. Compare guaranteed income with needs to see how much additional income is required.

3. Look at assets to see what can be done with them, how much risk to assume to get additional income computed in Step 2. At the same time, consider possible reductions in "needs."

Peggy's "guaranteed" income will be only $4,000, including $2,000 each from social security benefits and self-employed retirement plan benefits. This will leave $16,000 income to come from various assets to meet her needs of $20,000 a year. Present investments would probably return about $14,000 of this amount.

To improve Peggy's income picture, one possibility would be to get rid of the special situation securities and unimproved real estate by gifts to the children. Removing these from Joe's estate would save about 40 percent of his one-half of these assets in the form of reduced death taxes and administration expenses. In addition, Peggy would be freed from any cash drain due to costs of keeping the real estate. Another suggestion would be to dispose of at least some of the lower yield securities and put the proceeds in high grade bonds yielding 8–9 percent. Since some of the securities are now yielding only 5 percent, a shift of $100,000 in principal would give Peggy an added $3,000 to $4,000 a year.

If Peggy wants to reduce her "needs" she should consider disposing of her home, or summer home, or both. She will have $115,000 tied up in non-income producing assets, with a mortgage on which to make payments. One word of caution, however. Recent studies have shown a marked physical effect on individuals from substantial changes in their affairs. Items such as the death of a family member, selling a home, moving to another city, etc., all have their effect. A death of a spouse is probably the most serious of all these events. As a result, there is considerable question as to whether the family home should be disposed of immediately and add further stress, regardless of the effect in dollars.

Joe and Peggy have no housing problems, except the possibility of disposing of some. This would be either in the event of Joe's death, or if he gets tired of maintaining the big house in addition to the summer home.

Savings are certainly more than adequate. There seems to be no need for life insurance, since Joe has no real liquidity problems. He is going to qualify for the maximum marital deduction by either leaving all of his assets to Peggy, or by leaving her at least one-half, with the other half in trust and the income to go to her. This will mean that his gross estate for tax purposes will be one-half of the $500,000 in assets, plus one-half of the $33,000 life insurance proceeds, or a gross estate of $266,-500. Cash needs might be something like $62,000 for taxes and $25,000 for administration expenses, or a total of $87,000. With bank accounts of $45,000 and listed securities of $245,000, there seem to be no liquidity problems. One improvement which might be considered would be to have Joe transfer all ownership of his life insurance to his wife, Peggy. This would mean that this asset would be out of the taxable estate, and there would be a saving in death taxes of about 35 percent of the amount of the insurance proceeds.

The Rolling Stonestons

In various chapters in this book, we have discussed the William Fitzgerald Stoneston family. Early in the book, you were introduced to Bill, age 40, and Sally, 37, and and their three children, aged 14, 13, and 3. We used the Stonestones to illustrate the analysis of present net worth in Chapter 1. Based on that analysis we determined that their net worth was $413,700.

We analyzed the Stonestons' income and expenses in Chapter 2 and determined that Bill was receiving approximately $50,000 from his consulting practice and almost $15,000 from royalties on books and videotape programs. The Stonestons committed expenses are approximately $34,000, and therefore they have substantial after tax dollars available for investment purposes.

In Chapter 2, we did a 10-year analysis of income and expenses for the Stonestons (see Exhibits 9 and 10 in Chapter 2), based on their goals, to determine the feasibility of their goals and to determine the possible net worth available when Bill is age 50.

The Four Firsts

We previously looked at the Stonestons' *income* prospects. Obviously the Stonestons do not appear to have an income problem. But, as is sometimes the case with financially secure and successful people, their financial success enables them to think of alternative careers, the establishment of a second career in the later stages of life—i.e., early fifties. This choice is sometimes a difficult one and involves an analysis of a complex set of variables as is briefly explored in the next and concluding chapter.

As to a *place to live,* again the Stonestons do not appear to have any problems. Their primary residence is located in a community they and their children enjoy; the residence is one which provides ample room and privacy for the independent activities of each of the members of the family. A few years ago, the Stonestons purchased about four acres of wooded property with about 200 feet of no-bank waterfront property about an hour from their primary residence. This property has a well-maintained large wooden cabin which provides a retreat setting for the Stonestons with fishing, clam digging, tree fort design, and boating activities available. In addition, the Stonestons are thinking about building a primary residence on the property in their later years and using the cabin for the children and guests. The property can also be used as income producing property for nine months a year if the Stonestons only wish to use it in the summertime.

As to *savings,* the Stonestons believe that a balance of between $3,000 to $5,000 in a regular savings account in a savings and loan association is sufficient as an emergency fund. Lately, they have also increased their liquidity by investing in bankers' acceptance notes for three primary reasons—high interest rates to be obtained on such short-term investments, need for funds to cover the European trip they are planning in the near future, and liquid funds to cover the remaining debt on the waterfront property.

Since the waterfront property still has a balance of $24,000 to go, the Stonestons are interested in having funds to cover that debt in the event an economic crisis reduces Bill's consulting income. As long as the short-term money market rates exceed the 7½ percent interest rate on the note, investments with liquidity make some sense in this case. However, if the money market rates fall below the 7½ percent level, it seems that the Stonestons may want to evaluate the level of their liquid funds.

As to the *insurance* picture of the Stonestons, we performed an analysis of the Stonestons' program in Chapter 4. In that analysis, we determined that the total insurance needed was approximately $212,000, and the Stonestons' insurance coverage is approximately $270,000. The Stonestons have at least two alternatives *if* they wish to reduce the insurance coverage. One, they can continue to borrow on the increasing cash value of the policies, thereby reducing the insurance coverage by the amount of the borrowing. The Stonestons are currently paying 5 percent on the amount they have already borrowed on the cash value of the policies. They certainly can find alternative investments yielding greater than 5 percent return. Two, they could reduce the amount of group coverage by $55,000 and thus save the premium on that amount.

Marketable Securities

About two years ago, the Stonestons decided to use an investment counseling firm to manage the stock portfolio that they had developed up to that time. The portfolio was about $50,000 at that time, a size which was sufficient for some diversification and which was about the minimum handled by the reputable investment counselors in the Stonestons area.

In selecting the firm, the Stonestons visited with several firms recommended by CPAs and brokerage houses in the area. The Stonestons wanted to select a local firm because they felt that personal attention was an important factor in such a financial relationship. The firm they selected was a small firm managing about $10 million of assets with a minimum fee of $500 or 1 percent of the portfolio assets. The portfolio manager is one of the two principals in the firm and can be called on investment policy questions at any time.

The portfolio has changed over the last two years both in composition and in value. During the first year, the portfolio dropped about 22 percent —from $50,000 to $38,000 (marketable securities of $33,300 and a special situation security of $5,000)—while the Dow Jones Industrials had dropped about 13 percent; Standard & Poors 500 had dropped about 14.3 percent. However, during the second year the portfolio increased in value from $38,300 to almost $44,000, primarily through the strategy of short selling of high multiple securities. So, during the period during which the Stonestons basic securities portfolio has been managed by an investment counselor, the value of the portfolio decreased approximately 12 percent, while the Dow Jones Industrials average decreased almost 45 percent with the Standard & Poors 500 down about 46 percent. The portfolio has yielded about 2.5 percent of dividends during most of the period. The current portfolio has an annual yield of about 6 percent.

Real Estate

Almost 45 percent of the Stonestons' net worth is related to real estate. This is consistent with the model we presented in the introduction to Section II. Here, we suggested real restate should comprise a substantial, if not the most substantial, part of the net worth of an individual in his forties. Real estate may provide the greatest possibilities for appreciation and it also provides significant tax advantages to people with high tax brackets.

The Stonestons' real estate investments consist of three individual properties and real estate investments through two limited partnerships. The three individual properties consist of the Stonestons personal residence, the summer waterfront property, and a home which the Stonestons are renting to Bill's parents. All provide some tax shelter since the personal residence is used by Bill for some of his consulting work, most of his writing, and videotaping. The summer waterfront property is rented for a portion of the year.

The investments through the limited partnerships also provide tax shelter. One of the limited partnerships has invested in income-producing properties in California, Colorado, Utah, and Washington. The Stonestons have invested $25,000 in the last four years, but the net cost of the investment after the tax shelter provided has been $11,500. The economic value of the properties at the date the net worth statement was prepared was $31,000.

The other investment through a limited partnership is investment in raw land, with prospects for industrial development in the metropolitan area in which the Stonestons live. Since the investment is in raw land, the tax shelter aspects are not as great as those in depreciable properties. The Stonestons have invested $15,000 over the last five years with net cost after tax deductions of $13,250. The appraised value of the property is approximately $23,000 per partner.

Given the Stonestons' tax bracket and the nature and amount of their other more liquid assets, real estate probably makes considerable sense. As the Stonestons grow older, liquidity may become more important, and the liquidation of some real estate may be wise. Certainly as the two children finish college and become financially independent, the Stonestons may wish to sell their primary residence and build on their waterfront property. We certainly do not recommend the purchasing of a significant amount of additional real estate at this point.

Investments in Closely-Held Situations

Investments in closely-held situations or special situations are advisable only if liquidity, income, and safety are not important. Normally such investments are not advisable for most people. Sometimes, they are unavoidable. In the case of the Stonestons, the investment of $35,000 in Bill's consulting practice is absolutely essential. It may appreciate in value if the practice grows and a management succession program is implemented to carry on the practice when Bill retires or dies.

The other closely-held investments ($16,400) include securities in companies with whom Bill is directly involved, either as a board member, consultant, or author. In each of these cases, he is familiar with the companies involved and believes that their products have a long run growth potential.

We recommend that the Stonestons do not commit any more funds into special situations other than Stoneston & Associates, primarily because of the risk involved.

Self-Employment Trust

Bill Stoneston established a self-employment trust (Keogh plan) several years ago and has contributed $20,000 to the trust. As we discussed in Chapter 10, the contributions to such a plan are deductible. Bill initially invested the funds in a no-load growth mutual fund but recently decided to transfer the program to a Keogh plan offered by a local bank which allows Bill to exercise quite a bit of discretion in the investment decisions. In the last year, Bill has invested the funds primarily in natural resources securities—gold mining, finance company, and forest product company stocks. With the recent appreciation in gold, the trust fund's value has increased to over $27,000.

Educational Trust

Sally Stoneston's deceased father set up an educational trust for the benefit of the Stoneston children. The trust was established about four years ago, and a large metropolitan bank was appointed trustee. The trust funds of approximately $50,000 were commingled with funds of other small trust accounts of the bank. The fund grew to a value of $65,000 about a year ago and declined to a recent value of $35,000—a drop of about 46% reflecting the performance of the stock market during the period. Because of the provisions of the trust, it is almost impossible to change the management of the trust and possibly out-perform the general stock market averages. Thus, we cannot recommend any change in this portion of the Stonestons' net worth. However, this example and other similar cases we have witnessed involving large bank trust funds have led us to the opinion that you should try to gain some knowledge of a bank's performance before you appoint a bank as a trustee, or set up the trust in such a way that there is some process by which a trustee can be changed if the performance is not good.

Chapter 19

INTEGRATING
LIFE PLANNING AND
FINANCIAL PLANNING

Although much of the discussion in this book has focused on the accumulation of financial resources, we firmly believe that the key to personal financial planning is the accumulation and utilization of financial resources to obtain maximum *utility*. We would hope that maximum utility relates to the ends for which money represents the means. We do not believe that the accumulation of wealth has any social virtue and quite agree with a passage from Keynes:

"The love of money as a possession—as distinguished from love of money as a means to the enjoyments and realities of life—will be recognized for what it is, a somewhat disgusting morbidity, one of those semi-criminal, semi-pathological propensities which one hands over with a shudder to the specialists in mental disease." [1]

The accumulation of wealth should be the means to reach lifetime objectives of providing funds for a home; for schooling and educational travel; for healthful pursuits and other leisure time activities which broaden one's mind and vision; for creating new occupational opportunities; and for helping others who are not so financially fortunate. Thus, the most important aspect of financial planning has to be the integration of such plan-

---

[1] John M. Keynes, *Economic Possibilities for our Grandchildren,* taken from the *Money Game* by Adam Smith (New York: Dell Publishing Co., Inc., 1969), page 253.

ning with the formulation of objectives related to occupation, health, professional and personal development, and the development of others.

Focus on Your Passion

We are not advocating a new sex life but merely suggesting that you focus on the things you really want to do. Too many people are chained to regular pay checks in jobs they do not enjoy by the complex tyranny of credit cards, monthly payments and possessions, social pressures to spend, and the propensity to consume all, if not more, than we earn. This drive for more and more income in order to spend more and more money for more and more things appears to create more and more stress with *distress*.

The subject of stress has gained increasing attention lately as developed wealthy societies are characterized by increasing alcoholism, heart attacks, psychiatric treatments, and harried lifestyles. Dr. Hans Selye, one of the foremost authorities on stress, suggests that stress *without* distress comes not from having financial wealth but from finding, among the jobs you are capable of doing, the one you really like best—and that people appreciate.[2]

But to determine what you really want to do and to construct a plan to get there is another matter all together. Too many of us go about our daily lives dreaming about what we might do, what we might have done, and drifting through life in what some have called the range of mediocrity. To do anything else than dream requires an identification of some lifetime goals and a plan for doing something about accomplishing these goals.

How to Get Control of Your Life

One way to integrate life planning and financial planning is to go through a series of exercises that force you to reassess your objectives and values every so often. There are many exercises that have been constructed, a few of which we have included here as examples.

Alan Lakein, in his book *How to Get Control of Your Time and Life*,[3] suggests you take two minutes with a pad and pencil and write down every-

---

[2] Hans Selye, *Stress Without Distress* (Philadelphia: J. B. Lippincott, 1974).

[3] Alan Lakein, *How to Get Control of Your Time and Life* (New York: McKay, 1973).

thing you can think of including money, career, physical, family, social, community, spiritual, and personal goals. It may take two extra minutes to add and subtract and think again, but you must fill up the entire sheet of paper, a creative act in itself (unless you are using a very small pad or a very big pencil). He then suggests that you select three of the goals you feel are most important. Next, taking two minutes each, be specific about each of the three goals. Identify sub-goals, logical next steps, immediate plans. Put down as much as possible. Then from each of the three goals, select one item to do next week. Thus you create an action program. This exercise probably indicates that you have some conflicting goals, and forces you to think about those that are most important.

Unfortunately, however, this exercise may lead to your suggesting some fairly general kinds of goals "to make your wife happy," "to be rich," "to be successful," etc. To be more specific, he suggests you go through a second exercise—again in two minutes—jotting down what you think is most important for you in the next 3–5 years. By attaching a specific time-frame to your goals, you should be more concerned about specific action to accomplish these goals. He then suggests one more exercise—a real hooker. Answer the question "How would you like to live if you knew you would be dead six months from today?" The answer to this question forces you to prioritize, to really concentrate on those things that you feel are most important. In answering these questions you are forced to focus on particular life events that you really consider important, and many times these events have nothing to do with your present occupation. For example, many young executives that we have discussed this exercise with in the recent past mentioned things like spending at least an afternoon a week with my wife, have some uninterrupted time with each of my children; get my tired, somewhat flabby body in a better shape; learn more about international money markets; study life in the Galapagos Islands; write poetry; learn a foreign language; and beat my "goddam" partner in tennis. Lakein further suggests that if you really believe these goals are important you should do something about them. Construct activities to accomplish the goals and set aside time to perform the activities. Confront your goals each week and formulate next week's time plan to make sure you achieve what you set out to do.

Another goals and values exercise is one that has been developed by Sidney B. Simon, Professor of Humanistic Education at the University of Massachusetts. He also suggests beginning with a piece of paper and a pencil and then simply put down 20 things in life that you really *love to do*—any 20 things at all. The only requirements are that you truly love to do what you jot down and that you don't list the same lovely thing 20 times. Some of us who are narrow-minded and specialized are going to have difficulty in jotting down 20 things, so this exercise may require some extra thought and perhaps even some imagination. After you have taken five minutes, five hours, or five weeks to list the 20 things you love to do, you should code your list in the following ways:

1. Put a $ (dollar) sign next to every item that requires an expenditure of at least $5 every time you do it. (Don't count the money it costs to buy the equipment. For example, if you were into bike riding, you wouldn't put a dollar sign in front of it even though your bike cost more than $5. The issue here is that it costs you $5 *each* time you do it.)

2. Use the letters A (for alone), P (for people), and S (for a special person) and record which is your preference. For each activity, do you *prefer* to do it alone, or with people, or with some special person (not necessarily the same special person for each activity)? Note that you can often do a certain activity alone, or with people, or with a special person. The coding here, however, records your *preference*.

3. Put an R next to every item that has an element of *risk* to it. It can be physical risk, emotional risk, or intellectual risk. It doesn't have to be risky for anyone else. Just get in touch with which of your 20 passions are risky for you.

4. Think of someone you love. Place an X in front of every item on your list which you hope would appear on his or her list if he or she had made a list of 20 passions, also. (In fact, you might want to get that person to do just such a thing. It could form a very significant data bank for both of you. . . .)

5. Place the number 10 next to any item that probably would not have been on your list 10 years ago.

6. Place a 5 next to anything you love to do which you think might not remain on your list five years from now.

7. Finally, date each item to show when you did it last. You need not be perfectly accurate. It is OK to say something like, "During August of 1974." [4]

After this is done, Simon then suggests that you write down or say to someone you trust a series of "I've learned's." "I've learned's" are sentences that always have two first-person pronouns in them. Here are some examples:

I learned that I . . . .
I re-learned that I . . . .
I see that I need to . . . .

---

4 Don Biggs, *Breaking Out*. (New York: McKay, 1973), pp. 215–216.

I was disappointed to notice that I . . . .

I feel ready to affirm that I . . . .

It surprised the hell out of me to see that I . . . .[5]

By putting together a series of "I've learned's" this exercise should become a real change agent. You may see life more clearly than you did before and determine what passions you really have.

After you go through these exercises, you may decide to do a number of things differently or a number of different things. You may decide to change your occupation. In this regard, we suggest you read several recent books. The first, *The Seven Laws of Money,* contains some refreshing comments for the vast majority who have committed expenses in excess of income and who feel trapped by the "growing like topsy" pressure to keep spending. Although the author's seven laws are all relevant to most of us, his first law is most appropriate to our present discussion regarding occupation. The First Law of Money is "Do it!" "Money will come when you are doing the right thing." The author suggests that what is most important is to pick a livelihood that you feel strongly about and that you are able to perform well. The rest of the book follows the same view—follow the rules of money (credit, budgets, net worth planning, etc.), handle money with respect for the system it represents, but don't let it be the force which keeps you from doing the thing you feel you do best.[6]

In a very witty book, *How to Retire at 41,* the author challenges conventional wisdoms regarding work patterns, occupational identities, and spending habits. As to retirement he suggests:

> "If you want to retire at 41, it seems to me that there are at least three absolute prerequisites. (It always turns out somehow that there may be more, is why I say "at least.") First and foremost is that you *be* 41 and have a job to retire *from.* Second, you should be somewhat fed up with your work; otherwise there wouldn't be much point (in fact, no point whatsoever) in quitting, not if you were enjoying it. Third, you should have done fairly well when you were working, so you won't feel your retreat is some kind of defeat. Fourth—and this may not seem as important as the others, but is pretty much what all that follows is about—you should have some idea of how you are going to use up all of the time that will suddenly become available.
>
> 'And fifth,' you say, 'is that I have to have some money to live on,'.
>
> What a fraud you are. I discount this money business more or less entirely.

---

[5] Biggs, *Breaking Out,* p. 217.

[6] Michael Phillips, *The Seven Laws of Money.* (New York: Word Wheel and Random House, 1974.)

If you *really* wanted to quit work, you could do it tomorrow—you know you could. Certainly you could do it within 6 months, after simplifying your life and making certain arrangements you've got in the back of your mind. Anybody can quit work—even if it means drawing unemployment insurance, camping out, and living on welfare. But you probably have some better ideas: you'd never have picked up this book if retiring wasn't at least a possibility.

The thing is, it's far more expensive to work than we ever realize. The place you live, the way you move around, the kind of entertaining you do, the taxis you take and the taxes you pay, all the things you pay others to do because you don't have time to do them yourself, even those fancy schools you've got your children in, the very clothes on your back—all these, and in fact virtually all aspects of your life, financial and otherwise, but financial is what I am talking about now—all are determined by your work. And they are—just about all of them—more expensive because you are working than they would be if you were not." [7]

The author's last comments on the expenses of work are equally applicable to most of us who are not contemplating retirement just yet.

Develop a Financial Plan to Support Your Objectives

Now that you know what you really want to do, determine the financial implications and develop a financial plan. Thus, we are back where we started in Chapter 1 (believe it or not), and we can afford to do a little summary and bring this book to a close. The following step-by-step procedure may assist you to develop the financial plan.

1. Get your assets in shape by first determining how much net worth you have using the worksheets discussed in Chapter 1.

2. Analyze your income prospects and your expenditure patterns. Many economists indicate that inflation may be a fact of life in the decades ahead. With such a possibility, we have recommended in Chapter 2 that you analyze your current spending habits.

3. Keep your committed expenses reasonable. Determine what spending can be cut back. Our guess is that we all have fat built into our budgets and could reduce our expenditures by 20 percent without

---

[7] A short portion of the "Prologue appeared in Esquire magazine, March 1973, under the title, "Living Alone in Bad Company." Copyright © 1973 by Esquire, Inc. from the book *How to Retire at 41* by L. Rust Hills. Reprinted by permission of Doubleday & Company, Inc.

seriously changing our basic lifestyle. Separate the basics from the nice-to-have and be ingenious in ways by which your consumption patterns can be altered to combat the effect of rising inflation.

As starters, we pass along some ways West Europeans are trying:

"To make perfume last, shake a little on a small piece of cotton wool and drop this inside your bra. The scent lingers longer.

Always have a meal or snack before shopping for groceries.

Shop one day later each week. Every seven weeks you'll have one week's housekeeping money left over.

If only a drop of lemon juice is required, pierce the lemon with a knitting needle and squeeze. The lemon will keep indefinitely as the hole closes again.

Other housewives suggest that hair shampoo is cheaper than bubble bath and does the same job, that dad's old pajamas make good ironing-board covers, and that telephone directories can become children's scrapbooks." [8]

4. Maintain flexibility by keeping your debt in control. Take a look at your current debt and ask the question "What would happen if incomes generally—including your own were reduced by 20 percent for a prolonged period of time." Good times are not here to stay, as we once may have imagined, and the pyramiding of debt may be extremely hazardous in the times ahead.

5. Determine how much life insurance protection must be provided for anyone important to you. Use the worksheets discussed in Chapter 4 to make your analysis.

6. Tailor your investments to fit your personality and your view of the world, the economy, your job, your wife, anything else that is an important consideration in evaluating investment alternatives. We have suggested many investment alternatives in Sections II and III of this book and have set forth some basic rules on tax planning in Section IV to help you succeed financially. However, you have to invest in those opportunities which make you comfortable. For example, many people we know prefer to invest in tangible items such as art, antiques, wine, and maybe even baked beans,[9] primarily because they can directly *use* such investments and because they really enjoy the process of finding out about

---

[8] "West Europeans, Rich and Poor, Tightening Belts," *International Herald Tribune,* Oct. 22, 1974, p. 1.

[9] You may laugh but Fred Coleman reported in the *International Herald Tribune* Oct. 22, 1974: In these days soaring inflation, British millionaire, Jim Slater, advises investing in cans of baked beans. You cannot eat stock certificates or fine art but even if the bottom falls out of the baked bean market Mr. Slater claims you won't starve. The (London) Sunday Telegraph took Mr. Slater seriously and spent £100 ($233) on canned food and plans to see if that investment does better than the London Stock Exchange.

such objects of investment. A mountain cabin, a summer retreat, and of course your own business, falls into the same category. These investments necessarily involve the investor to a much greater degree than investments which are much more impersonal such as a stock certificate, a mutual fund, or a savings certificate. Others believe assets such as gold mining stocks, silver, natural resources, real estate, and productive land are appropriate because such investments represent classic tangible wealth.

7. Get directly involved in developing your plan. There is just no substitute for your involvement in financial planning. If you have read this far and have completed the worksheets and exercises, you have started your plan. Once you have prepared your basic plan, you may wish to seek out competent advisors to *react* to your plan, but not to prepare it, to recommend changes that you understand, and to assist you in tailoring a plan to meet your needs. But don't lean on advisors. In fact, have a healthy skepticism about any of the advice you receive. By all means, don't make a decision on recommendations you don't understand. A good advisor should make sure you understand his or her recommendations and should welcome questions about any advice he or she gives.

8. Implement your plan—spend according to your plan, invest in those assets that are tailored to your personality, and periodically check your progress against your plan. Evaluate your plan at least once a year and update it for changes in your personal objectives, the economic situation, and other events that affect you financially. But, by all means, remember to have a good life. May you grow old gracefully and with a great deal of prosperity.

PERSONAL FINANCIAL PLANNING WORKSHEETS

The accompanying worksheets are designed to assist you in performing a comprehensive analysis of your financial affairs. The worksheets are grouped according to the major phases of the analysis:

Worksheet 1—Basic Information

Worksheet 2—Present Net Worth

Worksheet 3—Asset Details

Worksheet 4—Income and Expense Analysis

Worksheet 5—Committed Expenditures

Worksheet 6—Discretionary Expenditures

Worksheet 7—Insurance Analysis

WORKSHEET 1
BASIC INFORMATION

I. YOU AND SPOUSE

Name	Age Birthdate	Marital Status

You _____ ___ _____ Married ___ Single ___

Spouse _____ ___ _____ Divorced ___ Widowed ___

Residence _____ Head of Household ___

Occupation _____ Phone _____

Business Address _____ Phone _____

Social Security Number: Husband _____; Wife _____

Military Identification Number _____

II. CHILDREN

Name	Age	Birthdate	Spouse	Age	Occupation	No. of Children

III. PARENTS OF FINANCIAL PLANNER AND SPOUSE

List names, dates of birth, and whether you are providing support for parents of either spouse.

_____

_____

_____

_____

IV. OTHER DEPENDENTS

Name	Relationship	Age	Residence	Occupation

V. ADVISORS

	Name	Address	Telephone No.
Attorney			
Accountant			
Bank Officer			
Insurance Agent			
Investment Advisor			
Broker			
Tax Advisor			
Trust Officer			
Others (with nature of data involved)			

VI. DOCUMENTS

Identification No.
(where applicable)   *Location*   *Date*

Your Will _____

Spouse's Will _____

Trust Agreements _____

Mortgages _____

Property Deeds _____

Car Titles _____

Stock Certificates _____

Stock Purchase
Agreements _____

Bonds & C.D.'s _____

Checking Accounts _____

Saving Account
Passbooks _____

Life Insurance
Policies _____

Other Insurance
Policies _____

Contracts _____

Set of Last Instructions _____

Retirement Agreements _____

Pension or Profit
Sharing Plans _____

Birth Certificates _____

Marriage Licenses _____

Divorce and
Settlement Papers _____

Notes Receivable _____

Notes Payable _____

Employment Contracts _____

Income Tax Returns
(last 3 years) _____

Personal and Business
Income Tax Returns
(if applicable) _____

Gift Tax Returns _____

Military Discharge
& Documents _____

Financial or
Insurance Surveys _____

Other Records
and Valuables _____

_____

_____

_____

WORKSHEET 2
PRESENT NET WORTH
As of _____

	Estimated Current Value
I. ASSETS	
Liquid:	
Cash (checking and regular savings accounts)	$_____
Term savings accounts	$_____
Short-term investments—Treasury bills, certificates of deposit, etc.	$_____
Marketable securities	$_____
Accounts receivable	$_____
Cash value of life insurance	$_____
Not so Liquid:	
Real estate	$_____
Investment partnerships	$_____
Special situations	$_____
Retirement Funds:	$_____
Personal:	
Residence	$_____
Furnishings	$_____
Automobile	$_____
Boats	$_____
Other:	$_____
TOTAL ASSETS	$_____

II. LIABILITIES

Estimated Current Value

Short-Term Obligations:
Current bills $_____

Borrowings on life insurance $_____

Automobile(s) $_____

Notes and contracts payable $_____

Other $_____

Personal loans (give details on back) $_____

Accrued taxes $_____

Long-Term Obligations:
Mortgages on real estate investments $_____

Mortgage on personal residence $_____

Other obligations $_____

TOTAL LIABILITIES $_____

ASSETS — LIABILITIES = NET WORTH $_____

WORKSHEET 3
Asset Details

I. Cash & Short-Term Investments

Checking and Savings Accounts

Institution	Type (Regular = e 90 Day, 1 yrs.)	Rate of Interest	Restrictions on Withdrawal

Certificates of Deposits/Treasury Bills/Bankers' Acceptances

Institution	Type of Investment	Maturity Date	Rate of Interest

II. STOCKS & BONDS

(Indicate if stocks are common or preferred. Give interest rate and maturity of bonds.)

No./Shares or Par Value	Name of Issue	Exchange	Date Acquired	Cost	No./Shares or Par Value	Name of Issue	Exchange	Date Acquired	Cost

III. LIFE INSURANCE

Company & Policy Number	Issue Date	Plan	Face Amount	Special Provisions	Cash Value

WORKSHEET 3—Continued

ASSET DETAILS

IV. REAL ESTATE

Description, Street No. and Location	Title in Name of	Cost	Present Valuation		Mortgages or Liens			Annual Taxes	Lien Holder
			Land	Improve-ments	Monthly Payment	Interest Rate	Amount		

V. INVESTMENT PARTNERSHIPS

Name of Partnership	Nature of Partnership	Original Investment		Annual Contribution	
		Date	Amount	Years	Amount

WORKSHEET 4

INCOME & EXPENSE ANALYSIS

_____ MONTHS ENDED _____ _____ _____
(Number)   (Month)   (Day) (Year)

The analysis of income and expense will provide a useful tool to determine whether your standard of living will permit additional accumulation of wealth. Some financial counseling may be beneficial at this time to pinpoint areas requiring attention so that you may rearrange your affairs in a more advantageous manner. The analysis for a particular year, not necessarily a calendar year, should also provide the basis for budgets and forecasts of requirements in future years.

	Previous Year	Current Year	Estimated Next Year
INCOME			
Salary:			
Yourself	$_____	$_____	$_____
Your spouse	_____	_____	_____
Other persons	_____	_____	_____
Self-employment income:			
(net of expenses)	$_____	$_____	$_____
Other income:			
Interest	_____	_____	_____
Dividends	_____	_____	_____
Capital gains & (losses)	_____	_____	_____
Rents (net of expenses)	_____	_____	_____
Royalties (net of expenses)	_____	_____	_____
Partnerships, estates, or trusts	_____	_____	_____
Other	_____	_____	_____
	$_____	$_____	$_____

WORKSHEET 5
Committed Expenditures

COMMITTED EXPENDITURES

	Previous Year	Current Year	Estimated Next Year
Housing (includes mortgage or rental payments, repairs, insurance, taxes, fuel, and utilities)	$_____	$_____	$_____
Transportation (includes payments on installment purchase, insurance, licenses, gas and oil, repairs)	_____	_____	_____
Food	_____	_____	_____
Household supplies and furnishings	_____	_____	_____
Phone	_____	_____	_____
Clothing and personal	_____	_____	_____
Education and recreation	_____	_____	_____
Medical (includes health insurance)	_____	_____	_____
Insurance (life)	_____	_____	_____
Total before taxes, interest and installment payments	$_____	$_____	$_____
Taxes (Social Security and income)	$_____	$_____	$_____
Interest (other than on installment payments)	_____	_____	_____
Installment payments Major purchases (other than automobile)	_____	_____	_____
Repayment of principal on borrowings	_____	_____	_____
Investment plans	_____	_____	_____

WORKSHEET 6
DISCRETIONARY EXPENDITURES

	Previous Year	*Current Year*	*Estimated Next Year*
DISCRETIONARY EXPENDITURES:			
Somewhat discretionary—			
Entertainment	$_____	$_____	$_____
Regular vacations	_____	_____	_____
Church and charities	_____	_____	_____
Hobbies	_____	_____	_____
Organizations—fraternal	_____	_____	_____
—civic	_____	_____	_____
—social	_____	_____	_____
Personal gifts	_____	_____	_____
Emergency fund	_____	_____	_____
Total	$_____	$_____	$_____
Very discretionary—			
Home or home improvements	$_____	$_____	$_____
Auto, boat, etc.	_____	_____	_____
Personal property (home furnishings, etc.)	_____	_____	_____
Trips—extended	_____	_____	_____
Investments	_____	_____	_____
Special goals	_____	_____	_____
Other (give details on back)	_____	_____	_____
Total	$_____	$_____	$_____
TOTAL EXPENDITURES	$_____	$_____	$_____

WORKSHEET 7
INSURANCE ANALYSIS

Time Period	Widow's Age From To	Number of Years	Income Required	Income Analysis Monthly Less Social * Security Available	Less Widow's Earnings	Balance Needed	Yearly Amount Needed	Insurance Required
1. Period during which *more than one child* is less than 18 and dependent upon your widow.								
2. Period in which *only one child* is less than 18 and dependent upon your widow.								
3. Period after your youngest child reaches 18 and until your spouse reaches 60								
4. Period after your spouse reaches 60 and until her death.								

TOTAL INCOME REQUIREMENTS
ADDITIONAL CASH REQUIRED
(FROM STEPS 1 TO 4) $ _____
TOTAL INSURANCE NEEDED $ _____

* In 1974, the benefits for a widowed mother and one child were $606.80; family maximum $707.90; check with your local social security office for current benefits.

In 1974, the full benefits for a widow at age 65 were $404.50; reduced benefits begin at age 60 for widows and the reduction factor is 19/40 of 1% for each month of entitlement age 60–65. For example, the reduction factor at age 62 would be 19/40 × 36 months or .171; thus

330

INDEX

American average, 143-144
American Institute Counselors Inc., on gold-related investments, 210-211
American Institute of Economic Research
  on gold-related investments, 214-216
  on inflation, 189-190
Analysis, financial
  described, 30-36
  sample worksheet, 34-35
Annual gifts, 297
Apartment houses, as investment, 154-155
Assets. *See also* Liquid assets; Long term assets
  and inflation rate, 38-40
Attorney, as financial advisor, 271-272

Balanced funds, 134
Bank accounts, 97-99. *See also* Swiss bank accounts
Banker's acceptances, 109
Bank trust department, as financial advisor, 272
Biggs, Don, on life planning, 312-313
Bond funds, 136

Bondholders' rights, 117-118
Bonds, 119-121
Borrowing, 292
  on insurance, 304-305
  during period of hyperinflation and depression, 200
Browne, Harry
  on gold-related investments, 214-216
  on Swiss bank accounts, 195-196
Business
  owning your own, 179-188, 278-279, 293-294
  sources of additional information, 262-263
Business interests, in estate planning, 251-252

Capital, removing from your own business, 187-188
Capital gains. *See* Investments; Tax favored income
Capital sources, for management of your own business, 181
Cash flow, for management of your own business, 184
Cash forecast, 99-103, 104-105
Certificates of deposit, 109-110